科技英语口语教程

总主编　黄锦华
主　审　Johnathon William Ferguson
主　编　董月琳　卢淑玲
副主编　韦　俊　孙远用　盛捷柯
　　　　王芳芳　韦艳梅　陆梅华
　　　　宋琳琳　刘甜甜　杜　卉
　　　　陈士芳　邝江红　胡春华
　　　　李　丽　邓先超　吉文婕

苏州大学出版社
Soochow University Press

图书在版编目(CIP)数据

科技英语口语教程/董月琳,卢淑玲主编. —苏州:
苏州大学出版社,2015.8(2023.7重印)
 ISBN 978-7-5672-1462-0

Ⅰ.①科… Ⅱ.①董…②卢… Ⅲ.①科学技术—英语—口语—高等学校—教材 Ⅳ.H319.9

中国版本图书馆 CIP 数据核字(2015)第 196420 号

本书配有录音,可在苏州大学出版社官网
(http://www.sudapress.com)"下载中心"下载。

书　　名：	科技英语口语教程
主　　编：	董月琳　卢淑玲
责任编辑：	杨　华
封面设计：	刘　俊
出版发行：	苏州大学出版社(Soochow University Press)
地　　址：	苏州市十梓街1号　邮编：215006
印　　装：	苏州工业园区美柯乐制版印务有限责任公司
网　　址：	http://www.sudapress.com
E - mail：	yanghua@suda.edu.cn
邮购热线：	0512-67480030
销售热线：	0512-67481020
开　　本：	787mm×1092mm　1/16　印张：16　字数：367千
版　　次：	2015年8月第1版
印　　次：	2023年7月第13次印刷
书　　号：	ISBN 978-7-5672-1462-0
定　　价：	36.00元

凡购本社图书发现印装错误,请与本社联系调换。服务热线:0512-67481020

前 言
Preface

目前,培养本科层次的应用型人才已成为许多高等院校的办学定位和培养目标。作为一线教师,我们也日益感受学生所需的英语实际应用能力的紧迫性,尤其是切合学生专业的专门用途英语的应用能力。考虑实际教学之需要,我们编写了这本教材。该教材可作为专门用途英语课程的相关教材,重在科技英语口语练习,同时加强专业词汇、常用句型和相关科技英语知识的学习。

该教材由7个单元组成,包括汽车工程、机械电控、土木建筑、生物化工、经济管理、艺术、计算机科学与技术等学科方向,其特点在于融合文、理、工学科,综合编写,方便学生进行交叉学科资料的查阅和学习。每个单元包含2—4个相关话题和一篇科技英语知识的介绍,每个话题由两篇对话、生词表、专有名词、常用句型和练习组成。全书共有25个话题和7篇科技英语知识介绍。

该教材由广西科技大学鹿山学院外国语言文学系的老师共同完成,黄锦华教授任总主编。具体分工如下:Topic 1 及科技英语的阅读技巧由陈士芳编写;Topic 2,Topic 3,Topic 19 及科技英语词汇的特点(一)由董月琳、卢淑玲共同编写;Topic 4,Topic 5 由刘甜甜编写;Topic 6 由吉文婕编写;Topic 7 及科技英语词汇的特点(二)由杜卉编写;Topic 8,Topic 9 由宋琳琳编写;Topic 10 由李丽编写;Topic 11 及科技英语词汇的翻译技巧由邝江红编写;Topic 12,Topic 13 由韦俊编写;Topic 14 及科技英语的句法特点由王芳芳编写;Topic 15 由董月琳编写;Topic 16,Topic 17 由孙远用编写;Topic 18 及科技英语的篇章特点由韦艳梅编写;Topic 20 由邓先超编写;Topic 21,Topic 22,Topic 23 由陆梅华编写;Topic 24 及科技英语的翻译原则和策略由盛捷柯编写;Topic 25 由胡春华编写。词汇表汇总由盛捷柯、韦艳梅完成。董月琳、卢淑玲、韦俊、孙远用、王芳芳、盛捷柯参与了该教材的审校工作。外籍专家 Johnathon William Ferguson 参与了全书的英文审核工作。全书由董月琳、卢淑玲汇总完成。

在本教材编写过程中,广西科技大学鹿山学院其他系部的专业教师及一些企业专家也为本教材的编写提出了宝贵的意见,他们是陈玲玲、管菁、黄艳玲、梁慧、梁宗国、王镜瑜、杨欢、易青等老师,在此表示衷心的感谢!

由于时间紧迫,加之作者水平有限,本教材难免有所疏漏,敬请读者批评指正。

编者

2017 年 5 月

目 录
Contents

Unit 1　Automotive Engineering　/ 1
　Topic 1　Automotive Design and Manufacturing　/ 1
　Topic 2　Car Sales　/ 8
　Topic 3　After-Sale Service and Repairing　/ 15
　科技英语知识——科技英语词汇的特点(一)　/ 21

Unit 2　Mechanical and Electric Control Engineering　/ 22
　Topic 4　Product Design　/ 22
　Topic 5　Mould Machining　/ 29
　Topic 6　Electrical Automation　/ 35
　Topic 7　Automation Equipment　/ 42
　科技英语知识——科技英语词汇的特点(二)　/ 49

Unit 3　Civil and Architectural Engineering　/ 50
　Topic 8　Civil Engineering　/ 50
　Topic 9　Building Structural Design　/ 58
　Topic 10　Architectural Design and Decoration　/ 66
　Topic 11　Transportation Construction　/ 72
　科技英语知识——科技英语词汇的翻译技巧　/ 78

Unit 4　Biochemical Engineering　/ 80
　Topic 12　Food Engineering　/ 80
　Topic 13　Environmental Engineering　/ 87
　Topic 14　Chemical Engineering　/ 94
　科技英语知识——科技英语的句法特点　/ 101

Unit 5　Economy Management　/ 103
　　Topic 15　Management　/ 103
　　Topic 16　Finance and Economics　/ 110
　　Topic 17　Logistics　/ 117
　　Topic 18　Marketing Management　/ 125
　　Topic 19　Tourism　/ 131
　　科技英语知识——科技英语的篇章特点　/ 138

Unit 6　Art　/ 139
　　Topic 20　Industrial Design　/ 139
　　Topic 21　Environmental Art Design　/ 146
　　Topic 22　Dress and Costume　/ 152
　　Topic 23　Animation and Cartoons　/ 159
　　科技英语知识——科技英语的阅读技巧　/ 166

Unit 7　Computer Sciences and IT　/ 168
　　Topic 24　Internet　/ 168
　　Topic 25　E-Business　/ 175
　　科技英语知识——科技英语的翻译原则和策略　/ 181

Appendix Ⅰ　Words and Phrases　/ 184
Appendix Ⅱ　Keys to Exercises　/ 208
Appendix Ⅲ　Translation of Dialogues　/ 216

Unit 1

Automotive Engineering

Topic 1 Automotive Design and Manufacturing

Section A Dialogues

Dialogue 1

Morton: Engineer   Henry: Designer

Morton: As everyone knows, Liuzhou is a city of **automobiles**. Though there are a lot of taxis on the street, people dream of having their own cars. It has become a **trend**.

Henry: Every time I come to Liuzhou, I have the feeling that there are more and more automobiles, and the roads are better and better. Automobiles will surely become an **indispensable** part of our lives.

Morton: With the development of society, your **concept of design** is **converting** as well.

Henry: Every **era** has its unique design ideas while design principles that **comply** with the **requirements** of customers remain unchanged.

Morton: Customers expect the auto designs are capable of **indicating** the spirit of the times. What's the present design idea of Audi A8L?

Henry: That is to build the best car. Let me introduce more details. This time the popular outlook is still kept in the latest design; moreover, some brand new issues such as "economical **consumption**, **high efficiency**, fashion, and safety" are also addressed.

Morton: We are aware that the automobile is composed of four sections such as the **engine**, **chassis**, **body** and **electrical system**. Please tell me which sections have been changed.

Henry: First of all, let's start from the engine. Nowadays, due to the **diminishing gasoline** supply, we need to develop a completely new engine in order to **maximize** the efficiency of energy, "1.0 liters EcoBoost" three-**cylinder** engine, i.e. the lowest **displacement** engine.

Morton: Sounds **fantastic**! What about the price?

Henry: Don't worry! In order to be more attractive and get more shares in the market, Ford motor company has signed a contract with us. They will invest and **sponsor** us for half a year before this car starts selling.

Morton: Got it. Here comes a simple question, what is the **transmission** of this car, **manual** or automatic?

Henry: **Based on** customers' requirements, we offer two options, manual and auto, and the **ratio** is 5:1.

Morton: You've got a wonderful design idea!

Henry: Thanks a lot!

Vocabulary

automobile	/ˈɔːtəməbiːl/	n.	汽车
trend	/trend/	n.	趋势
indispensable	/ˌɪndɪˈspensəbl/	adj.	必不可少的
convert	/kənˈvɜːt/	v.	转变,改变
era	/ˈɪərə/	n.	时代
comply	/kəmˈplaɪ/	v.	遵从,服从
requirement	/rɪˈkwaɪəmənt/	n.	要求
indicate	/ˈɪndɪkeɪt/	v.	表明,反应
consumption	/kənˈsʌmpʃn/	n.	消耗
engine	/ˈendʒɪn/	n.	发动机
chassis	/ˈʃæsi/	n.	底盘,底座
body	/ˈbɒdi/	n.	车身
diminish	/dɪˈmɪnɪʃ/	v.	减少,减小,减弱
gasoline	/ˈgæsəliːn/	n.	(美)汽油
maximize	/ˈmæksɪmaɪz/	v.	最大化
cylinder	/ˈsɪlɪndə(r)/	n.	气缸
displacement	/dɪsˈpleɪsmənt/	n.	排量

fantastic	/fæn'tæstɪk/	adj.	极好的
sponsor	/'spɒnsə(r)/	v.	赞助
transmission	/træns'mɪʃn/	n.	传动装置,变速器
manual	/'mænjuəl/	adj.	手动的
ratio	/'reɪʃiəʊ/	n.	比例
concept of design			设计理念
high efficiency			高效
electrical system			电气系统
base on			基于

Dialogue 2

James: Engineer   David: Designer

James: Hi, David, what are you doing these days?

David: I'm working on designing a new car.

James: Wonderful! How is it going?

David: The exterior has been finished, but the problem comes in the designing of its **interior layout.**

James: Oh, what's the problem?

David: I want to design a seven-seat **passenger car**, but the **inner space** will be very small and inconvenient for luggage carrying. Can you help me solve this problem?

James: I've got an idea. The two **rear** rows of seats can be designed as **foldable** ones. Meanwhile, a storage space could be designed under the seats. Therefore, the seats can be folded and stored in the space while carrying huge luggage. And when luggage is small, the seats can be pulled out for holding more passengers.

David: Really nice advice! Thanks a lot!

James: You're welcome! (*Checked the car.*) There is something wrong with your cylinder design. With this designed position for the cylinder, the car will **sag** heavily when you make a turn, consequently lowering its safety.

David: This design is based on the limitation of the space within the car, which will **make the best use of** the space of the car and reduce the production cost, making it more compact and effective.

James: As for the sagging problem, why not make an experimental car to have a test drive, to see whether this problem exists, and furthermore, any solutions are available?

David: OK, let's have a try.

(*After an hour, the two completed the test drive and came back.*)

David: Although the design of the car is pretty good, when the car is **steering**, the **gravity** of it really **deviates**, without locating in the center.

James: Considering the sagging problem caused by gravity center, we can **hit back** by designing the cylinder position, **rendering** the car's gravity center stay stable.

David: Yeah, you give me a nice piece of advice. Thank you so much!

James: My pleasure!

Vocabulary

interior	/ɪnˈtɪəriə(r)/	adj.	内部的
layout	/ˈleɪaʊt/	n.	安排,设计,布局
rear	/rɪə(r)/	adj.	后面的
foldable	/ˈfəʊldəbl/	adj.	可折叠的
sag	/sæg/	v.	中间下垂,弯曲
steer	/stɪə(r)/	v.	驾驶,行驶,引导
gravity	/ˈgrævəti/	n.	重力
deviate	/ˈdiːvieɪt/	v.	偏离,背离
render	/ˈrendə(r)/	v.	使成为,使变得
passenger car			小客车
inner space			内在空间
make the best use of			最大限度利用
hit back			回击,反击

Section B Notes

1. Audi A8L(奥迪 A8L):奥迪 A8L 是奥迪车系中最高档的豪华车,其市场定位是用以跟奔驰 S600 及宝马 7 系列竞争的。奥迪 A8L 率先使用了全铝车身,不仅坚固耐用,而且减轻了车身重量,为汽车带来更加强劲的动力表现。奥迪 A8L 目前有三种车型可选,分别是 A8L2.8、A8L4 和 A8L 加长型。目前,奥迪 A8L 为其所属系列中的最新车系。

2. "1.0 liters EcoBoost" three-cylinder engine("1.0 升 EcoBoost"三缸发动机):这是福特工程师历经 20 多年创新实验的完美杰作,可媲美 1.6 升自然吸气发动机,是排量最小的发动机。其最大功率达 120 马力,最大转矩输出 152 牛·米,比绝大部分 1.6 升自然吸气发动机性能更加优越。该发动机采用多项先进技术,由柄连杆机构采用偏置曲轴布局,活塞往复运动所在的轴线的延长线不经过曲轴中心,可减少做功冲程期间活塞与缸壁的摩擦,能使燃烧更充分。

Section C Exercises

Ⅰ. **Translate the following words or phrases into Chinese.**

1. automobile
2. chassis
3. cylinder
4. electrical system
5. layout
6. foldable
7. deviate
8. hit back

Ⅱ. **Translate the following words or phrases into English.**

1. 必不可少的
2. 高效
3. 排量
4. 设计理念
5. 内部的
6. 小客车
7. 重力
8. 最大限度利用

Ⅲ. **Role play.**

A is an engineer of automobiles, and B is a designer who wants to design one part of a car (such as the outlook, body, or chassis). They encounter some problems in the process of designing. Try to use the words and phrases you have learned to make a conversation between them.

Section D Related Words and Phrases

1. body — 车身
2. clutch — 离合器
3. styling — 式样,款式
4. brake — 刹车,制动器
5. gearbox — 变速器,变速箱
6. drive shaft — 传动轴
7. differential — 差速器
8. horn — 喇叭
9. starter — 起动机,起动装置
10. charge — 充电
11. alternator — 交流发电机
12. principal component — 主要部件
13. internal combustion engine — 内燃机
14. power unit — 动力装置
15. trunk deck — 行李箱盖
16. loading room — 货厢
17. driving room — 驾驶室
18. petrol tank (AmE. gas tank) — 汽油箱
19. auto manufacturer — 汽车制造商
20. drain off — 排出,流出
21. steering wheel — 方向盘
22. engine block — 发动机气缸体
23. engine performance — 发动机性能
24. engine displacement — 发动机排量
25. roof paned — (车身)顶板

Section E Useful Expressions and Sentences

1. Though there are a lot of taxis on the street, people dream of having their own cars. It has become a trend.

    虽然大街上有很多的出租车,但是,老百姓还是希望拥有自己的小汽车,而且现在

已然成为一种潮流。

2. Automobiles will surely become an indispensable part of our lives.
   汽车肯定会成为我们生活中不可缺少的一部分。

3. Every era has its unique design ideas while design principles that comply with the requirements of customers remain unchanged.
   设计理念会因时代而异,而满足消费者需求的设计原则是不会改变的。

4. Customers expect the auto designs are capable of indicating the spirit of the times.
   消费者所期望的是能反映时代精神的汽车款式。

5. Now let me introduce more details.
   现在让我详细地介绍一下。

6. This time the popular outlook is still kept in the latest design; moreover, some brand new issues such as "economical consumption, high efficiency, fashion, and safety" are also addressed.
   这一次的设计除了保留了近几年热销的车款以外,还强调了"经济环保、高效、时尚、安全"等全新的设计理念。

7. We are aware that the automobile is composed of four sections such as the engine, chassis, body and electrical system.
   我们都知道,汽车是由发动机、底盘、车身及电气系统四大部分组成。

8. Nowadays, due to the diminishing gasoline supply, we need to develop a completely new engine in order to maximize the efficiency of energy.
   当前在石油资源日趋紧张的环境下,我们应当开发全新的发动机,使之能最高效地利用燃料。

9. The purpose of an automobile engine is to supply the power needed to move the vehicle.
   汽车发动机的功用是提供汽车行驶所需的动力。

10. In order to be more attractive and get more shares in the market, Ford motor company has signed a contract with us.
    为了增强吸引力,提高市场份额,福特汽车公司已经和我们签订了合同。

11. What is the transmission of this car?
    这款汽车采用什么样的变速器?

12. Based on customers' requirements, we offer two options, manual and auto, and the ratio is 5∶1.
    基于客户的需求,我们提供两种选择,即手动挡与自动挡,按照5∶1的比例制造。

13. Hi, David, what are you doing these days?
    您好,大卫,最近在忙什么呢?

14. The exterior has been finished, but the problem comes in the designing of its interior layout.

    外观基本设计好了,不过,内饰空间的布置上遇到了点问题。

15. I want to design a seven-seat passenger car, but the inner space will be very small and inconvenient for luggage carrying.

    我想设计成七人座小客车,可是这样的话,内部空间就非常小,不方便携带行李。

16. The two rear rows of seats can be designed as foldable ones.

    可以将后两排的座椅设计成折叠式。

17. With this designed position for the cylinder, the car will sag heavily when you make a turn, consequently lowering its safety.

    气缸设计在这个位置的话,汽车在转弯的时候会产生严重的倾侧,因而会降低汽车的安全性。

18. This design is based on the limitation of the space within the car.

    这次设计的位置是根据汽车的有限空间设计的。

19. Although the design of the car is pretty good, when the car is steering, the gravity of it really deviates, without locating in the center.

    虽然汽车的设计不错,可是每当汽车在转弯的时候,汽车的重心确实会偏离,没有位于汽车的中心。

20. Considering the sagging problem is caused by gravity center, we can hit back by designing the cylinder position, rendering the car's gravity center stay stable.

    考虑汽车倾侧问题是重心偏离问题造成的,我们可以重新设计一下气缸的位置,使汽车的重心保持稳定。

Topic 2   Car Sales

Section A   Dialogues

 Dialogue 1

Kevin: ***Customer***   Alex: *Sales manager*

Kevin: I like the Ford Focus you showed me before. I think it is pretty much what I need.

Alex: Sure. You are making a good choice. There are so many improvements with the design of the new Ford Focus.

Unit 1 Automotive Engineering

Kevin: What does the **standard** option include?

Alex: For the new cars, the standard option includes the air condition, **ABS**, dual air bags, and radio with DVD player. Moreover, the **cruise control system** is loaded for Focus.

Kevin: What're the differences compared with the old **model**?

Alex: The new model has got the improvements in **styling** and **coating**. It would be more comfortable and **eye-catching**.

Kevin: Nice. What about the **sunroof**? Is that a standard option?

Alex: Sorry, the sunroof is **optional**, sir.

Kevin: I see. Another important question is when I can get this car. I need a new car ASAP.

Alex: It might take two weeks. If you order now, it would be **available** by May.

Kevin: That's good enough, I think. What colors does the new Focus come in?

Alex: We have this new model in red, white, blue, yellow or silver. These are the standard colors. Of course you could specially order from various other colors too.

Kevin: My colleague got one Focus that is last year's model. And his car is a kind of grey color **mixed with** silver. I really like that color. I wonder whether I can get that color on my Focus or not.

Alex: I know the color you mean. Is this it, sir? (*shows him a picture*)

Kevin: Yes, I think that's it. Can I get that?

Alex: Yes, you can. That color is very popular with most of our customers. So we've kept it available.

Kevin: Well, I think I want to order the new Focus then. It looks like an excellent car.

Alex: You have made a good choice, sir. I also have one. It is a **compact**, safe and **reliable** driving machine.

Kevin: Yes, I know. I think Ford is the most reliable car on the road. I would never **switch to** other choices. I don't have any service problems with my Ford. It runs smooth as silk.

Alex: Alright, sir. I will prepare the **paperwork** ready for you. Just a moment.

 Vocabulary

customer	/ˈkʌstəmə(r)/	n.	顾客
standard	/ˈstændəd/	n.	标准配置
model	/ˈmɒdl/	n.	型号,车型
styling	/ˈstaɪlɪŋ/	n.	造型,款式

coating	/ˈkəʊtɪŋ/	n.	涂层,外层
eye-catching	/aɪˈkætʃɪŋ/	adj.	引人注目的
sunroof	/ˈsʌnruːf/	n.	顶窗
optional	/ˈɒpʃənl/	adj.	可选择的
available	/əˈveɪləbl/	adj.	可获得的,可找到的
compact	/kəmˈpækt/	adj.	紧凑的
reliable	/rɪˈlaɪəbl/	adj.	可靠的
paperwork	/ˈpeɪpəwɜːk/	n.	表单
ABS (anti-lock braking system)			防抱死制动系统
cruise control system			巡行车速控制系统
ASAP (as soon as possible)			尽快
mix with			混合
switch to			转变,(使)改变

 Dialogue 2

Josh：Customer   Ellen：Sales manager

Ellen：Good morning, sir. How can I help you?

Josh：Morning. I'd like to buy a car. Would you recommend one for me?

Ellen：At such a young age, you deserve a car that has more technological sense.

Josh：I have been thinking of buying such a car. Any suggestions?

Ellen：Aha, you've come to the right person. I'll show you around. We have many models displayed here.

Josh：Great! Thank you.

Ellen：We have the new 3008 in our 4S store, and both its power and appearance are very impressive.

Josh：I guess it must be a really nice car. Show me more details.

Ellen：Yeah. Its STT (stop-start) is **fuel-efficient**, which can save as much as 15% of fuel under **urban traffic conditions**, and the **ultra-sized retractable full-view roof** is fantastic. Well, what impresses me most is its **MRN** (**multimedia radio navigation**), which is very **intuitive** and convenient for people who play iPhone or iPad all day long. 3D **photo navigation** and **full-view visual parking support system** are also loaded in this car. Furthermore, given the operating habits of Chinese, this system supports **handwriting** and pinyin input, making it very convenient to use. In general, it's a much **ergonomic** car.

Josh: Sounds interesting. I'd love to have a **test drive**.

Ellen: You definitely should. You can make an appointment with us for the test drive. And there's **fee- and interest-free policy** recently. If you buy now, all kinds of colors are available.

Josh: Aha, I'd better pick my favorite color.

Vocabulary

fuel-efficient	/ˈfjuːəl ɪˈfɪʃnt/	adj.	节油的
intuitive	/ɪnˈtjuːɪtɪv/	adj.	凭直觉得到的，直观的
handwriting	/ˈhændraɪtɪŋ/	n.	手写
ergonomic	/ˌɜːgəˈnɒmɪk/	adj.	人类工程学的
urban traffic condition			城市交通路况
ultra-sized retractable full-view roof			超大尺寸可伸缩全景天窗
MRN (multimedia radio navigation)			多媒体收音机导航
photo navigation			实景导航
full-view visual parking support system			全方位可视泊车辅助系统
test drive			试驾
fee- and interest-free policy			费率双零政策

Section B Notes

1. ABS（anti-lock braking system）（防抱死制动系统）：通过安装在车轮上的传感器发出车轮将被抱死的信号，控制器指令调节器降低该车轮制动缸的油压，减小制动力矩，经一定时间后，再恢复原有的油压，这样不断地循环（每秒可达5～10次），始终使车轮处于转动状态，且又有最大的制动力矩。没有安装ABS的汽车，在行驶中如果用力踩下制动踏板，车轮转速会急速降低。当制动力超过车轮与地面的摩擦力时，车轮就会被抱死，完全抱死的车轮会使轮胎与地面的摩擦力下降。如果前轮被抱死，驾驶员就无法控制车辆的行驶方向；如果后轮被抱死，就极容易出现侧滑现象。

2. cruise control system（CCS）（巡行车速控制系统）：又称为定速巡航行驶装置、速度控制系统、自动驾驶系统等。其作用是按司机要求的速度打开定速巡航之后，不用踩油门，踏板就自动地保持车速，使车辆以固定的速度行驶。采用了这种装置，当在高速公路上长时间行车后，司机就不用再去控制油门踏板，减轻了疲劳，同时减少了不必要的车速变化,从而节省燃料。

3. 4S store(4S 店):是一种以"四位一体"为核心的汽车特许经营模式,包括整车销售(sale)、零配件销售(spare parts)、销售服务(service)、信息反馈(survey)等。

4. full-view visual parking support system(全方位可视泊车辅助系统):显示屏显示倒车信息,全面掌握障碍物方位。前倒车雷达在前进泊车时也能探测低矮障碍物,保护车辆安全。带有倒车辅助线,图像清晰、响应快,在黑暗或低照明度情况下,图像显示依然效果良好。

5. fee- and interest-free policy(费率双零政策):指贷款购车时的免手续费、免利息的双免政策。

Section C Exercises

Ⅰ. Translate the following words or phrases into Chinese.

1. standard
2. anti-lock braking system
3. cruise control system
4. styling
5. sunroof
6. full-view visual parking support system
7. intuitive
8. compact

Ⅱ. Translate the following words or phrases into English.

1. 节油的
2. 多媒体收音机导航
3. 城市交通路况
4. 超大尺寸可伸缩全景天窗
5. 实景导航
6. 费率双零政策
7. 人性化的
8. 可靠的

Ⅲ. Role play.

A is a seller for automobiles, and B is a customer who wants to buy a car and knows something about the car. Try to use the words and phrases you have learned to ask and answer questions.

Section D Related Words and Phrases

1. instrument panel — 仪表板
2. indicator — 指示器
3. ignition key — 点火钥匙
4. accelerator pedal — 油门
5. air bag — 安全气囊
6. shift position — 档位
7. seat belt — 安全带
8. head restraint — 座椅头枕
9. windscreen — 挡风玻璃
10. rear window — 后窗玻璃
11. windscreen wiper — 挡风玻璃刮水器
12. rear mirror — 后视镜
13. front wheel — 前轮
14. rear wheel — 后轮
15. full-size spare tire — 全尺寸备胎
16. wing — 翼子板
17. hubcap — 毂盖
18. bumper — 保险杠,缓冲器
19. tire — 轮胎
20. radiator — 散热器
21. bonnet(AmE:hood) — 发动机罩
22. boot(AmE:trunk) — 轿车后部行李箱
23. headlight — 车头灯(车辆前部的大灯)
24. dipped headlight — 近光灯
25. electronic stability program(ESP) — 车身电子稳定系统

Section E Useful Expressions and Sentences

1. I'd like to buy a car.
   我想买辆车。

2. Is it for personal or business use?
   是私用还是商用?

3. Please tell me more details.
   请多给我介绍一些信息。

4. I think there is one type that suits you.
   我想总有一款适合你。

5. This car has excellent safety features, like air bags and ABS.
   这辆车有一流的安全性能,如安全气囊和防抱死制动系统。

6. Compared with the old model, this type is improved in styling and coating.
   与旧款相比,新款在外观设计和涂层上有所改进。

7. I need a new car ASAP.
   我需要尽快拿到新车子。

8. I prefer the red color.
   我更喜欢红色。

9. The silver ones of this type are out of stock.
   这款车银色已脱销。

10. I'll take the red one. I think it is just great for my wife.
    我要红色的。我想它刚好适合我太太。

11. What does the standard option include?
    它有哪些标准配置?

12. What colors does the new Focus come in?
    新福克斯都有哪些颜色?

13. I wonder whether I can get that color on my Focus or not.
    我想知道我的福克斯是否也能选那个颜色。

14. It is a little more than I expected. Would you allow me a special discount?
    这比我预想的价格稍微高了些。你能给个特别的折扣吗?

15. The best I can do is 3% discount.
    我最多能给3%的折扣。

16. Here are our latest price sheets.
    这是我们最新的价格单。

17. Our price is without further discounts.

    我们的价格不再打折。

18. This is really a bargain.

    这才叫价格低廉。

19. This quote has minimized our room for profits.

    这个报价已经最大限度地压缩了我们的利润空间。

20. OK, I can accept the price.

    好吧,我可以接受这个价格。

Topic 3 After-Sale Service and Repairing

Section A Dialogues

Dialogue 1

A: *Receptionist in a 4s store*　　B: *Car owner*

A: Good morning. What seems to be the problem?

B: No problem at all! I'm taking a long distance trip and I want to make sure my car is in good mechanical condition.

A: Very wise decision. When was the last time you had a check-up?

B: Not that long. I think it was four months ago.

A: We usually recommend that you bring your car in every five thousand kilometers.

B: Why? I mean, what exactly do you do to a car that you need to check it so often?

A: First of all, we change the motor oil and oil filter. If you don't do this, it can cause your engine to run faster and that means you would probably have to change the **pistons** and **intake valves**.

B: I see. What else?

A: We also check your **spark plug**, **fuel filter**, and other oil levels such as **hydraulic fluid**. We also check the clutch and **brake** to determine when you need replacement.

B: OK, well, when you put it that way, it doesn't seem like a waste of time and money.

A: Trust me, **regular check-up** will keep your car running **smoothly** and avoid **breakdowns**.

B: Sounds reasonable.

A: Please take your valuables with you and give me your **spare key**. I'll take you to our **reception room**. Please write down your **plate number**, your name and telephone number in the form.

B: OK. How soon can I get my car?

A: You may get it at 2:00 tomorrow afternoon. Here is my business card with my number. We are ready to help at any time.

B: Thank you very much.

A: My pleasure.

 Vocabulary

piston	/ˈpɪstən/	n.	活塞
brake	/breɪk/	n.	刹车
smoothly	/ˈsmuːðli/	adv.	平稳地
breakdown	/ˈbreɪkdaʊn/	n.	故障
intake valve			进气阀
spark plug			火花塞
fuel filter			燃油滤油器
hydraulic fluid			液压油
regular check-up			定期保养
spare key			备用钥匙
reception room			接待室
plate number(= number plate)			车牌号

 Dialogue 2

Both A and B are car owners.

A: Where are you going?

B: I'm taking the car to the garage. It needs **lubrication** and oil-changing. And the brakes are grabbing. I'm going to send it to the **mechanic** for checking.

A: I thought you just had it in the **garage**.

B: That was last month. I had a new transmission put in. I've only had it for six months, and I've already spent a lot of money on repairs.

Unit 1　Automotive Engineering

A：I think it is good to buy a car rather than to **maintain** it. What's worse, I just don't trust those vehicle maintenance shops. Sometimes, they **overcharge** or don't replace those **parts** I have been paying for. Last week, they even tried to persuade me to buy some of the new but not necessary parts for replacement. You know, I just have this car for half a year and it's a reliable brand too. I was just wondering about all these.

B：There are such shops living on selling parts. I don't like their service either. All they want is your money. But in the long run, they will be losing customers. Anyway, the car service business is new in China. We all have to control what they are doing. Otherwise, they will not improve.

A：Is it possible to make a **complaint call** to some organization if someone gets **rip-off** from these garages?

B：Yes, it is. Those organizations exist. You can call a lawyer if you need legal help.

A：As for some small problems, you don't need to go to the garage. The garage is profiting a lot. We need to have basic knowledge about car service.

Vocabulary

lubrication	/ˌluːbrɪˈkeɪʃn/	n.	润滑
mechanic	/məˈkænɪk/	n.	机修工
garage	/ˈɡærɑːʒ/	n.	汽车保修行，汽车修理店
maintain	/meɪnˈteɪn/	v.	维修，维护
overcharge	/ˌəʊvəˈtʃɑːdʒ/	v.	收费过高
part	/pɑːt/	n.	零件，部件
rip-off	/ˈrɪpɒf/	n.	索要高价，敲竹杠
complaint call			投诉电话

Section B　Notes

1. clutch（离合器）：位于发动机和变速箱之间的飞轮壳内，用螺钉将离合器总成固定在飞轮的后平面上，离合器的输出轴就是变速箱的输入轴。在汽车行驶过程中，驾驶员可根据需要踩下或松开离合器踏板，使发动机与变速箱暂时分离或逐渐接合，以切断或传递发动机向变速器输入的动力。离合器是机械传动中的常用部件，可将传动系统随时分离或接合。基本要求为：接合平稳，分离迅速而彻底；调节和修理方便；外廓尺寸小；质量小；耐磨性好，有足够的散热能力；操作方便省力。常用的离合器分为牙嵌式与摩擦式两类。

2. spark plug(火花塞):俗称火嘴,它的作用是把高压导线送来的脉冲高压电放出,击穿火花塞两电极间空气,产生电火花,以此引燃气缸内的混合气体。主要类型有准型火花塞、缘体突出型火花塞、电极型火花塞、座型火花塞、极型火花塞、面跳火型火花塞等。

3. transmission(变速器):是能固定或分档改变输出轴和输入轴传动比的齿轮传动装置,又称变速箱。变速器由传动机构和变速机构组成,可制成单独变速机构,或与传动机构合装在同一壳体内。传动机构大多用普通齿轮传动,也有的用行星齿轮传动。

Section C Exercises

Ⅰ. Translate the following words or phrases into Chinese.

1. engine
2. mechanic
3. brake
4. maintain
5. garage
6. breakdown
7. rip-off
8. spark plug

Ⅱ. Translate the following words or phrases into English.

1. 活塞
2. 备用钥匙
3. 收费过高
4. 零件,部件
5. 平稳地
6. 接待室
7. 投诉电话
8. 车牌号

Ⅲ. Role play.

A is a receptionist in a 4S store, and B is a car owner who wants to have his car checked. Try to use the words and phrases you have learned to ask and answer questions.

Section D Related Words and Phrases

1. vehicle maintenance — 汽车维护
2. vehicle repair — 汽车修理
3. manufacturing defect — 制造缺陷
4. design defect — 设计缺陷
5. wear of vehicle part — 汽车零件磨损
6. normal wear — 正常磨损
7. wear rate — 磨损率
8. partial failure — 局部故障
9. critical failure — 致命故障
10. dieseling (after run) — 自燃现象
11. clogged filter — 滤油器阻塞
12. cylinder sticking — 咬缸
13. noisy brake — 制动器发响
14. brake fade — 制动失效
15. abnormal knocking — 异响
16. check up — 检查,审查
17. assy repairing — 总成修理
18. running-in period — 磨合期
19. screwdriver — 螺丝刀
20. ring spanner — 花扳手
21. hub puller — 轮毂拆卸器
22. wheel wrench — 车轮拆卸器
23. silencer — 消音器
24. tire pump — 打气筒
25. pressure gauge — 胎压力计

Section E Useful Expressions and Sentences

1. Valuable cars require more maintenance.
   昂贵的汽车需要更多的维护。

2. How much does the car maintenance cost?

保养汽车需要花多少钱?

3. The brakes are not working as well as they used to be.

   (这辆车的)刹车不如以前灵敏了。

4. The car is much quieter after the maintenance.

   这辆车经过保养后噪声小多了。

5. Check the function of your car regularly.

   要定期对汽车的性能进行测试。

6. The engine of the car needs fixing.

   这辆车的发动机需要修理。

7. Maintaining your car regularly can guarantee your safety.

   定期对汽车进行保养,可以确保行驶安全。

8. Car maintenance can be divided into regular and irregular maintenance.

   汽车保养分为定期保养和非定期保养两大类。

9. First fill in the car maintenance manual.

   先填写汽车维护手册。

10. This car maintenance is free of charge.

    这次汽车保养是免费的。

11. He replaced with the imported tires for his new car.

    他为新车换上了进口轮胎。

12. The air-conditioner of the car doesn't work.

    这辆车的空调不管用了。

13. How about the after-sale service of this car?

    这辆车的售后服务怎么样?

14. Something is wrong with the exhaust system.

    汽车的排气系统出了故障。

15. Summer is the peak period of car breakdown.

    夏天是汽车故障高发期。

16. Could you help me repair my car?

    可以帮我修理一下汽车吗?

17. This garage has a good reputation.

    这家汽车维修店口碑很好。

18. How much does it cost for repairing the car?

    修这辆车需要多少钱?

19. I want to replace with the imported components.

    我想换进口的零件。

20. How long will it take to repair the car?

多长时间可以修好这辆车？

科技英语知识

科技英语词汇的特点（一）

科技英语是英语的一种特殊文体，尤其在词汇方面具有比较突出的特点。准确把握词义是理解新科技英语文章的前提和基础。以下简要介绍科技英语词汇的3个特点。

1. 常用词汇专业化

科技英语大量使用科技术语，其中有相当数量的科技术语借鉴自基础英语的常用词汇。这些普通的常用词汇用在某一专业科技领域中却成了专业技术用语。例如：

wing 翅膀—机翼/前翼子板　　　coat 外套—镀层

mouse 老鼠—鼠标　　　　　　　package 包裹—软件包

2. 广泛使用缩略词

缩略法，即提取一词语组合主要词汇（多为实词）的第一个字母组成新词的构词方法。科技英语中广泛使用缩略词是因为它们简略、方便。例如：

CCS（cruise control system）巡行车速控制系统

ABS（anti-lock braking system）防抱死制动系统

ESP（electronic stability program）车身电子稳定系统

CAD（computer-aided design）计算机辅助设计

3. 大量使用合成词

合成词，即将两个或两个以上的旧词组合成一个新词。在英语发展过程中，用合成法构成的复合词为科技英语提供了大量的新词汇。例如：

framework 构架，框架　　　　hardware 硬件

website 网站　　　　　　　　videophone 可视电话

screensaver 屏保　　　　　　　wavelength 波长

Unit 2

Mechanical and Electric Control Engineering

Topic 4 Product Design

Section A Dialogues

Dialogue 1

Alan: Interviewer   Zhang Qiang: Applicant

Alan: Come in, please.

Zhang: Good morning, sir.

Alan: Good morning. Please take a seat. You are Mr. Zhang?

Zhang: Yes. I'm Zhang Qiang.

Alan: I've read your resume. Why did you choose **Mechanical** Engineering as your major?

Zhang: Many factors led me to do so. One of them is that I like **tinkering with** machines.

Alan: I know you have worked for two years. As for **mechanical engineering**, what are you **primarily** interested in and good at?

Zhang: I like designing products most, and I have been awarded with my designs. In addition, I'm familiar with **CAD**. I believe I can do well if I'm employed.

Alan: As far as I know, CAD is the useful **software** for **product design**. Can you give me a brief introduction to CAD?

Zhang: Yes. CAD is short for **computer-aided design**. It is the software that can help designers to design by computer and **graphic device**. Usually, different design schemes need a lot of **calculation**, analysis and comparison by computer, to decide whether it is an **optimal** decision.

Unit 2　Mechanical and Electric Control Engineering

Alan: Wonderful. Just now, you said you have got an award on design. Can you introduce your design?

Zhang: OK. I have designed a **hydrogen-boosted gasoline engine**, which greatly improves **vehicle fuel** economy. Hydrogen is not available at **gas stations** at present, so this powerful gasoline engine hasn't been introduced to the market. However, I believe the consumers will see the type of engine in cars in the near future.

Alan: Great. Do you have any more questions to ask about this job?

Zhang: No further questions.

Alan: Thank you very much, Mr. Zhang. I will inform you of the result of the interview as soon as possible. Goodbye.

Zhang: Thank you, bye.

Vocabulary

mechanical	/məˈkænɪkl/	adj.	机械的
primarily	/praɪˈmerəli; ˈpraɪmərəli/	adv.	主要地
software	/ˈsɒftweə/	n.	软件
graphic	/ˈɡræfɪk/	adj.	绘画的,图案的
device	/dɪˈvaɪs/	n.	装置,设备
calculation	/ˌkælkjuˈleɪʃn/	n.	计算
optimal	/ˈɒptɪməl/	adj.	最佳的
vehicle	/ˈviːəkl/	n.	交通工具,车辆
fuel	/ˈfjuːəl/	n.	燃料
tinker with			小修补,小修理
mechanical engineering			机械工程
product design			产品设计
CAD(computer-aided design)			计算机辅助设计
hydrogen-boosted gasoline engine			氢助燃汽油发动机
gas station			加油站

Dialogue 2

Mark: *Customer*　　*Gary*: *Salesman*

Gary: Good afternoon, sir. How can I help you?

Mark: Good afternoon. I'd like to know something about your company.

Gary: OK. We are a design company, cooperating with some professional furniture **manufacturers**, such as wooden, **hardware**, **fiberglass** and so on.

Mark: That sounds great. Do you have a **catalogue** of your products?

Gary: Yes. Besides the catalogue we also have the website. You can also search the Internet to know our products in detail.

Mark: All right. Can I have a look around your design office?

Gary: Maybe after cooperation, but you can meet all design samples in our **showroom**. What products are you interested in?

Mark: I want to **customize** a set of genuine leather sofas. Well, this set looks nice. The leather is better than that of your competitors.

Gary: You are **discerning**. The **piping** and the back **cushion** are **semi-aniline leather**.

Mark: But the cushion doesn't look very thick, and why is there fabric under the cushion?

Gary: The cushion is made of **polyurethane foam**. It is very comfortable. Moreover, the bending between **saddle leather straps** and seat cushions that you see conforms to the standard of the human body curve, and this type of design has been applied for a **patent**. Please try and feel it.

Mark: Very nice. Can I see its back?

Gary: You see, the technique of hot **seaming** is adopted here, and this **mould** is an **aluminum alloy** sheet forming. Please check the **polish** work and piping.

Mark: Sure. Clear curve and clean connection. Can you do any other colors?

Gary: We can do ten colors together. There are **swatches** at our website.

Mark: Yes. The sofa is of high quality. I'm very satisfied. I will reply to you tomorrow if I decide to place an order.

Gary: Thank you, sir. I do hope the answer will be favorable.

 Vocabulary

manufacturer	/ˌmænjuˈfæktʃərə(r)/	n.	生产者,制造者
hardware	/ˈhɑːdweə/	n.	硬件
fiberglass	/ˈfaɪbəglɑːs/	n.	玻璃纤维
catalogue	/ˈkætəlɒg/	n.	目录,目录簿
showroom	/ˈʃəʊruːm/	n.	展厅
customize	/ˈkʌstəmaɪz/	v.	定制,定做

discerning	/dɪˈsɜːnɪŋ/	adj.	眼光敏锐的,有识别力的,有洞察力的
piping	/ˈpaɪpɪŋ/	n.	绲边
cushion	/ˈkʊʃn/	n.	坐垫
patent	/ˈpætnt/	n.	专利
seaming	/ˈsiːmɪŋ/	n.	线缝,接缝
mould	/məʊld/	n.	模具
polish	/ˈpɒlɪʃ/	n.	抛光,上光
swatch	/swɒtʃ/	n.	样品,布样
semi-aniline leather			半苯胺真皮
polyurethane foam			聚氨酯泡沫
saddle leather strap			鞍皮带
aluminum alloy			铝合金

Section B Notes

1. CAD（computer-aided design）（计算机辅助设计）：指利用计算机及图形设备帮助设计人员进行设计工作。

在设计中通常要用计算机对不同方案进行大量的计算、分析和比较,以决定最优方案;各种设计信息,不论是数字的、文字的或图形的,都能存放在计算机的内存或外存里,并能快速地检索;设计人员通常用草图开始设计,将草图变为工作图的繁重工作可以交给计算机完成;由计算机自动产生的设计结果,可以快速做出图形,使设计人员及时对设计做出判断和修改;利用计算机可以进行与图形的编辑、放大、缩小、平移和旋转等有关的图形数据加工工作。

2. mechanical engineering（机械工程）：机械工程是一门涉及利用物理定律为机械系统作分析、设计、生产及维修的工程学科。机械工程是以有关的自然科学和技术科学为理论基础,结合生产实践中的技术经验,研究和解决在开发、设计、制造、安装、运用和修理各种机械中的全部理论和实际问题的应用学科。

3. polyurethane foam（PU foam）（聚氨酯泡沫塑料）：是异氰酸酯和羟基化合物经聚合发泡制成,按其硬度可分为软质和硬质两类,其中软质为主要品种。一般来说,它具有极佳的弹性、柔软性、伸长率和压缩强度;化学稳定性好,耐许多溶剂和油类;耐磨性优良,较天然海绵大20倍;还有优良的加工性、绝热性、黏合性等性能,是一种性能优良的缓冲材料,但价格较高。聚氨酯软泡常用于沙发家具、枕头、坐垫、玩具、服装和隔音内衬。

4. semi-aniline leather（半苯胺真皮）：半苯胺真皮选用上好牛皮,并且要加工60天以上,它比普通的真皮更有细腻感,而且通风性也好。

5. aluminum alloy（铝合金）：铝合金是工业中应用最广泛的一类有色金属结构材料,已在航空、航天、汽车、机械制造、船舶及化学工业中大量应用。工业经济的飞速发展,对铝合金焊接结构件的需求日益增多,铝合金的焊接性研究也随之深入。

Section C Exercises

Ⅰ. Translate the following words or phrases into Chinese.

1. optimal   2. computer-aided design
3. polyurethane foam   4. piping
5. swatch   6. customize
7. tinker with   8. fiberglass

Ⅱ. Translate the following words or phrases into English.

1. 制造者   2. 展厅
3. 模具   4. 产品设计
5. 加油站   6. 可获得的
7. 装置,设备   8. 铝合金

Ⅲ. Role play.

A is a recruitment manager of a mechanical product design company, and B is an applicant who wants to work in this company. Try to use the words and phrases you have learned to ask and answer questions.

Section D Related Words and Phrases

1. three-dimensional — 三维的,立体的
2. hatching — 剖面线
3. spindle — 杆轴,心轴
4. sample — 样品
5. drawing — 图样,草图
6. draft taper — 拔模锥度
7. instruction manual — 说明书
8. coupon — 测试样品
9. coefficient of friction — 摩擦系数
10. barcode scanner — 条形码扫描器
11. assembly drawing — 装配图
12. bending moment — 弯矩
13. channel — 凹槽,槽铁
14. sand paper — 砂纸
15. projector — 投影仪
16. fit tolerance — 配合公差
17. tracing — 摹图,映描图
18. surface roughness — 表面粗度
19. straightness — 直度
20. sketch — 草图
21. plane strain — 平面应变
22. roughness — 粗糙度
23. undercut — 底切,底部掏槽
24. robot — 自动机,自动控制装置
25. production line — 生产(装配)线
26. major defect — 主要缺陷
27. minor defect — 次要缺陷
28. performance — 动作性能

Section E Useful Expressions and Sentences

1. This engineer is familiar with both English and Japanese.
   这位工程师精通英语和日语。

2. All the steel will be used to make formwork.
   所有的钢材将被用来做模板。

3. The better you do the job, the more pay you'll get.
   你工作做得越好,工资就越高。

4. I'm afraid we will not be able to finish the work within this week.
   我担心本周内我们将无法完成工作。

5. Why always ask the workers to work overtime?
   为什么总让工人加班呢?

6. Why not make a call to the engineer and ask him about it?
   为什么不给工程师打个电话问一问呢?

7. How long will it take you to design this project?
   你们需要多久来设计这个项目?

8. I think it will take us at least one more month to finish the product design.
   我想我们至少还需要一个月的时间来完成产品设计。

9. Please go to the design department to pick up the manager.
   请去设计部接经理。

10. Please do welding, cutting and grinding.
    请做好焊接、切割和削磨的工作。

11. I'd like to draw your attention to the variation order issued by you on March 9.
    我想提醒你注意你方在3月9号下达的变更订单。

12. We are going to contract to build a project about the product design.
    我们准备承接一个关于产品设计的项目。

13. We are executing a railway construction project.
    我们正在执行一个铁路建设项目。

14. I do hope that this can be settled in a friendly way.
    我特别希望这个问题可以友好解决。

15. We could provide relevant information for you, but you must promise to keep it secret.
    我方可以提供相关信息,但你方必须承诺保守秘密。

16. The new design method is worth trying.

新的设计方法值得尝试。

17. We plan to export over ten million dollars' worth of materials and equipment.

    我们计划出口价值 1000 多万美元的材料和设备。

18. Please tell us the facts. Don't elaborate on them.

    请告诉我们事实，不要多做解释。

19. Is the design in accordance with the latest version?

    是按照最新的版本来设计的吗?

20. We will try our best to meet your design requirement.

    我们将尽力满足您的设计要求。

Topic 5 Mould Machining

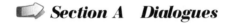 **Section A Dialogues**

 Dialogue 1

Joe：Professor   Grace：Manufacturer

Joe： Have you any questions on this set of mould machining?

Grace： Yes. I need to ask you some questions. Now, we have the basic information about this mould, such as the type of **mould machine**, **cavity** number, product material, **gating system** and so on. But we don't have the **gating requirements**, surface requirements of the product and the standard of spare parts. Firstly, can you tell me whether the product surface is a visible one? How to do surface treatment, **texture** or **polishing**?

Joe： Yes, it is. Please make the texture on this side.

Grace： Well, I know. In addition, the 2D and **3D drawing** provided by you is not the same. Can you tell me which one is correct?

Joe： Please use the 3D drawing. In fact, I have already copied mould **specification**, 3D drawing and customer's data to your leader. Have you received them?

Grace： Yes, we have. We found there was no **draft angle** in the 3D drawing, and in some places the glue is too thick. So we need to check it with you again.

Joe： Is that? I remember the draft angle in the 3D drawing has been added except for some **ribs**. But it will not affect the mould structure. Is your work in accordance with the latest **version**?

Grace: Sorry, I'm not sure. I will double check this and tell you later, OK?

Joe: All right. Moreover, is the mould fully **automatic** running?

Grace: Maybe. The part may hang on the **angle lifter**. If needed, we will consider two stage **ejections**. But we need to make some pictures later and confirm with you again.

Joe: OK. Any other questions?

Grace: No further questions. Thank you, professor.

Joe: You are welcome.

 Vocabulary

cavity	/ˈkævəti/	n.	腔,凹处,洞
texture	/ˈtekstʃə(r)/	n.	晒纹
polishing	/ˈpɒlɪʃɪŋ/	n.	抛光
specification	/ˌspesɪfɪˈkeɪʃn/	n.	规格,规范,工程设计(书)
rib	/rɪb/	n.	骨状物,肋骨,翼助
version	/ˈvɜːʃn/	n.	版本
automatic	/ˌɔːtəˈmætɪk/	adj.	自动的
ejection	/iˈdʒekʃn/	n.	喷出,射出,喷出物
mould machine			注塑机
gating system			浇注系统
gating requirement			浇口要求
3D drawing			三维绘图
draft angle			拔模角
angle lifter			斜顶

 Dialogue 2

Peter: *Professor*   Steven: *Student*

Steven: Professor, may I ask you some questions about my curriculum design if you are free?

Peter: Sure. What can I do for you?

Steven: The following is the mould information I will design. Could you check whether it is

Unit 2　Mechanical and Electric Control Engineering

right? The length of this part is 310.02 mm, width 68.47 mm, height 36 mm, thickness 1.8 mm, weight 59.93 kg. The mould machine is 230 T, and the material is black. The outside of the part makes texture, inner side needs polishing, and it also needs a **date stamp**.

Peter: Well, it is correct.

Steven: Is this mould dimension measured in **inch** or **meter**? Does it need spare parts?

Peter: I think it should be measured in meter. Moreover, you had better prepare a complete set of **spare parts** in case of need.

Steven: Yes, professor. In addition, there is an **undercut** at this position and I will make the angle lifter and **slide** in this position. Is that OK?

Peter: Yes, that's OK. After finishing it, you will find it will also have **parting line** on this side.

Steven: The rib here is too thick and on the low side, so it will be difficult to fill here when we do the injection. Can I reduce the thickness of this rib?

Peter: There are two options if you choose to reduce, that is to make **inserts** or **welding**.

Steven: It is a pity that I have made the texture on this side. If I **reduce plastic**, it will take about five days to redo the texture. Then I can not hand in my work on time. Do I have your **permission**?

Peter: I need to discuss this problem with other professors and then I will reply to you.

Steven: Thank you, professor.

Vocabulary

inch	/ɪntʃ/	n.	英寸
meter	/ˈmiːtə(r)/	n.	米
undercut	/ˌʌndəˈkʌt/	n.	底切,底部掏槽
slide	/slaɪd/	n.	行位,滑板,滑道
insert	/ɪnˈsɜːt/	n.	镶嵌物,镶块
welding	/ˈweldɪŋ/	n.	焊接
permission	/pəˈmɪʃn/	n.	许可
date stamp			日期戳,邮戳
spare part			备用零件
parting line			分型线
reduce plastic			减胶

Section B Notes

1. mould machine（注塑机）：注塑机又名注射成型机或注射机。它是将热塑性塑料或热固性塑料利用塑料成型模具制成各种形状的塑料制品的主要成型设备，分为立式、卧式、全电式。注塑机能加热塑料，对熔融塑料施加高压，使其射出并充满模具型腔。注塑机是塑料加工业中使用量最大的加工机械，不仅有大量的产品可用注塑机直接生产，而且还是组成注拉吹工艺的关键设备。中国已成为世界塑机台件生产的第一大国。

2. gating system（浇注系统）：是为将液态金属引入铸型型腔而在铸型内开设的通道。浇注系统包括：

（1）浇口杯。承接浇包倒进来的金属液，也称外浇口。

（2）直浇口。连接外浇口和横浇口，将金属液由铸型外面引入铸型内部。

（3）横浇口。连接直浇口，分配由直浇口来的金属液。

（4）内浇口。连接横浇口，向铸型型腔灌输金属液。

3. angle lifter（斜销）：塑胶模具中的一种附件，是用来成型塑胶产品中的侧边成型面。斜销分多面斜销和直面斜销等几种。

4. draft angle（拔模角）：为了让工件更好地脱离模具而人为地设定的工件与模具分模面相交的侧面切向与模具分模面法向之间的夹角。在锻造造型时，为了易于把模型从砂型中取出，通常沿铸件拔模标目的的内、外壁上均制有约1：20的斜度，叫拔模斜度。拔模斜度通常较小，并且须在图纸上进行标注。

Section C Exercises

I. Translate the following words or phrases into Chinese.

1. polishing
2. ejection
3. 3D drawing
4. angle lifter
5. specification
6. undercut
7. permission
8. spare part

II. Translate the following words or phrases into English.

1. 自动的
2. 晒纹
3. 浇注系统
4. 拔模角
5. 镶嵌物
6. 邮戳
7. 减胶
8. 焊接

Ⅲ. **Role play.**

A is a student majoring in Mould Machining, and B is a professor. A wants to ask B some questions about his curriculum design. Try to use the words and phrases you have learned to ask and answer questions.

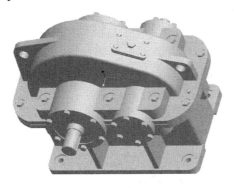

Section D Related Words and Phrases

1.	manufacture	制造
2.	machining	用机器制造,对……进行机械加工
3.	workshop	车间
4.	work piece	工件
5.	cutting machine	切割机
6.	cutting piece	切片
7.	grinding machine	磨削机
8.	lathe	车床
9.	numerical control lathe	数控车床
10.	lathe tool	车刀
11.	laser marking machine	激光标刻机
12.	fitter	钳工
13.	grinding wheel	砂轮
14.	bore	钻削,镗孔
15.	turning	车削工作
16.	tapping machine	攻丝机
17.	punch	冲床
18.	shaping machine	成形机
19.	saw tooth	锯齿

20.	electrical welding	电焊
21.	welding torch	焊接枪
22.	spindle	主轴,杆,轴
23.	lubricating oil	润滑油
24.	linear cutting	线切割
25.	welder	焊机
26.	waste	废料
27.	rust	生锈
28.	deformation	变形

Section E Useful Expressions and Sentences

1. Please read the operation manual carefully.
   请仔细阅读操作手册。

2. Please observe the instructions in the manual strictly.
   请严格遵照手册中的说明。

3. Please check all the machines at fixed periods.
   请定期检修机器。

4. Please turn off the main power switch.
   请切断主电源开关。

5. It is time to have lunch. Let's discuss this project later this afternoon.
   午饭时间到了,我们下午再继续讨论这个项目吧。

6. Please use good quality diesel fuel.
   请使用优质柴油。

7. Please check the position wetted with oil on the gauge.
   请检查一下油标尺的油湿位置。

8. Please apply a thin coat of lubricating oil on the inside of the outside oil hoses by brush every other day.
   请每隔一天用刷子在外露油管内侧涂上一层薄薄的润滑油。

9. Please put a cover on the oil hoses.
   请将油管盖好。

10. Please place a fire extinguisher near at hand.
    请在身边备一个灭火器。

11. The compressor automatic change snap switch is set at "Auto".

压缩机自动转换开关处于自动位置。

12. Please press the compressor run push-button switch.

    请按下压缩机启动开关按钮。

13. You should have finished welding last week.

    你们本应上周就该完成焊接工作。

14. What if the steel bars get rusty?

    钢板生锈了怎么办?

15. Water and power will be made available on the site by March 13.

    工地将在 3 月 13 号前通水通电。

16. We are in urgent need of 20 tons of steel sheet.

    我们急需 20 吨钢板。

17. I happened to see him when I negotiated the contract in the mould factory yesterday.

    昨天我在模具厂洽谈合同时正好看到他。

18. About this problem, I need to discuss with other colleagues, and then I will reply to you.

    就这个问题,我需要和其他同事商议后,再答复您。

19. Can we modify these production problems by ourselves?

    我们可以自己更改这些产品问题吗?

20. This action will not affect the mould structure.

    这种做法不会影响模具结构。

Topic 6　Electrical Automation

Section A　Dialogues

Dialogue 1

Abby: I have a **LED** (**light emitting diode**). Can you help me design a **circuit** to **light** it **up**?
Betty: Sure. What is the **voltage** of the **power**?
Abby: I have a 12 V **automobile battery**.
Betty: Could you tell me the **working parameters** of your LED?
Abby: Let me see. Oh, the **working voltage** is 2 V and the **working current** is 10 mA.

Betty: We need to install a **voltage dropping resistor**.

Abby: What is it? How does it work?

Betty: The opposition to current is called electrical resistance and is represented by the letter symbol R. The unit of resistance is the ohm, a term that is often expressed by using Ω. One ohm is defined as that amount of resistance that will limit the current in a conductor which is one ampere when the voltage applied to the **conductor** is one volt.

Abby: Well, what is the value of the **resistor**? How do we **figure** it **out**?

Betty: Have you learned **Ohm's Law**?

Abby: Got it. The resistor and diode are **in series**, and the current is both 10 mA. But what is the voltage of the resistor?

Betty: The voltage of the resistor should be the voltage of the automobile battery minus LED's working voltage.

Abby: Yes. It is 10 V (12 V – 2 V).

Betty: Absolutely. Based on Ohm's Law, we can use the **formula** (R = U/I) to calculate the value of the resistor which equals 1,000 ohms.

Abby: I have learned a lot. Thank you very much for your help.

Betty: You are welcome!

Vocabulary

circuit	/ˈsɜːkɪt/	n.	电路
voltage	/ˈvəʊltɪdʒ/	n.	电压,伏特数
power	/ˈpaʊə(r)/	n.	电源
battery	/ˈbæt(ə)ri/	n.	电瓶
parameter	/pəˈræmɪtə/	n.	参数
current	/ˈkʌrnt/	n.	电流
conductor	/kənˈdʌktə(r)/	n.	导体
resistor	/rɪˈzɪstə(r)/	n.	电阻
formula	/ˈfɔːmjələ/	n.	公式
LED(light emitting diode)			发光二极管
light up			照亮,点亮
automobile battery			汽车电瓶
working parameter			工作参数

working voltage	工作电压
working current	工作电流
voltage dropping resistor	降压电阻
figure out	计算,解决
Ohm's Law	欧姆定律
in series	串联

Dialogue 2

Gary: Hi, what are you doing?

Paul: I'm reading a book about **robots**.

Gary: Oh, I am also interested in intelligent robots.

Paul: Really? It is said that robots are very useful in industry, and robots can do some things more efficiently than people. Do you think so?

Gary: Yes, I think so. For example, robots never get sick or need to rest, so they can work 24 hours a day, 7 days one week.

Paul: Oh, I see. When the task would be dangerous and risky for a person, robots can do the work instead.

Gary: What else have you learned from the book?

Paul: I also got that although robots cannot do every type of job, there are certain tasks they do very well: **assembling operations, continuous arc welding and spot welding, packaging, spray coating, material removal, machine loading, material transfer, cutting operations, part inspection, part sorting, part cleaning** and **part polishing**.

Gary: Wow! It is unbelievable. Can you elaborate on the robot welding?

Paul: Yes. Welding is one of the most common uses for industrial robots and robot welded car bodies could enhance safety since a robot never misses a welding spot and does equally well all through the day.

Gary: It is really a hard-working robot. Well, how does a robot perform in the part sorting? I cannot imagine it! How can it tell the different parts?

Paul: Well, let's first talk about the **visional sensory** with which the robot is able to determine the location and recognize the parts to be picked up.

Gary: Visional sensory is amazing! What about the **tactile sensory**? How does it work?

Paul: It is a complex question. To simulate tactile like in human hands, a tactile-sensing system must perform some fundamental operations, such as (1) the joint face sensor that senses the force applied to the robot's hand, wrist and arm points; (2) the touch sensor which senses the pressure applied to various points on the hands' surface.

Gary: Oh, I've got it. Thank you so much for your patience and explanation. I will have a date with my girlfriend. Let's talk more next time.

Paul: It's my pleasure. See you.

 Vocabulary

robot	/ˈrəʊbɒt/	n.	机器人
welding	/ˈweldɪŋ/	v.	焊
packaging	/ˈpækɪdʒɪŋ/	n.	包装
assembling operation			装配业务
continuous arc welding and spot welding			连续电弧焊和点焊
spray coating			喷涂
material removal			物料去除
machine loading			机器装载
material transfer			物料传送
cutting operation			切割作业
part inspection			部件检验
part sorting			零件筛选
part cleaning			零件清洗
part polishing			零件抛光
visional sensory			视觉传感器
tactile sensory			触觉传感器

Section B Notes

1. voltage dropping resistor(降压电阻):电荷在导体中运动时,会受到分子和原子等其他粒子的碰撞与摩擦,碰撞和摩擦的结果形成了导体对电流的阻碍,这种阻碍作用最明显的特征是导体消耗电能而发热(或发光)。物体对电流的这种阻碍作用,称为该物体的电阻。

2. Ohm's Law(欧姆定律):在同一电路中,导体中的电流跟导体两端的电压成正比,跟导体的电阻成反比,这就是欧姆定律。

3. working voltage(工作电压):电压,也称作电势差或电位差,是衡量单位电荷在静电场中由于电势不同所产生的能量差的物理量。其大小等于单位正电荷因受电场力作用从 A 点移动到 B 点所做的功,电压的方向规定为从高电位指向低电位。电压的国际单位制为伏特(V),常用的单位还有毫伏(mV)、微伏(μV)、千伏(kV)等。

4. working current(工作电流):科学上把单位时间里通过导体任一横截面的电量叫作电流强度,简称电流。通常用字母 I 表示。它的单位是安培。安德烈·玛丽·安培(1775—1836),法国物理学家、化学家,在电磁作用方面的研究成就卓著,对数学和物理也有贡献。电流的国际单位安培即以其姓氏命名,简称"安",符号为"A"。

Section C Exercises

Ⅰ. Translate the following words or phrases into Chinese.

1. working voltage
2. working current
3. conductor
4. Ohm's Law
5. voltage dropping resistor
6. robot
7. visional sensory
8. tactile sensory

Ⅱ. Translate the following words or phrases into English.

1. 点亮
2. 点焊
3. 电路
4. 切割作业
5. 包装
6. 装配业务
7. 零件筛选
8. 零件抛光

Ⅲ. Role play.

Your major is Electrical and Computer Automation, and A is your classmate. Now you are confused about Ohm's Law. First, try to use the words and phrases you have learned to ask A some questions, and then exchange the roles between you and A.

Section D Related Words and Phrases

1. distribution circuit		直流配电线路
2. emergency lighting circuit		事故照明线路
3. control circuit		控制线路
4. signal circuit		信号线路
5. flashing-signal circuit		闪光信号回路

6.	precipitator	催化剂
7.	transformer	变压器
8.	lightning protector	避雷器
9.	three-phase alternating current	三相交流电
10.	power distribution cabinet	动力配电箱
11.	control cabinet	控制箱
12.	fuse	保险丝
13.	voltage regulator	电压调节器
14.	internal resistance	内电阻
15.	transmission and distribution system	供配电系统
16.	circuit breaker	电路断路器
17.	capacitor	电容
18.	rectifier	整流器
19.	power loss	功率损耗
20.	oscilloscope	示波器
21.	ammeter	电流表
22.	voltmeter	电压表
23.	ohmmeter	欧姆表
24.	multimeter	万用表
25.	positive pole	正极
26.	negative pole	负极
27.	cross section area	截面积
28.	continuous load	连续负荷
29.	constant speed	恒定转速
30.	three-phase winding	三相绕组
31.	rotating magnetic field	旋转磁场

Section E Useful Expressions and Sentences

1. The current is dependent on the voltage of the battery, on the dimensions of sample, and on the conductivity of the material itself.
   流过材料的电流取决于电池的电压、材料的截面积和材料自身的电阻率。

2. When a current passes through the coil, a magnetic field is set up around it that tends to oppose rapid changes in current intensity.

当电流通过线圈时,线圈周围将产生磁场,它将对抗电流的快速变化。

3. The control program is the computer program stored in the PLC memory that tells the PLC what's supposed to be going on in the system.

控制程序是储存在 PLC 存储器内的计算机程序,它指示 PLC 在系统中下一步应该继续做什么。

4. Providing power to the microcontroller is the last piece of the mechatronic system.

在机电一体化系统,微处理器的动力源也不能漏掉。

5. Installing robots is often a way by which business owners can be more competitive, because robots can do some things more efficiently than people.

因为机器人工作比人更有效率,安装机器人往往使企业家更有竞争力。

6. The most popular technology for realizing microcircuits makes use of MOS transistor.

用来实现微电路的最通用的技术是利用 MOS 管。

7. It is easier to perform quality assurance by a spot-check instead of checking all parts.

通过抽检代替全检,质量更容易得到保证。

8. CAM main functions include: digital control, process design, robotics and factory management.

CAM 主要功能包括:数字控制、工艺设计、机器人技术和工厂管理。

9. Numerical control uses coded information to control machine tool movements.

数控就是使用编码信息来控制加工机器的运动。

10. Process planning is involved with the detailed sequence of production steps from start to finish.

工艺设计是指从开始到结束的详细生产步骤。

11. CAD is an acronym of computer-aided design, and CAM stands for computer-aided manufacturing.

CAD 是计算机辅助设计的缩写形式,而 CAM 则代表计算机辅助制造。

12. In brief, the operation of the plant is as follows: coal is taken from storage and fed to a pulverizer (or mill), mixed with preheated air, and blown into the furnace, where it is burned.

简单地说,电厂的运行是这样的:煤从仓库取出,送入一个粉碎机,与预先加热的空气混合后喷入锅炉,在锅炉中燃烧。

13. Since the power transmitted is equal to the product of the current, the voltage and power factor, the same amount of power can be transmitted with a lower current by increasing the voltage.

因为所传输的有功功率等于电流、电压和功率因数的乘积,因此,通过增加电压,减少电流可以传输相同的功率。

Topic 7 Automation Equipment

Section A Dialogues

 Dialogue 1

A: *Interviewer*   B: *Candidate*

A: Come in, please.

B: Good morning, sir.

A: Morning. Have a seat, please. I'm the interviewer, John White.

B: Thank you. I'm Li Jun.

A: I have read your **CV**. Why did you choose to major in **Mechanical Automation**?

B: Many factors led me to make the choice. The most important one is that I always have a dream of people's adoption of the machines that I've designed one day.

A: Do you think you can be **qualified** for this job?

B: Yes! I have been studying for 4 years in the Department of Mechanical Engineering, and it has helped me to build a solid rationale foundation. Moreover, I have been working at another company for 4 years, which enables me to gain lots of practical experience. I came here for broader development space.

A: So, what do you know about our company?

B: Of course. Jinyuan Science and Technology Company was founded in 2003. It focuses on **comprehensive** manufacturing service, for example, robotics, mechanical design, customized assembly line, automation equipment and so on. With **abundant** experience, Jinyuan has become a leader in the research and development of automation equipment and customized **fixtures** in China.

A: Great. You prepared a lot for today's interview. What is your **technical title** now?

B: I'm a **senior mechanical engineer**.

A: Do you have any **certificate** with you?

B: Here it is. And, these are my designs. Some of them have been **applied for patents**.

A: Can you briefly introduce one of your designs?

B: OK. This is my favorite—4 workstations integrated equipment. It includes a twelve-axis robot module, four feeders and eight trays for precise positioning. Meanwhile, it is

Unit 2 Mechanical and Electric Control Engineering

equipped with automated ejectors and Chinese-English operating interface.

A: That sounds pretty good! How do you see your career development?

B: I would like to be a manager of the Research and Development Department after **accumulating** enough experience and furthering my profession.

A: That's fine.

 Vocabulary

CV (curriculum vitae)	/ˌsiːˈviː/(/kəˈrɪkjələm ˈviːtaɪ/)		履历
qualified	/ˈkwɒlɪfaɪd/	adj.	合格的,有资格的
comprehensive	/ˌkɒmprɪˈhensɪv/	adj.	综合的,广泛的
abundant	/əˈbʌndənt/	adj.	丰富的
fixture	/ˈfɪkstʃə(r)/	n.	装置器,固定装置
certificate	/səˈtɪfɪkət/	n.	证书,执照
accumulate	/əˈkjuːmjəleɪt/	v.	积累
mechanical automation			机械自动化
technical title			技术职称
senior mechanical engineer			高级机械工程师
apply for patents			申请专利

 Dialogue 2

A: Customer service staff   B: Client

A: Hello! This is Taidong Science and Technology Company. What can I do for you?

B: Hello! I'm looking for some equipment for my **assembly line**. Someone recommended your company to me. But I'm afraid I'm not familiar with your company or products.

A: Please let me do a brief introduction of our company. Taidong, founded in 2003, is **specialized** in designing and manufacturing the most advanced and **innovative** automation equipment in computer and communications. We have more than 2,000 employees around the world, and 200 sets of machining equipment.

B: I would like to know what your core business and services are.

A: Focused on continuous investigation in new technologies, Taidong has been a leader in robotics, mechanical design, and automation equipment. We can even customize a fully automated assembly line for you.

B: Actually, I'm quite interested in automation equipment because I'm preparing a new assembly line. I just need some machines.

A: Well then, we are your best choice. Taidong uses the latest **CCD** (**charge coupled device**) inspection systems, laser measure techniques, and **multi-axis** robots to achieve accurate and high-speed assembly. What kind of equipment do you need?

B: I need equipment which can assemble a small-sized light diffuser onto a screen instead of manual assembly.

A: We can certainly meet your requirement—light diffuser and cover glass automated assembly machine. This is a whole new product from Taidong.

B: Can you tell me more details about this machine?

A: It includes a four-axis robotic arm, two **conveyors**, and three CCD cameras for more precise positioning. The machine's motion control system is fully **programmable**. **Application program** is easy to **optimize**. And you can update all data at any time. It largely promotes saving in labor, production, and **FPY** (**first pass yield**).

B: You have mentioned the CCD camera. What is the strong point of it?

A: The integrated CCD vision system can monitor the robot **real-time** motion with high precision.

B: OK. I want to **place an order** now!

Vocabulary

specialize	/ˈspeʃəlaɪz/	v.	专门从事,专门研究
innovative	/ˈɪnəveɪtɪv/	adj.	革新的,新颖的
multi-axis	/ˈmʌltɪæksɪs/	adj.	多轴的
conveyor	/kənˈveɪə(r)/	n.	传送带,传递带
programmable	/prəʊˈɡræməbl/	adj.	可编程序的
optimize	/ˈɒptɪmaɪz/	v.	使优化,使最佳化
real-time	/ˈriːəltaɪm/	adj.	实时的
assembly line			装配线
CCD(charge coupled device)			电荷耦合装置
application program			应用程序
FPY(first pass yield)			直通率,一次性通过的成品率
place an order			订购,下单

Section B Notes

1. CV(curriculum vitae)(履历)：和 resume 相比较，CV 通常更加详细（一般都要两页纸及以上），涵盖更加全面。在美国，CV 主要用于申请学术、教育、科研职位，或者申请奖学金等，而在欧洲、非洲和亚洲等地，CV 则更常用于应征工作。现在常常有人把 CV 和 resume 混起来，统称为"简历"，其实精确而言，CV 应该是"履历"，resume 才是"简历"。resume 概述了与求职有关的教育准备和经历，是对经验技能的摘要，其主要目的在于说服用人单位老板雇用自己；curriculum vitae 则集中说明学术工作，不重视与文化程度和学习成绩无直接关系的资料。

2. CCD(charge coupled device)(电荷耦合装置)：作为一种集成电路，电荷耦合装置上有许多排列整齐的电容，能感应光线，并将影像转变成数字信号，经由外部电路的控制，每个小电容都能将其所带的电荷转给它相邻的电容。它是代替照相像底，用来记录影像的电子元件。CCD 像素所含的电量和入射到像素的光强度成正比。CCD 记录光的效率约是 70%，远高于传统底片的 2%，所以广泛应用在数码摄影、天文学等领域。

3. FPY(first pass yield)(直通率)：是衡量生产线出产品质水准的一项指标，用以描述生产质量、工作质量或测试质量的某种状况。具体含义是指，在生产线投入 100 套材料中，制作过程中第一次就通过了所有测试的产品数量。因此，经过生产线的返工(rework)或修复才通过测试的产品，将不被列入直通率的计算中。通常有以下两种形式（依生产取样不同而异）计算 FPY：(1)直通率 = [进入过程件数 − (返工 + 返修数 + 退货数)]/过程件数 × 100%；(2)直通率 = (直通合格数/投入总数) × 100%。

4. multi-axis robot(多轴机器人)：又称单轴机械手、工业机械臂、电缸等，是以 XYZ 直角坐标系统为基本数学模型，以伺服电机、步进电机为驱动的单轴机械臂为基本工作单元，以滚珠丝杆、同步皮带、齿轮齿条为常用的传动方式所架构起来的机器人系统，可以完成在 XYZ 三维坐标系中任意一点的到达，也可遵循可控的运动轨迹。多轴机器人采用运动控制系统实现对其驱动及编程控制，直线、曲线等运动轨迹的生成为多点插补方式，操作及编程方式为引导示教编程方式或坐标定位方式。

Section C Exercise

Ⅰ. **Translate the following words or phrases into Chinese.**

1. mechanical engineering
2. certificate
3. core business
4. automation equipment
5. manufacture
6. programmable
7. technical title
8. place an order

Ⅱ. **Translate the following words or phrases into English.**

1. 理论基础
2. 革新的,新款的
3. 机械工程师
4. 操作界面
5. 定制
6. 使优化,使最佳化
7. 装配线
8. 申请专利

Ⅲ. **Make an introduction of the following machine by using the following words and phrases.**

LED die-bonding machine
LED 固晶机(把需要固晶的产品固晶在治具上面)

1. assemble … onto … 在……上装备……
2. increase productivity 提高生产力
3. operate at a high speed 以高速运转
4. three-axis robot arms 三轴机械臂
5. ensure the stability of … 确保……的稳定性
6. guarantee its long-running accuracy 保证长期准确性

Section D Related Words and Phrases

1. admissible error		容许误差
2. annunciator		信号器
3. assignment problem		配置问题,分配问题
4. bottom-up development		自下而上开发
5. control accuracy		控制精度
6. data acquisition		数据采集
7. digitization		数字化
8. economic effectiveness		经济效益
9. effectiveness		有效性

10. feasibility study	可行性研究
11. frequency converter	变频器
12. industrial automation	工业自动化
13. input-output model	投入产出模型
14. linear programming	线性规划
15. man-machine coordination	人机协调
16. MAP (manufacturing automation protocol)	制造自动化协议
17. MB (model base)	模型库
18. on-line assistance	在线帮助
19. peak time	峰值时间
20. production budget	生产预算
21. real-time telemetry	实时遥测
22. rectifier	整流器
23. robot programming language	机器人编程语言
24. signal detection and estimation	信号检测和估计
25. tachometer	转速表

Section E Useful Expressions and Sentences

1. Why did you choose to major in Mechanical Automation?
   为什么选择机械自动化专业？

2. Many factors led me to choose this major.
   很多因素导致我选这个专业。

3. Do you think you can be qualified for this job?
   你觉得你能胜任这份工作吗？

4. It focuses on comprehensive manufacturing services.
   它致力于综合制造业服务。

5. It has become a leader in the research and development of automation equipment.
   它已经是自动化设备研发领域的领导者了。

6. Some of my designs have been applied for patents.
   我的一些设计已经申请了专利。

7. It is equipped with automated ejectors and the Chinese-English operating interface.
   它装载了自动进出器和中英文操作界面。

8. I'm looking for some equipment for my assembly line/production line.

我正在为我的装配线/生产线寻找一些设备。

9. What is your core business or service?

   你的核心商业或服务是什么?

10. We can even customize a fully automated assembly line for you.

    我们甚至可以为你定制一条完全自动的装配线。

11. The machine's motion control system is fully programmable. Application program is easy to optimize. And you can update all data at any time.

    这款机器的运动控制系统是完全编程的,应用程序很容易优化。你还可以在任意时间更新你的数据。

12. It largely promotes saving in labor, production, and FPY(first pass yield).

    它大大节省了劳动力,增加了产量和直通率。

13. I want to place an order now!

    我现在就想下订单了。

14. The machine adopts imported automatic control; labor intensity is low.

    本机采用进口全自动控制,工人劳动强度低。

15. The system may include a processor, a memory, and an operation interface.

    该系统将包含一个处理器、一个储存器和一个操作界面。

16. This paper introduces a kind of real-time telemetry and tele-monitoring system.

    这篇文章介绍了一种实时遥测与监护系统。

17. I would like to be a manager of the Research and Development Department after accumulating enough experience and furthering my profession.

    我希望能在积累足够经验和专业知识后,成为研发部的管理人员。

18. When the device is placed on the pad, the two recognize each other through built-in sensors.

    当把这种装置放在平板上时,二者通过内置传感器相互识别。

19. The customization products, service with low cost, and high equality are the core competence of the mass customization pattern.

    定制化的产品,其低成本、高质量的服务是批量定制生产模式的核心竞争力。

20. There remains a direct and intimate connection between automated equipment and production management software.

    自动化设备和生产管理软件之间保持着直接和密切的联系。

科技英语知识

科技英语词汇的特点(二)

上一单元我们已经讨论过科技英语词汇的 3 个特征,它们分别是常用词汇专业化、广泛使用缩略词、大量使用合成词。本单元将会从科技英语词汇的来源和结构方面谈谈它的特点。

1. 多来源于希腊语和拉丁语

在科技英语词汇中,有将近一半的科技词汇直接来源于希腊语和拉丁语。还有一部分,则是根据希腊语和拉丁语的词素新造出来的。尽管这两种语言的使用早已不再流行,但它们的词素还广泛用于科技词汇,特别是化学、生物学、药物学和医学中。例如:

semi-(半)→semi-metal(半金属)　　　di-(二,双)→diode(二极管)
meth-(甲基)→methane(甲烷)　　　　mono-(单一)→mono-plus(单脉冲)

2. 借用其他学科词汇

某些新兴学科常会从相关学科借用一些词汇,再赋予它们新的内涵,从而孕育出该学科的一些新词汇,这也极大地丰富了现代英语词汇。例如:

bit(钻头【石油】)→bit(刨刀【机械】)
input(输入电路【无线电】)→input(输入【计算机】)

3. 广泛使用前缀、后缀

科技英语词汇主要是通过缀合法派生的,派生法是形成科技英语词汇的一种主要手段。根据词根所加词缀的位置,派生法有添加前缀(prefixion)和后缀(suffixation)两种。例如:

de-(脱,除)→degreaser(脱脂剂)
anti-(防,抗)→anti-acid(抗酸的)　　anti-age(防老化的)
-meter(计,仪)→mega-meter(兆米)　spectrometer(分光计)

Unit 3

Civil and Architectural Engineering

Topic 8   Civil Engineering

Section A   Dialogues

Dialogue 1

*Kevin: Headman   Joe: **Supervisor***

Kevin: Good afternoon, Joe.

Joe: Good afternoon. This afternoon our task is to install this receiving tower. Your team should follow the instruction. Please read the instruction and **erection drawing** carefully before you start. Here is the erection drawing and the **general drawing** of this tower.

Kevin: Thank you. Firstly, I would like to check some information about the receiving tower, such as the weight, height, and **center of gravity**.

Joe: The weight of this receiving tower is 40 tons. It's here.

Kevin: It's so heavy. How about the height? Is it over 50 meters?

Joe: Yeah, that's right.

Kevin: Supervisor, I don't understand the meaning of this **invisible** line.

Joe: It means that the center of gravity is 20 meters from the bottom of the receiving tower.

Kevin: Oh, thank you.

Joe: Please remember to check over the following tools: **electrical winch**, **wire ropes**, **pulleys**, etc., and make sure all of them are in good condition. And also don't forget to check the **anchor bolt** once more with the aid of the drawing.

Kevin: Thank you for reminding me of it.
Joe: It's my pleasure.
Kevin: Er ... I can't see this part clearly. Are there any **modifications** on this erection drawing?
Joe: Let me see. Oh, this is one **copy** of the **original**; these letters and the scale of the drawings are **blurred**.
Kevin: Could you please check these letters and the scale?
Joe: Let me check them. That's the original. Here you are.
Kevin: Thank you, supervisor. Everything is ready, and we have checked over them.
Joe: Good. Let's start, please.
Kevin: Pay attention, everyone! Listen to my order ... Good, the tower has been on its position. The **perpendicular tolerance** of the tower is less than one **thousandth** of its height. **Acceptable**!
Joe: OK. Tighten the **anchor nuts**. Take a rest, please.
Kevin: Thank you so much.

Vocabulary

supervisor	/ˈsjuːpəvaɪzə(r)/	n.	监督人,管理人
invisible	/ɪnˈvɪzəbl/	adj.	隐形的,看不见的
pulley	/ˈpʊli/	n.	滑轮
modification	/ˌmɒdɪfɪˈkeɪʃn/	n.	修改,修正
copy	/ˈkɒpi/	n.	副本,复制品
original	/əˈrɪdʒənl/	n.	原件,原型,原作
blurred	/blɜːd/	adj.	模糊不清的
thousandth	/ˈθaʊzənθ/	n.	千分之一
acceptable	/əkˈseptəbl/	adj.	可接受的
erection drawing			安装图
general drawing			总规划图
center of gravity			重心
electrical winch			电动绞车
wire rope			钢丝绳,钢索
anchor bolt			地脚螺栓

perpendicular tolerance	垂直偏差
anchor nut	地脚螺母

Dialogue 2

*Josh: **Sophomore**   Ellen: Freshman*

Ellen: Hello, my name is Ellen. I'm a freshman in this university.

Josh: Hi, my name is Josh. I'm a sophomore in this college. Glad to meet you!

Ellen: Oh, I'm so lucky. You are my **senior fellow**. What's your major?

Josh: My major is Civil Engineering. How about yours?

Ellen: The same as yours. Could you please tell me something about civil engineering?

Josh: Yeah. Firstly, I would like to tell you that our civil work includes construction of roads, buildings, **foundations** and **reinforced concrete structure**.

Ellen: What kinds of materials will we use to construct houses?

Josh: Sand, brick and stone are generally used.

Ellen: Got it. I know that **concrete** is one of the most important materials for buildings. How do construction workers get concrete?

Josh: The concrete material is mixed in a **rotating-drum batch mixer** of some construction company at the job site.

Ellen: Oh, how do we evaluate the quality of the concrete?

Josh: The quality of the concrete depends on proper **placing, finishing and caring**.

Ellen: If we want to enhance the strength of the concrete, what should we do?

Josh: Normally, concrete can be made stronger by **pre-stressing**.

Ellen: Please tell me something about the engineering materials. What are the most important construction materials used in civil engineering?

Josh: **Cement**, steel and **timber** are the most important construction materials used in civil engineering. As far as I know, there are four broad classifications of steel: **carbon steel, alloy steel, high-strength low-alloy steel** and **stainless steel**.

Ellen: Thanks! I have learned a lot. Can I have your telephone number and **WeChat ID**?

Josh: My telephone No. is 18878020006, and WeChat ID is 445566@hotmail.com.

Ellen: I really appreciate your kindness. Hope to see you again.

Unit 3 Civil and Architectural Engineering

Vocabulary

sophomore	/ˈsɒfəmɔː(r)/	n.	大学二年级学生
foundation	/faʊnˈdeɪʃn/	n.	地基,基础
concrete	/ˈkɒŋkriːt/	n.	混凝土
pre-stress	/priːˈstres/	v.	预加应力
cement	/sɪˈment/	n.	水泥
timber	/ˈtɪmbə(r)/	n.	木材
senior fellow			师兄,学长
reinforced concrete structure			钢筋混凝土结构
rotating-drum batch mixer			间歇式转筒搅拌机
placing, finishing and caring			浇筑、饰面(抹光)、养护
carbon steel			碳素钢
alloy steel			合金钢
high-strength low-alloy steel			高强度低合金钢
stainless steel			不锈钢
WeChat ID			微信号

Section B Notes

1. civil engineering(土木工程):是建造各类工程设施的科学技术的统称。它既指所应用的材料、设备和所进行的勘测、设计、施工、保养、维修等技术活动,也指工程建设的对象,即建造在地上或地下、陆上或水中,直接或间接为人类生活、生产、军事、科研服务的各种工程设施,例如房屋、道路、铁路、管道、隧道、桥梁、运河、堤坝、港口、电站、飞机场、海洋平台、给水排水及防护工程等。

2. perpendicular tolerance(垂直偏差):同一测站点上铅垂线与椭球面法线之间的夹角 u,即是垂直偏差。

3. reinforced concrete structure(钢筋混凝土结构):指用配有钢筋增强的混凝土制成的结构,其承重的主要构件是用钢筋混凝土建造的,包括薄壳结构、大模板现浇结构,以及使用滑模、升板等建造的钢筋混凝土结构的建筑物。这种结构中的钢筋承受拉力和混凝土承受压力,具有坚固、耐久、防火性能好、比钢结构节省钢材和成本低等优点。

4. concrete(混凝土):简称为"砼(tóng)",是指由胶凝材料将集料胶结成整体的工程复合材料的统称。通常讲的混凝土一词是指用水泥作胶凝材料,沙、石作集料,与水(可含外加剂和掺合料)按一定比例配合,经搅拌而得的水泥混凝土,也称普通混凝土。它广

53

泛应用于土木工程。

5. carbon steel(碳素钢)：是近代工业中使用最早、用量最大的基本材料。广泛应用于建筑、桥梁、铁道、车辆、船舶和各种机械制造工业,在近代石油化学工业、海洋开发等方面也得到大量使用。

6. alloy steel(合金钢)：钢里除铁、碳外,加入了其他的合金元素,就叫合金钢。在普通碳素钢基础上添加适量的一种或多种合金元素而构成的铁碳合金。根据添加元素的不同,以及采取的加工工艺,可获得高强度、高韧性、耐磨、耐腐蚀、耐低温、耐高温、无磁性等特殊性能。

7. high-strength low-alloy(HSLA)steel(高强度低合金钢)：通过加入少量合金元素以获得所需的强度水平的一类特定的钢。最常见的合金元素有铌、钒、钛等。常见的高强度低合金结构钢一般在钢号前加注其屈服强度,如 Q345,表明强度为 345 的高强度低合金结构钢。

Section C Exercises

Ⅰ. Translate the following words or phrases into Chinese.

1. freshman
2. reinforced concrete structure
3. finishing
4. concrete
5. cement
6. stainless steel
7. foundation
8. timber

Ⅱ. Translate the following words or phrases into English.

1. 大学二年级学生
2. 监理人
3. 浇筑、抹光、养护
4. 高强度低合金钢
5. 预加应力
6. 总规划图
7. 千分之一
8. 间歇式转筒搅拌机

Ⅲ. Match the Chinese with the following English.

1. general drawing	A. 滑轮
2. pulley	B. 模糊不清的
3. invisible	C. 总规划图
4. acceptable	D. 电动绞车
5. wire rope	E. 钢丝绳
6. perpendicular tolerance	F. 看不见的
7. modification	G. 垂直偏差

Unit 3 Civil and Architectural Engineering

（续表）

8. blurred	H. 原件
9. original	I. 可接受的
10. electrical winch	J. 修改,修正
11. anchor nut	K. 地脚螺母

Ⅳ. Role play.

Your major is Civil Engineering, and A is your classmate. Now you are confused about the construction materials for high buildings. First, try to use the words and phrases you have learned to ask A some questions, and then exchange the roles between you and A.

Section D Related Words and Phrases

1. procurement	采购,购买
2. technical proposal	技术方案,技术报价书
3. reference material	参考资料
4. preliminary (final) technical document	初步(最终)技术文件
5. plot plan	平面布置
6. truck crane	起重机
7. air (electric) powered grinder	气(电)动砂轮
8. double insulated	双重绝缘的
9. electrode holder	焊钳
10. welder	焊工,焊机
11. parallel-jaw vice	平口钳
12. grease gun	油枪
13. oiler	注油器,加油器

14. torque wrench 力矩扳手
15. bolt 螺栓
16. cast iron 铸铁
17. piling 打桩,桩
18. insulation 绝缘,隔热,隔音
19. cracker 破碎机,破碎器
20. cooler 冷却器,制冷装置
21. pressure vessel 压力容器
22. distilling column 蒸馏塔
23. pressure blower 高压鼓风机
24. screw jack(＝jackscrew) 螺旋千斤顶,螺旋起重器
25. overhaul 拆修,解体检修

Section E Useful Expressions and Sentences

1. A working drawing must be clear and complete.
   工作图必须简明完整。

2. Data on equipment can be found in the related information.
   有关设备的数据可从相关资料中找到。

3. The water has been treated (softened), but it is not drinkable water.
   这水经过处理(软化),但不是饮用水。

4. There is a switch board (control panel, distribution box) mounted on the wall.
   墙上装有一个开关板(控制盘、配电箱)。

5. Put on your safety helmet, please.
   请戴上安全帽。

6. Shall we go to the warehouse to check the equipment?
   我们去仓库去检查设备吗?

7. We must avoid as far as possible the damage of equipment during storage.
   我们必须尽量避免设备在储存期间损坏。

8. This is a working (plot plan, vertical layout, structure plan, floor plan) general plan drawing.
   这是施工(平面布置、竖向布置、结构、屋间平面)总图。

9. To maintain the best quality of the construction work is the important responsibility of the field controllers.

保持施工工作的优良质量是现场管理人员的重要职责。

10. I want to see the certificate of quality (certificate of manufacturer, certificate of inspection, certificate of shipment, material certificate, and certificate of proof).

    我要看看质量证书(制造厂证书、检查证明书、出口许可证书、材料合格证和检验证书)。

11. The welds passed the examination of radiographic test.

    这些焊缝通过射线透视检查为合格。

12. Cast iron cannot compare with steel in tensile strength.

    铸铁在抗拉强度上比不上钢。

13. Erection of the equipment will be carried out according to the specifications and drawings.

    设备安装将按照说明书和图纸进行。

14. The cooler is a pressure vessel. It is subject to the pressure vessel code.

    这台冷却器是一个压力容器,它必须服从压力容器法规。

15. This low pressure blower (pump) will be assembled in No. 3 Workshop.

    这台低压鼓风机(泵)将在三号车间予以装配。

16. We can adjust the levelness of the machine by means of shim and screw jack.

    我们可以利用垫铁和螺丝千斤顶来调整机器的水平度。

17. The bolt does not match the nut.

    螺栓与螺母不配。

18. We prefer welding to riveting.

    我们认为焊接比铆接好。

19. Piping erection work includes: prefabrication, placing, aligning, welding and bolting.

    管道安装工作包括预制、安置、对准、焊接和用螺栓装配。

20. This pipe is made of carbon steel (stainless steel, cast iron, plastic).

    这根管子是碳素钢(不锈钢、铸铁、塑料)制成的。

Topic 9 Building Structural Design

Section A Dialogues

Dialogue 1

Kevin: College student   Joe: Kevin's classmate

Kevin: Good evening, Joe.

Joe: Good evening, Kevin. I heard that a 6-**magnitude** earthquake happened in Japan when we had dinner last night.

Kevin: Yeah. Millions of people got **injured** and died, and quite a lot of buildings and houses were destroyed.

Joe: How **distressing**! I knew that the Japanese government is taking some actions to improve the sustainability of buildings. Why did so many buildings and houses **collapse**? Do you know?

Kevin: I have no idea about the earthquake in Japan, but my roommates and I have done a lot of study on the earthquakes that happened in Wenchuan County, Sichuan Province.

Joe: Really? Please tell me more.

Kevin: After a lot of research and data analysis, we found that the **seismic performance** of these buildings with **steel structure** is the best, and the **seismic force** during the whole earthquake is small since the quality of the steel structure is quite light.

Joe: Oh, I'm beginning to understand why the three steel frame factories were between slightly damaged and basically **intact** at Beichuan County, the meizoseismal area.

Kevin: Yeah, you are quick to learn.

Joe: Thank you for your compliment. I saw lots of buildings with reinforced concrete structures. How about their seismic performance compared with the steel structure?

Kevin: Good question. Did you discover that those buildings with reinforced concrete structures were seriously damaged and collapsed at Yingxiu County?

Joe: Sorry, I didn't.

Kevin: That's all right. Although the quality of reinforced concrete structures are heavier, they have good **ductility**, which means that they can **withstand** larger **deformation**.

Therefore, the seismic performance of the reinforced concrete structure is better than buildings with **brick and concrete structures**.

Joe: Do you mean that the seismic performance of steel structures is better than that of reinforced concrete structures? And the seismic performance of reinforced concrete structures is better than brick and concrete structures?

Kevin: Yeah, quite right.

Joe: But I don't understand why the seismic performance of brick and concrete structures is worse than that of reinforced concrete structures.

Kevin: Because brick and concrete are heavy and **brittle**, the **tensile**, **shear** and **bending strength** are relatively low; therefore, the seismic performance of **masonry buildings** is relatively poor.

Joe: Got it!

 Vocabulary

magnitude	/ˈmæɡnɪtjuːd/	n.	震级
injured	/ˈɪndʒəd/	adj.	受伤的
distressing	/dɪˈstresɪŋ/	adj.	令人苦恼的
collapse	/kəˈlæps/	v.	倒塌,坍塌
intact	/ɪnˈtækt/	adj.	完整的
ductility	/dʌkˈtɪlɪti/	n.	延展性
withstand	/wɪðˈstænd/	v.	经受,承受
deformation	/diːfɔːˈmeɪʃn/	n.	变形
brittle	/ˈbrɪtl/	adj.	易碎的
tensile	/ˈtensaɪl/	adj.	可伸展的,可拉长的,张力的
shear	/ʃɪə(r)/	n.	切断,修剪,剪断
seismic performance			抗震性能
steel structure			钢结构
seismic force			地震力
brick and concrete structure			砖混结构
bending strength			抗弯强度
masonry building			砖石建筑

Dialogue 2

Josh: General manager   Ellen: Businessman

Ellen: Hello, Josh. I haven't seen you for a long time. Where did you go in the summer holiday?

Josh: Hi, Ellen. Nice to see you! I traveled to Shenzhen.

Ellen: Shenzhen? A beautiful and developed **special economic district**. Did you visit **the Window of the World(WOTW)**?

Josh: Yeah. My daughter insisted on it.

Ellen: Really? Why does she like the Window of the World so much?

Josh: She said that she hoped to take a close look at **Egyptian pyramids**.

Ellen: She got what she hoped for! What do you think of Egyptian pyramids?

Josh: They are very beautiful—a beauty of strength. That's what the designers expect to express. Do you know the **Marseille Apartments** in France and the **Chandigarh Convention Center** in India? They have the similar design style.

Ellen: I have never seen them. But I have seen **the Louvre Pyramid** in Paris designed by Ieoh Ming Pei and the **Apple concept store** in Shanghai that are famous for their **gentle beauty**. These buildings are completely made of **transparent** glass.

Josh: Yes, you are right. Today many Japanese **architects** such as Kazuyo Sejima and Junya Ishigami are in **pursuit** of gentle beauty.

Ellen: You are just like a **Jack of all trades**.

Josh: Thank you, Ellen. Have you ever heard of the **Villa Savoye** in Paris?

Ellen: Yeah, I have heard from my business friends in France. They had invited me to visit the most easily **recognizable** and **renowned** examples of the international style.

Josh: You **broaden** my eyes.

Ellen: Ha-ha, it's a bit **exaggerated**.

Josh: Do you have any plan for a journey during the Spring Festival next year?

Ellen: Yes. Do you want to join in our plan?

Josh: That's perfect! My wife and I have been expecting a long journey with your family for some time.

Ellen: The same as us. Let's make a detailed plan in the next month.

Unit 3 Civil and Architectural Engineering

 Vocabulary

transparent	/træns'pærənt/	adj.	透明的
architect	/'ɑːkɪtekt/	n.	建筑师
pursuit	/pə'sjuːt/	n.	追求
recognizable	/'rekəgnaɪzəbl/	adj.	可辨认的,可认识的
renowned	/rɪ'naʊnd/	adj.	著名的,知名的
broaden	/'brɔːdn/	v.	使扩大,使变阔,使变宽
exaggerated	/ɪɡ'zædʒəreɪtɪd/	adj.	夸张的,言过其实的
special economic district			经济特区
the Window of the World (WOTW)			世界之窗
Egyptian pyramid			埃及金字塔
Marseille Apartments			马赛公寓
Chandigarh Convention Center			昌迪加尔会议中心
the Louvre Pyramid			卢浮宫金字塔
Apple concept store			苹果概念店
gentle beauty			柔美
Jack of all trades			万事通
Villa Savoye			萨伏伊别墅

Section B Notes

1. seismic force(earthquake load)(地震力):又称地震荷载。结构物由于地震而受到的惯性力、土压力和水压力的总称。由于水平振动对建筑物的影响最大,因而一般只考虑水平振动。

2. steel structure(钢结构):主要由钢制材料组成的结构,是主要的建筑结构类型之一。结构主要由型钢和钢板等制成的钢梁、钢柱、钢桁架等构件组成,各构件或部件之间通常采用焊缝、螺栓或铆钉连接。因其自重较轻,且施工简便,广泛应用于大型厂房、场馆、超高层建筑等领域。

3. brick and concrete structure(砖混结构):指建筑物中竖向承重结构的墙、柱等采用砖或者砖块砌筑,横向承重的梁、楼板、屋面板等采用钢筋混凝土结构。适合开间进深较小,房间面积小,多层或低层的建筑,对于承重墙体不能改动,而框架结构则可以对墙体进行改动。

4. Marseille Apartments(马赛公寓):1952年建,它代表现代建筑大师勒·柯布西埃对于住宅和公共住居问题研究的高潮,尤其是关于个人与集体之间关系的思考。

5. Chandigarh Convention Center(昌迪加尔会议中心):由现代建筑大师勒·柯布西埃设计,1955年竣工,设计非常具有想象力,形状非常奇特。它宛如一个巨人的大脑、心脏、躯干、器官等,巨人的大脑把其他器官紧密地联系在一起。

6. the Louvre Pyramid(卢浮宫金字塔):由美籍华人建筑大师贝聿铭设计建造。他在设计中借用古埃及的金字塔造型,并采用了玻璃材料,金字塔不仅表面积小,而且还可以反映巴黎不断变化的天空,并为地下设施提供良好的采光。

7. Junya Ishigami(石上纯也):日本建筑师,毕业于东京艺术大学,之后在SANAA建筑事务所工作4年,2004年成立自己的事务所。在比利时展出了他的家具作品野餐(picnic)系列。

8. Kazuyo Sejima(妹岛和世):日本知名女建筑师,出生于日本茨城县,现任庆应义塾大学理工学部教授。妹岛和世的作品多带有重要的穿透性风格,她大量运用玻璃外墙等材质,让建筑感觉轻盈、飘浮。

9. Villa Savoye(萨伏伊别墅):现代主义建筑的经典作品之一,位于巴黎近郊的普瓦西,由现代建筑大师勒·柯布西埃于1928年设计,1930年建成,使用钢筋混凝土结构。这幢白房子表面看来平淡无奇,简单的柏拉图形体和平整的白色粉刷的外墙,简单到几乎没有任何多余装饰的程度,唯一可以称为装饰部件的是横向长窗,这是为了能最大限度地让光线射入。第二次世界大战后,萨伏伊别墅被列为法国文物保护单位。

Section C Exercises

I. Translate the following words or phrases into Chinese.

1. seismic performance
2. brick and concrete structure
3. bending strength
4. masonry building
5. gentle beauty
6. transparent
7. architect
8. recognizable

II. Translate the following words or phrases into English.

1. 受伤的
2. 倒塌,坍塌
3. 易碎的
4. 拉长的
5. 延展性
6. 著名的,知名的
7. 追求
8. 万事通

III. Role play.

You and your desk-mate are talking about the following architecture——Villa Savoye, which you have already learned. What do you think of its beauty, design, materials, etc.? One asks more questions about this building, and the other answers the questions. Then exchange the roles.

Section D Related Words and Phrases

1. architectural form	建筑形式
2. environment art	环境艺术
3. architectural design methodology	建筑设计方法
4. historical building preservation	古建筑保护
5. building optics	建筑光学
6. building thermology	建筑热学
7. building acoustics	建筑声学
8. solar building	太阳能建筑
9. building safety	建筑安全
10. building energy conservation	建筑节能
11. building fire protection	建筑防火
12. building anti-seismic	建筑抗震
13. building surveying	建筑测量
14. architectural construction	建筑构造
15. building facility	建筑设施
16. building finishing	建筑装修
17. interior decoration	室内装饰
18. classical architecture	古典建筑
19. multistory building	多层建筑
20. high-rise building	高层建筑

21.	skyscraper	摩天楼
22.	mobile house	活动房屋
23.	mezzanine	夹层,夹楼
24.	information desk	问询处
25.	janitor's room	收发室

Section E Useful Expressions and Sentences

1. A structure must be well built; it must have permanence.
   一座建筑的结构必须良好,必须具有永久性。

2. In stone buildings, windows, doors, and the spaces between columns are almost compelled to be taller than their width.
   石建筑中的窗、门、支柱空间的高度必须比宽度高。

3. It is necessary to plant grass all over the road close to cross-border traffic to form a surface for the wheel of the cars.
   有必要在临近过境交通的路上种植草坪,为通过的汽车提供铺面。

4. Do you like the design style of Birds Nest in Beijing?
   你喜欢北京鸟巢的设计风格吗?

5. The design of fire proof, water proof, energy conservation, sound insulation, anti-seismic and safety protection are perfect in this building.
   这栋建筑物的防火、防水、节能、隔音、抗震、安全保护设计做得非常好。

6. Are the design of this building's type, plane layout and structure suitable for the anti-seismic principle?
   这个建筑的体型、平面布置及构造符合抗震设计原则吗?

7. What do you think of the environmental design of this community?
   你认为这个社区的环境设计如何?

8. The design of this company's property management is so bad.
   这个公司物业管理的设计真糟糕。

9. Every real estate development company pays much attention to the design of environmental greening.
   每一家房地产开发商都非常关注环境绿化的设计。

10. Do you know the structure in space of this house?
    你知道这个房子的空间结构吗?

11. What are the characteristics of cantilever?

悬臂梁的特征是什么?

12. A perfect marriage and interweaving have been combined between architecture and landscape, or man-made and nature in this community.

    这个小区的建筑和园景、人工和自然巧妙地结合了起来。

13. The careful management of the artificial lake will bring an unforgettable experience for visitors.

    人工湖的细心管理将为游客带来一次难忘的经历。

14. The rich entertainment facilities and outdoors gathering space will attract millions of people.

    丰富的娱乐设施和户外聚会空间将吸引数百万人流。

15. This villa makes guests enjoy the natural wildness and recover the original simplicity of green life.

    这栋别墅能让顾客享受自然野趣和返璞归真的绿色生活。

16. The Christian church at the shore of the ocean will bring an incomparable new wedding experience for the bridegroom- and bride-to-be.

    位于海岸边的基督教堂将要给新人一个无与伦比的新婚体验。

17. The preliminary design of this project isn't reasonable.

    这个方案的初始设计不合理。

18. The final design is done.

    最终设计已经弄好了。

19. The design of warm in winter and cold in summer is very popular.

    这种冬暖夏凉的设计很受欢迎。

20. By building the house underground, the architects were able to almost completely eliminate the need for heating or cooling in the winter and summer months.

    由于房屋建造在地下,设计师们能够几乎完全免去冬日制暖、夏日制冷的需求。

Topic 10　Architectural Design and Decoration

Section A　Dialogues

Dialogue 1

Calvin: Designer　　Alex: Customer

Calvin: Good afternoon. Welcome to P. C. Interior Design.
Alex:　 Hi. I just saw the sign outside, and it says that you do all kinds of **interior design**.
Calvin: Yes, we do. What can I do for you?
Alex:　 Well, I'm thinking about **remodeling** my kitchen.
Calvin: What particular kind of design do you have in mind?
Alex:　 Currently, my kitchen is in a **traditional** style, and I want an **open-plan** kitchen.
Calvin: That sounds great. Do you mind if I **recommend** myself for the job?
Alex:　 No, that will be great!
Calvin: So, let's talk about what you need **in more detail**. What do you need or want in your new kitchen?
Alex:　 I'd like to have a spacious kitchen with a lot of **counter space** for food preparation and a large table for entertaining my friends.
Calvin: Good idea. Do you prefer any special style?
Alex:　 Yes, I prefer **contemporary design**.
Calvin: Have you **settled on** any **color scheme**?
Alex:　 No, not yet. My kitchen needs to be brightened up. Here are some pictures of my kitchen. How about a yellow and red color scheme?
Calvin: I don't think that color scheme goes very well with your **furniture**. It is too busy.
Alex:　 Can you suggest a color scheme that might match my furniture?
Calvin: I think **dove white** and **grey marble** would **lighten** the room and the colors will **compliment** your furniture.
Alex:　 Dove white and grey marble? Hmm ... That sounds great.
Calvin: What kind of **ambience** do you want in your kitchen?
Alex:　 I'd like it to look simple, **neat** and relaxing.
Calvin: Got it.

Unit 3 Civil and Architectural Engineering

 Vocabulary

remodel	/ˌriːˈmɒdl/	v.	改造,改变
traditional	/trəˈdɪʃənl/	adj.	传统的
open-plan	/ˌəʊpənˈplæn/	adj.	开放式的,敞开式的
recommend	/ˌrekəˈmend/	v.	推荐,介绍
furniture	/ˈfɜːnɪtʃə(r)/	n.	家具
lighten	/ˈlaɪtn/	v.	使照亮,变亮
compliment	/ˈkɒmplɪmənt/	v.	恭维,称赞
ambience	/ˈæmbiəns/	n.	气氛,布景,格调
neat	/niːt/	adj.	整洁的,干净的
interior design			室内设计
in more detail			更详细地
counter space			灶台空间
contemporary design			当代设计
settle on			选定
color scheme			配色方案,色彩设计
dove white			鸽子白
grey marble			云灰大理石

 Dialogue 2

Josh: Designer   Ellen: Customer

Josh: Good afternoon, Ellen. I'll **show** you **around** the office.

Ellen: Thanks. I hope my office has good **feng shui**.

Josh: Sure. Feng shui makes you more conscious of how your environment influences your **state of mind**.

Ellen: Yes. It's very important today, especially for businessmen.

Josh: That's true. Here we have a **double action frosted glass door**, as you asked for.

Ellen: Nice. Can I have another door over there?

Josh: You'd better not. An office with two doors is not good for feng shui, because the energy will come into one door and out through the other door.

Ellen: Whoops. That sounds terrible.

Josh: This way please. The windows on the ground floor are **stained glass** and the rest of the floors have **plate glass** windows.

Ellen: Stained glass on the ground floor and plate glass on the rest of the floors. OK. When are you going to fix the **curtains**?

Josh: Tomorrow, if nothing else needs to be redone.

Ellen: What color have you chosen for the curtains?

Josh: I think the blue curtains will go very well in your office. What do you think?

Ellen: I think it will be great.

Josh: This is your office. I have positioned the desk **diagonally** because the desk must face the door according to the feng shui guidelines.

Ellen: Oh, I see. Can I move the desk to face the **doorway** directly with the chair backing up against the wall?

Josh: Sure. I will move the desk into that position later.

Ellen: Thank you. I think you've done a very good job.

Josh: I'm very happy you like it.

 Vocabulary

curtain	/ˈkɜːtn/	n.	窗帘
diagonally	/daɪˈæɡənəli/	adv.	对角地,斜对地
doorway	/ˈdɔːweɪ/	n.	出入口,门道
show ... around			带领……参观
feng shui			风水
state of mind			心态
double action door			双向平开门
frosted glass			磨砂玻璃,毛玻璃
stained glass			彩色玻璃,有色玻璃
plate glass			平板玻璃

Section B Notes

1. interior design（室内设计）：室内设计是根据建筑物的使用性质、所处环境和相应标准，运用物质技术手段和建筑设计原理，创造功能合理、舒适优美、满足人们物质和精神生活需要的室内环境。

2. feng shui（风水）：风水不仅仅是一些时间和数字，也是关于土木工程建设和设计的指导原则。

Unit 3 Civil and Architectural Engineering

Section C Exercises

I. Translate the following words or phrases into Chinese.

1. remodel
2. contemporary design
3. counter space
4. furniture
5. double action door
6. stained glass
7. plate glass
8. curtain

II. Translate the following words or phrases into English.

1. 室内设计
2. 配色方案
3. 开放式厨房
4. 更详细地
5. 带领……参观
6. 在门口的斜对面
7. 正对门
8. 心态

III. Role play.

A is an interior designer, and B is a customer who wants to rebuild the bedroom. They are talking about the specific details about it. Try to use the words and phrases you have learned to ask and answer questions.

Section D Related Words and Phrases

1. color tone		色调
2. folding door		折叠门
3. trapdoor		活板门,通气门
4. sliding door		推拉门,滑门

5.	lever gear door	提升门
6.	roll shutting door	卷帘门
7.	inward opening window	内开窗
8.	outward opening window	外开窗
9.	shed roof	单斜屋顶
10.	gable/comb roof	人字屋顶
11.	hip roof	四坡屋顶,斜截头屋顶
12.	arched roof	拱形屋顶
13.	flat roof	平屋顶
14.	stippled tile	斑点装饰砖
15.	wall tile	墙面砖
16.	floor tile	地面砖
17.	glazed tile	釉面砖
18.	circle	圆形
19.	square	正方形
20.	trapezium	梯形
21.	triangle	三角形
22.	cube	立方体
23.	cylinder	圆柱体
24.	cone	圆锥体
25.	pyramid	棱锥体

Section E Useful Expressions and Sentences

1. I'm thinking about redesigning my kitchen.
   我想重新设计我的厨房。

2. I'm thinking about repainting the walls and changing the pictures.
   我想把墙重新刷一遍,把墙纸也换掉。

3. How long did it take you to do the tiling?
   你贴瓷砖花了多长时间?

4. I need a small cupboard for toiletries.
   我需要一个小壁柜放盥洗用品。

5. They are in good condition and don't need to be replaced.
   它们现在还很好,不需要换。

6. I just had all the walls repainted last week and it has all the modern conveniences.

   房子的墙壁上周刚刚刷过,房内现代化的设备齐全。

7. We will offer you different blue prints to choose or you may make the design as you like.

   我们会给您各种图案供您选择,或者按您自己的喜好进行设计。

8. I'd like our deck to be at the same level as the back door.

   我希望我们的露天平台和后门一样高。

9. The roof has leaks in it, and the front steps need to be fixed.

   屋顶有漏洞,前面台阶也需要修整。

10. I'm worried about the appearance of the floor.

    我担心地板的表面。

11. What style of furniture do you have? Is it traditional?

    你有什么样式的家具?是传统型的吗?

12. Bad feng shui can bring us disease, illness or even quarrels in the family.

    不好的风水会给我们的家庭带来疾病甚至争执。

13. Mirrors should not be hung on walls opposite beds in case you may be scared by reflections at night.

    镜子不能挂在床的对面,否则你半夜会被镜中的影像吓到。

14. Keep plants and flowers outside of your bedroom. Plants are thought to possess too much *yang*, which creates too much energy and activity for you to get the rest that you need.

    把盆栽和花卉都放到卧室外面。人们通常认为植物有太多阳气,这些阳气会产生过多的能量和活力而影响你的休息。

15. In fact, one third of the time in our lives is spent in the bedroom, so it is vital for us.

    实际上,我们一生中有三分之一的时间是在卧室度过的,所以,卧室对我们而言非常重要。

16. The door of the bedroom cannot face the door of the house.

    卧室的房门不能朝向房子的大门。

17. According to feng shui theory, a bathroom is known as the dirty, wet land. If bathroom feng shui is ignored, then health problems may occur. Therefore, we need more special concern of bathroom in order to live a more comfortable family life.

    根据风水学,盥洗室是污秽、潮湿的地方。如果忽视盥洗室的风水,就有可能带来健康问题。我们需要特别关注盥洗室的设计,从而使我们的家庭生活更舒适。

18. The bathroom should not be located in the center of the house.

盥洗室不能位于房子的正中间。
19. Bathroom and kitchen's door must avoid the relative position.
盥洗室的门不能正对厨房的门。
20. The sofa should better face the door directly because in feng shui, the sofa facing the door means a good relationship with others.
沙发最好正对门。在风水学上,沙发正对着门有助于和他人保持良好的关系。

Topic 11 Transportation Construction

Section A Dialogues

Dialogue 1

George: Engineering supervisor with the construction company

Mark: Trainee with the construction company

Mark: Good morning, supervisor. You are so early today.

George: Good morning, Mark. I'm going to the job site to see how the **asphalt** pavement **maintenance** is going on.

Mark: Oh, can I go there with you? I would like to learn about asphalt from you.

George: Sure. Let's go together and talk on the way. Usually, asphalt **refers to** a mixture of **aggregate** and **bituminous binder**, with or without added **mineral filler**.

Mark: Supervisor, compared with other **pavement** materials, such as concrete pavement, what are the benefits of asphalt?

George: Good question! In addition to being **smooth**, **durable**, safe, and quiet, asphalt is the most **versatile** pavement material. Pavement structures can be designed to handle any load, from passenger cars to heavy trucks.

Mark: I hear that in many countries, like China and Australia, asphalt is mainly used in urban areas and on heavy trafficked routes.

George: That's right. Asphalt has many uses which includes construction of a new pavement, **strengthening** an existing pavement, correcting irregularities in an existing pavement and repairing an existing pavement.

Mark: Wow! Asphalt is really amazing material for pavement.

George: Yes. You can say that.

Mark: Supervisor, since we are going to check the asphalt pavement maintenance today, can you tell me how important and necessary the maintenance job is?

George: The useful life of asphalt pavements in many cases is lower than had been **originally** expected. This is mainly due to increased **volume** of traffic and increasing actual weight of commercial vehicles which combined have caused severe problems.

Mark: So, throughout the country the number of roads which require immediate maintenance is growing each year. Is there any machine that can help to extend the life of asphalt pavement?

George: Nowadays, large **road milling machines** are used as the main equipment in maintenance operations. Generally speaking, road milling machines consist of three basic system: **power unit**, **cutting drum** and **conveying system**. The use of milling machines have greatly lowered the maintenance cost of asphalt pavement. Mark, you can watch how the machine is operated at the job site.

Mark: Thank you, supervisor. I really appreciate your kindness.

George: You are welcome.

 Vocabulary

asphalt	/ˈæsfælt/	n.	沥青,柏油
maintenance	/ˈmeɪntənəns/	n.	维修,维护
aggregate	/ˈæɡrɪɡət/	n.	集料
bituminous	/bɪˈtjuːmɪnəs/	adj.	含沥青的,沥青的
binder	/ˈbaɪndə(r)/	n.	黏合剂,结合剂
pavement	/ˈpeɪvmənt/	n.	人行道,硬路面
smooth	/smuːð/	adj.	光滑的,平整的
durable	/ˈdjʊərəbl/	adj.	耐用的
versatile	/ˈvɜːsətaɪl/	adj.	多用途的
strengthen	/ˈstreŋθn/	v.	加强
originally	/əˈrɪdʒənəli/	adv.	起初,原来
volume	/ˈvɒljuːm/	n.	量,大量
refer to			指的是……
mineral filler			矿物质填料
road milling machine			路面铣削机

power unit	动力设备
cutting drum	切割滚筒
conveying system	输送系统

Dialogue 2

Jordan and Stephanie are college students majoring in Transportation Engineering. Now they are talking about bridge engineering.

Jordan: Stephanie, what are you doing?

Stephanie: Ah, nothing. I'm just looking up some information on the Internet.

Jordan: Like what? Let me see … **William R. Bennett Bridge**? Wow, the bridge is **spectacular**!

Stephanie: The William R. Bennett Bridge, completed on May 25, 2008, is the **centerpiece** of a **revitalized** road network in the Okannagan.

Jordan: You sounds like an expert, Stephanie.

Stephanie: You are exaggerated. To be frank, I'm very interested in bridge engineering.

Jordan: The William R. Bennett Bridge is a **pontoon** bridge, isn't it?

Stephanie: Yeah. The whole bridge is 1,060 metres long in total, which includes a 690-metre string of long poles holding pontoons supporting an elevated **deck**.

Jordan: How many pontoons are there totally?

Stephanie: There are totally 9 concrete pontoons. Like the original Okanagan Lake Bridge, the new structure is one of the few floating bridges in North America. The new bridge was renamed to the William R. Bennett Bridge in honor of the 27th Premier of British Columbia. The bridge have five **lanes**, an elevated **span** to allow for the passage of **marine traffic**, and improved access for **cyclists** and **pedestrians**.

Jordan: It's surely a great bridge. But I'm wondering how much it cost.

Stephanie: The cost of the bridge has increased from the previous estimate of $100 million CAD to $144 million CAD "**due to dramatic** increases in the cost of construction materials and labour", which includes significant increases in the cost of concrete, steel, and fuel.

Jordan: In spite of the huge cost, I think the bridge has greatly improved the transportation network.

Stephanie: Yes. The William R. Bennett Bridge is designed to handle up to 80,000 vehicles daily.

Unit 3 Civil and Architectural Engineering

Vocabulary

spectacular	/spekˈtækjələ(r)/	adj.	壮观的
centerpiece	/ˈsentəpiːs/	n.	中心装饰物,最醒目的物件
revitalize	/riːˈvaɪtəlaɪz/	v.	使复兴
pontoon	/pɒnˈtuːn/	n.	(架设浮桥用的)浮舟,浮桥平台
deck	/dek/	n.	桥面
lane	/leɪn/	n.	车道
span	/spæn/	n.	跨度,墩距
cyclist	/ˈsaɪklɪst/	n.	骑自行车的人
pedestrian	/pəˈdestriən/	n.	步行者,行人
dramatic	/drəˈmætɪk/	adj.	巨大的
William R. Bennett Bridge			威廉·R. 班尼特大桥
marine traffic			水上运输
due to			因为,由于

Section B Notes

1. asphalt:沥青是由不同分子量的碳氢化合物及其非金属衍生物组成的黑褐色复杂混合物,是高黏度有机液体的一种,呈液态,表面呈黑色,可溶于二硫化碳。沥青是一种防水、防潮、防腐的有机胶凝材料。沥青主要可以分为煤焦沥青、石油沥青和天然沥青三种。其中,煤焦沥青是炼焦的副产品;石油沥青是原油蒸馏后的残渣;天然沥青则是储藏在地下,有的形成矿层或在地壳表面堆积。沥青主要用于涂料、塑料、橡胶等工业以及铺筑路面等。

2. road milling machine:路面铣削机,对沥青路面和混凝土路面进行铣削等。主要的用途有:沥青路面涌包、车辙、网裂、坑槽部位的铣削清除;清除桥面和路面的冰雪;桥面表面防水处理凿毛,高速铁路箱梁的梁面平整度和防水处理;沥青砼新铺前对原有旧路面轻度拉毛;地面受损、积污需要翻新时,去除旧地坪表面;道路微表处施工,对原有旧路面面层进行铣刨清除;等等。

3. William R. Bennett Bridge:威廉·R. 班尼特大桥是一座浮桥,建于2008年,位于加拿大不列颠哥伦比亚奥肯娜干湖。这座桥取代了建于1958年的老奥肯娜干湖桥,横跨奥肯娜干湖,从基隆拿市中心连接到西基隆。2005年,为了纪念加拿大前总理威廉·理查兹·班尼特,更名为威廉·R. 班尼特大桥。

Section C Exercises

I. Translate the following words or phrases into Chinese.

1. complete
2. maintenance
3. pavement
4. volume
5. spectacular
6. expert
7. pontoon
8. lane

II. Translate the following words or phrases into English.

1. 沥青
2. 矿物质填充料
3. 光滑的
4. 桥面
5. 输送系统
6. 运输网络
7. 路面铣削机
8. 水上运输

III. Role play

A and B are two students majoring in Transportation Construction. They are talking about asphalt and its uses. Try to use the words and phrases you have learned to make a dialogue.

Section D Related Words and Phrases

1. aggregate   集料
2. seal   封铅,密封
3. gap   缺口,裂口
4. grade   等级,级配
5. bitumen   沥青(指纯沥青)
6. deformation   变形

7. filler   填充料
8. tar   焦油沥青
9. patching   补坑
10. void   空隙
10. texture   质地,纹理
11. durability   耐久性
13. fatigue   疲劳
14. resistance   抵抗
15. glossary   术语表
16. subgrade   路基,地基
17. grit   粗砂
18. oxidation   氧化
19. hardening   硬化
20. skid-resistant 抗滑的
21. revetment   护坡
22. handrail   栏杆,扶手
23. culvert   涵洞
24. cable   缆,索
25. cable-stayed bridge 斜拉桥

Section E Useful Expressions and Sentences

1. Asphalt is a sticky, black and highly viscous liquid or semi-solid form of petroleum.
   沥青是具有黏性的、黑色的、极为黏稠的液体或者是半液态状的石油。

2. Asphaltic concrete is most commonly used for the surfacing of a newly constructed or reconstructed pavement.
   沥青混凝土常用于铺设新建的路面或者是重新改造的路面。

3. The primary use (70%) of asphalt/bitumen is in road construction, where it is used as the glue or binder mixed with aggregate particles to create asphaltic concrete.
   沥青的主要用途(70%)是道路建设,它与岩石颗粒混合成沥青混凝土而作为黏合剂。

4. Asphaltic concrete may be used to strengthen a pavement by removal and replacement of portions of the existing pavement material and by overlaying.
   沥青混凝土可以通过清除、更改已有路面各材料比例和叠加在已有路面的方式来加固路面。

5. In the case of wearing course, it may be necessary to provide adequate surface texture and skid resistance.

对于道路的磨耗层而言,有充分的表面粗糙度和防滑性能是很有必要的。

6. Asphaltic concrete is a composite material commonly used to surface roads, parking lots, airports, as well as the core of embankment dams.

   沥青混凝土是一种混合材料,常用于地面道路、停车场、飞机场和土石坝心墙。

7. Highway bridges across valleys are generally designed as prestressed concrete bridges with spans in the range of 60 m.

   跨越山谷的公路桥梁一般设计为跨度在60米范围内的预应力混凝土桥梁。

8. Different types of asphaltic concrete have different performance characteristics in terms of surface durability, tire wear, braking efficiency and roadway noise.

   不同类型的沥青混凝土在路面的耐用性、轮胎磨损、刹车效率和道路噪音等方面的表现各不相同。

9. Hot mix asphaltic concrete (commonly abbreviated as HMAC or HMA) is produced by heating the asphalt binder to decrease its viscosity, and drying the aggregate to remove moisture from it prior to mixing.

   热拌沥青混凝土(通常缩略为HMAC或HMA)的制作方法是通过加热沥青黏合剂来降低其黏性,并在搅拌前干燥集料来除去水分。

10. Warm mix asphaltic concrete (commonly abbreviated as WMA) is produced by adding either zeolites, waxes, asphalt emulsions, or sometimes even water to the asphalt binder prior to mixing.

    温拌沥青混凝土(通常缩略为WMA)是在搅拌前往沥青黏合剂中加入沸石、石蜡、乳化沥青或者有时还加入水而制成的。

科技英语知识

科技英语词汇的翻译技巧

从事科技文献翻译和其他翻译一样,首先要解决的就是词汇的翻译。要处理好科技英语词汇的翻译,不仅要有足够的词汇量,同时还要了解科技英语词汇的来源与特点,掌握这些词的构成方式及翻译技巧。以下介绍科技英语词汇的几种翻译技巧。

1. 识别常用词的"专门化"

有很多常用的词汇运用在某一专业范围内,因而具有与该专业相关联的特定意义,翻译的时候要联系上下文,注意辨别。例如,carrier 是个常用词,它的通常含义是"搬运人/搬运公司"。但是,在不同的领域中,此词有不同的含义。例如:

| 计算机:媒体 | 集成电路:载体 | 机床:刀架 |
| 航空:运输机 | 军事:航空母舰 | 医学:带菌者 |

2. 词义引申法

词义引申法就是把一些难以直译的具体化的名称,根据字面意义加以引申。例如:

The report card has arrived from the largest ever scientific Earth analysis, and many of the planet's ecosystems are simply not making the grade.

有史以来对地球进行的最大规模的科学分析表明,地球上的许多生态系统都达不到标准。

分析:report card 原意是指"成绩单",在本例中引申为"科学分析的结果"。

3. 词义具体化

词义具体化是指把字面意思抽象笼统的词语译成意义具体、含义明确的汉语词语。例如:

People sometimes get caught up in cost-effectiveness.

人们有时候只考虑划算。

分析:cost-effectiveness 字面意思是"成本效用",该例中把意思具体化为"划算"。

We want to build factories that are as functional as they are aesthetic.

我们要建既实用又美观的工厂。

分析:functional 的字面意思是"功能的",aesthetic 指"审美的",该例中分别具体为"实用"和"美观"。

4. 省略法

根据科技文体简练的原则,英译汉时,有时可以把原文的一些动词、名词或表示同一事物不同的重复用词加以省略。例如:

Stainless steel possesses good hardness and high strength.

不锈钢硬度大,强度高。

分析:possess 是"拥有"的意思,该例中用来描绘不锈钢的性状,根据汉语表达的特点和简练的原则,可以省略不译。

The mechanical energy can be changed back into electrical energy by means of a generator or dynamo.

用发电机能把机械能转变为电能。

分析:generator 和 dynamo 意思重复,都是"发电机"的意思。重复用词,译出其中之一即可。

5. 还原法

拼缀词词形与组成词半隐半现,容易引起联想判断,翻译的时候宜用还原法,析出全称,再按顺序递加词义。例如:

A U. S. Environmental Protection Agency study found that geo-exchange systems can gave up to 70 percent of home-heating costs.

美国环保局的一项调查表明,地热交换系统可以节省高达70%的家庭取暖费用。

分析:geo-用作前缀,表示"地球的",exchange 表示"交换",根据上下文语境,geoexchange systems 可译为"地热交换系统"。

Unit 4

Biochemical Engineering

Topic 12 Food Engineering

Section A Dialogues

Dialogue 1

Elsa and Anna are classmates, and they are in a supermarket now.

Elsa: Anna, should we go now? The to-buy list is almost done.

Anna: Hey, wait a second. I still need some **sweeteners**. Let's go this way.

Elsa: Sweeteners? Do you always have them in your **diet**?

Anna: Definitely. I like sweet food. But sugar makes us fat. So sweetener is a perfect **alternative** without that much **calorie**. With it, I'm having a healthy diet now.

Elsa: Really? I happened to read an article a couple of days ago. The author may have a different opinion.

Anna: Oh yes? What did it say?

Elsa: Briefly, sugar is bad, but sweetener is **deadly**.

Anna: It seems **horrible** now. I'd like to know more about it.

Elsa: I believe it's a **convincing** research result as it reveals a 10-week study.

Anna: What exactly is the research?

Elsa: Two groups of volunteers are required to **consume glucose** sugar and **fructose** separately with their daily diet within 10 weeks.

Anna: OK, I got it. But how does the researcher come to the conclusion of bad sugar and deadly sweetener?

Elsa: Volunteers in Group 1, who consumed controlled amount of sweeteners, produced new fat cells around their heart, liver, and other digestive organs.

Anna: How about the other group?

Elsa: They don't seem to have these changes.

Anna: It's astonishing. I always believed sweeteners are much healthier than sugar. I'd better put these sweeteners back on the shelf. But I can't get rid of the sweets. I'm a real **sugarholic**. What should I do then?

Elsa: First, avoid all **artificial** sweeteners; they damage health and body even more quickly than fructose. Then, use **organic** cane sugar or **raw** honey in **moderation**. And in addition, **stevia** could be another option.

Anna: Thank you pretty much. That's a practical recommendation. I think I can find them easily somewhere in this supermarket.

Elsa: That's a smart decision. And by the way, you'd better get rid of sweet drinks, like soda. And enjoy more vegetables and fruits to get glucose rather than fructose.

Anna: Alright, then. I will strictly follow your advice to get healthier.

Vocabulary

sweetener	/ˈswiːtnə(r)/	n.	甜味剂
diet	/ˈdaɪət/	n.	饮食
alternative	/ɔːlˈtɜːnətɪv/	n.	可选择的东西,供替代的抉择
calorie	/ˈkæləri/	n.	卡路里
deadly	/ˈdedli/	adj.	致命的
horrible	/ˈhɒrəbl/	adj.	可怕的
convincing	/kənˈvɪnsɪŋ/	adj.	可信服的
consume	/kənˈsjuːm/	v.	消耗
glucose	/ˈgluːkəʊs; -kəʊz/	n.	葡萄糖
fructose	/ˈfrʌtəʊs; -kəʊz/	n.	果糖
sugarholic	/suːgəˈhɒlɪk/	n.	嗜甜食者
artificial	/ˌɑːtɪˈfɪʃl/	adj.	人工的
organic	/ɔːˈgænɪk/	adj.	有机的
raw	/rɔː/	adj.	生的,未加工的
moderation	/ˌmɒdəˈreɪʃn/	n.	适度,节制
stevia	/ˈstiːvɪə/	n.	甜菊

Dialogue 2

Taylor: Student   Ellie: Professor

Taylor: Good morning, professor. I'm collecting information for my dissertation on **GM food**. Is it possible that you can tell me some latest information about it?

Ellie: Sure. I'm very pleased to know that you young people would like to know more about **genetic engineering**.

Taylor: Well, as far as I know, the public are having a heated discussion about GM vegetables, like corns and beans. But my concern is whether the scientists are focusing on GM animals.

Ellie: Absolutely. Researchers have developed dozens of GM animals in recent years, including pigs, chickens, salmons and goats.

Taylor: What makes them different from the traditional animals?

Ellie: To be specific, they are **gene-edited** animals. They are different from not only traditional animals but also **genetically modified** ones. **Transgenic** animals carry **genes** from different **species** while gene-edited animals have a few DNA letters **tweaked** to **replicate** a gene found in the same species. Here the risk is much smaller.

Taylor: Oh, it's the first time that I heard the word "gene-edited animals".

Ellie: Yes, it's quite different. But we still need to wait for the public's positive reaction to them. We researchers strongly believe that a gene-edited animal is **demonstrably** too good to be **turned down**. It's an effective method to solve the problem of resource shortage. Otherwise, how to feed a **swelling** global population with **dwindling** natural resources?

Taylor: Sounds reasonable. We need to use all the tools we have to solve the global problem, and genetic engineering is one of them.

Ellie: Exactly. Hope these may help you.

Taylor: Thank you, professor. You've inspired me a lot.

 Vocabulary

gene-edited	/dʒiːn ˈedɪtɪd/	adj.	基因编成的
transgenic	/ˌtrænzˈdʒenɪk/	adj.	转基因的
gene	/dʒiːn/	n.	基因

species	/ˈspiːʃiːz/	n.	物种
tweak	/twiːk/	v.	对……做微调
replicate	/ˈreplɪkeɪt/	v.	复制，重复
demonstrably	/dɪˈmɒnstrəbli/	adv.	可论证地，明确地
swelling	/ˈswelɪŋ/	adj.	逐渐增加的，突出的
dwindling	/ˈdwɪndlɪŋ/	adj.	减少的，逐渐变小的
GM food (genetically modified food)			转基因食品
genetic engineering			遗传工程
genetically modified			转基因的
turn down			关闭

Section B Notes

1. sweeteners（甜味剂）：是指赋予食品或饲料以甜味的食物添加剂。目前甜味剂按其来源可分为天然甜味剂和人工合成甜味剂；按其营养价值分为营养性甜味剂和非营养性甜味剂；按其化学结构和性质分为糖类和非糖类甜味剂。葡萄糖、果糖、蔗糖、麦芽糖、淀粉糖和乳糖等糖类物质，虽然也是天然甜味剂，但因长期被人食用，且是重要的营养素，通常视为食品原料，在我国不作为食品添加剂。天然非营养型甜味剂日益受到重视。

2. genetically modified food(GMF)（转基因食品）：是利用现代分子生物技术，将某些生物的基因转移到其他物种中去，改造生物的遗传物质，使其在性状、营养品质、消费品质等方面向人们所需要的目标转变的食品。转基因生物直接食用，或者作为加工原料生产的食品，统称为转基因食品。

3. genetically modified animal（转基因动物）：转基因动物是指将特定的外源基因导入动物受精卵或胚胎，使之稳定整合于动物的染色体基因组，并能遗传给后代的一类动物。

4. gene-edited（基因编成的）：一项先进的生物基因改良技术。通过计算机编程的方式将基因片段进行重组和修饰，可以对人类一些遗传疾病的治疗起到重要作用。

Section C Exercises

I. **Translate the following words or phrases into Chinese.**

1. genetic engineering
2. replicate
3. genetically modified
4. healthy diet
5. DNA letter
6. species
7. gene
8. daily diet

Ⅱ. Translate the following words or phrases into English.

1. 基因编成的　　　　　　　　2. 转基因的
3. 果糖　　　　　　　　　　　4. 葡萄糖
5. 可选择的东西　　　　　　　6. 嗜甜食者
7. 人造甜味剂　　　　　　　　8. 未加工的蜂蜜

Ⅲ. Role play.

A is an investigator, and B is a spokesman of food safety department. A is trying to get the information about current food safety situation in the country. Try to use the words and phrases you have learned to ask and answer questions.

Section D Related Words and Phrases

1. wild yeast	野生酵母
2. spoilage yeast	败坏酵母
3. evaporation	蒸发
4. alcoholic fermentation	酒精发酵
5. liquefy	（使）液化
6. byproduct	副产品
7. undesired (excessive) tannin	劣质丹宁酸
8. distillation	蒸馏
9. bottling line	灌装线
10. vacuum filtration	真空过滤机
11. blending	调配
12. oxidative ageing method	氧化陈酿法

13. stabilization 稳定性
14. nutrition 营养素,营养物
15. blanket 隔氧层,覆盖物,覆盖层
16. crusher 破碎机,碾碎机
17. atmosphere presser 气囊压榨机
18. polysaccharide 多糖,聚糖,多聚糖
19. cane sugar 蔗糖
20. invert sugar 转化糖
21. pigment 色素
22. ageing 陈化,熟化
23. primary fermentation 前发酵/主发酵
24. reduction smell 还原味
25. odor 气味

Section E Useful Expressions and Sentences

1. The problem of domestic food safety is constantly appearing. Have you heard about the drug problem?

   国内食品安全问题不断显现,你听说过药物的问题了吗?

2. Illegal businessmen only produce food that do harm to human bodies.

   不法商人只生产对人体有害的食品。

3. The consumers should learn to protect themselves and choose the products with high quality.

   消费者应该学会自我保护,学会选择质量好的商品。

4. This experiment is about how to use the amino acid for the synthesis of proteins.

   这个实验是关于氨基酸如何合成蛋白质的。

5. Is this a very complicated process?

   这个过程非常复杂吗?

6. We need some experimental apparatus and materials.

   我们需要一些实验设备和材料。

7. We should learn to analyze the experimental results.

   我们要学会分析实验结果。

8. Some contaminated foods led to irreversible and chronic diseases.

   一些被污染的食物会导致不可逆和慢性疾病。

9. The yogurt they produced contains a large amount of heavy metals.

   他们生产的酸奶含有大量的重金属。

10. The government should strengthen management.

    政府应该加强管理。

11. How to prevent food poisoning?

    如何防止食物中毒？

12. What are the symptoms of food poisoning?

    食物中毒的症状是什么？

13. I've got a terrible stomachache. It may be food poisoning.

    我肚子痛得厉害，可能是食物中毒了。

14. We think that meat and fried foods are not healthy.

    我们认为肉和油炸食品不健康。

15. Pickled food contains high content of salt, which easily induces gastric cancer.

    腌制食品含盐量太高，易诱发胃癌。

16. Microorganisms are a vital factor in food safety.

    微生物是影响食品安全的重要因素。

17. Canned food should be kept in a clean, dry and cool place.

    罐装食品应该保存在干净、干燥和阴凉的地方。

18. Milk tea contains high calories, high oil and no nutrition at all.

    奶茶含热量高、高油，并且没有营养。

19. Olive oil is a healthy ingredient.

    橄榄油是一种健康的食物。

20. Cod liver oil has benefits for the brain, joints and heart.

    鱼肝油胶囊对大脑、关节和心脏有好处。

Topic 13 Environmental Engineering

Section A Dialogues

Dialogue 1

Kerry: Journalist   Tim: Mayor

Kerry: Good morning, Mr. Mayor. Welcome to our radio programme today.

Tim: It's my pleasure to be here.

Kerry: A few days ago we saw a **documentary** called *Under the Dome* released on the Internet. It's filmed and **funded** by a Chinese **investigative** journalist. Her action reminds me of our own air pollution problem. Therefore, Mr. Mayor, could you please introduce the "**air pollutant**" issue to the audience?

Tim: Sure. It's a serious problem which appeared in London for the first time in the 18th century. Luckily, the situation is getting better here in our London now.

Kerry: You once mentioned to make London the "**Ultra Low Emission Zone**" (**ULEZ**). That seems ideal. Could you tell us more about the details?

Tim: Referring to this, I would like to introduce "diesel cars" first. It's the major pollutant. Once we solve this problem, it's easy to achieve ULEZ.

Kerry: Nice. What's the problem about diesel cars? In the past, diesel is highly praised by the government for its **higher efficiency** and **less emission** of CO_2 than petrol.

Tim: Yes, indeed. Concerning efficiency and less emission of CO_2, diesel is obviously better than petrol. But we all ignore another pollutant it can bring us also: NO_2. NO_2 is the trigger of **lung function decrease** and other serious heart-related diseases.

Kerry: I see. That's why certain organizations call for the government to upgrade their diesel engines.

Tim: Yes. We realize this as well. But we prefer a stricter rule that helps to **accelerate** the achievement of ULEZ.

Kerry: You mean the **charge** of £20 for each diesel car driving in central London?

Tim: Yes. We hope this would work.

Kerry: Don't you, sir, ever think of the possibility of this rule? We have a large number of diesel cars.

Tim: We've noticed the difficulties in launching this new regulation. But we are also aware of the harm of diesel. Diesel burning causes serious threats to human health. For instance, its burning emits **particulate matter** (**PM**), Ozone (O_3), NO_2, **polyaromatic hydrocarbons** (**PAHs**). The potential outcomes may be lung diseases, heart attack, **arrhythmias**, and even **premature death.**

Kerry: Impressive. Maybe we need another expert next time to let us know more about these serious diseases caused by air pollutants.

Tim: Yes. The **outcome** would be **dreadful** if the pollutants are out of control. So that's why I **appeal to** the public to take more care of the environment and our **offspring**.

Kerry: Absolutely. Thanks, Mr. Mayor.

Vocabulary

documentary	/ˌdɒkjuˈmentri/	n.	纪录片
dome	/dəʊm/	n.	穹顶
fund	/fʌnd/	v.	投资,拨款给
investigative	/ɪnˈvestɪɡətɪv/	adj.	调查研究的
accelerate	/əkˈseləreɪt/	v.	加快,加速
charge	/tʃɑːdʒ/	n.	收费
arrhythmia	/əˈrɪθmɪə/	n.	心律失常,心律不齐
outcome	/ˈaʊtkʌm/	n.	结果
dreadful	/ˈdredfl/	adj.	可怕的
offspring	/ˈɒfˌsprɪŋ/	n.	后代
air pollutant			大气污染物
Ultra Low Emission Zone (ULEZ)			超低排放区
higher efficiency			更高效
less emission			更少排放
lung function decrease			肺功能降低
particulate matter (PM)			颗粒物
polyaromatic hydrocarbons (PAHs)			多环芳烃
premature death			过早死亡
appeal to			呼吁

Dialogue 2

James: Marine scientist   Lee: Reporter

Lee: Nice to see you, James. I've read one of your reports about **ocean acidification**. I would like to get more information about it. It must be an **inspiration** for the public on environmental protection.

James: Well, I'm very pleased to help. What would you like to know?

Lee: You've conducted a study recently on **marine** snails?

James: Exactly. The result indicates that snails in sea around **Antarctic** are being affected by ocean acidification.

Lee: That means …

James: Snails' shells are being **corroded**.

Lee: What is ocean acidification, exactly?

James: It's the result of burning fossil fuels.

Lee: **Fossil fuel burning**? In the ocean?

James: Hahaha … Not in that way. Fossil fuel' burning produces CO_2, and the ocean **absorbs** the CO_2 in the atmosphere. The ocean has absorbed half of the CO_2 in the atmosphere. The process makes the ocean acidic. And the changes to ocean's pH levels will have severe consequences for marine wildlife and ecosystem.

Lee: That seems serious. But how indeed will the acidification affect marine wildlife?

James: You really care about the problem. I do appreciate it. The acidification reduces the **availability** of carbonate ions, which is a major element for **marine creatures** to build shells and skeletons.

Lee: Now I see the link between your study and some marine scientists' calls for **stabilizing** and **ultimately** reducing emissions.

James: Yes, that's right. CO_2 affects not only the atmosphere but also the ocean. Without control of its emission, the consequences would be deadly.

Vocabulary

inspiration	/ˌɪnspəˈreɪʃn/	n.	启发
marine	/məˈriːn/	adj.	海产的, 海洋的
Antarctic	/ænˈtɑːktɪk/	n.	南极洲
corrode	/kəˈrəʊd/	v.	侵蚀, 腐蚀

absorb	/əbˈsɔːb/	v.	吸收
availability	/əˌveɪləˈbɪləti/	n.	利用的可能性,有效性
stabilize	/ˈsteɪbəlaɪz/	v.	使稳定,保持……的稳定
ultimately	/ˈʌltɪmətli/	adv.	最终,最后
ocean acidification			海洋酸化
fossil fuel burning			矿物燃料燃烧
marine creature			海洋生物

Section B　Notes

1. Ultra Low Emission Zone（ULEZ）（超低排放区）：为了提高空气质量,伦敦市长计划到2020年在伦敦市中心建立一个超低排放区,只有零排放或者是低排放车辆才能进入。

2. ocean acidification（海洋酸化）：海水吸收了空气中过量的二氧化碳,导致酸碱度降低。酸碱度一般用pH来表示,范围为0—14,pH值为0时代表酸性最强,pH值为14时代表碱性最强。蒸馏水的pH值为7,代表中性。海水应为弱碱性,海洋表层水的pH值约为8.2。当空气中过量的二氧化碳进入海洋中时,海洋就会酸化。科学研究表明,受人类活动影响,2012年时过量的二氧化碳排放已将海水表层pH降低了0.1,这表示海水的酸度已经提高了30%。预计到2100年,海水表层酸度将下降到7.8,到那时海水酸度将比1800年高150%。

3. fossil fuel burning（矿物燃料燃烧）：矿物燃料包括煤、石油、天然气等。煤是可以燃烧的含有机物的矿石。其化学组成主要是碳、氢、氧等元素。石油一般生成在古代的沉积盆地、浅海或湖泊中。其中的生物与有机物经过漫长的地质变化及一系列的物理化学变化,逐渐变成无数细小的油珠,再汇成细流,集中迁移到地壳中有封闭构造的地层储藏起来,形成了油田。天然气是一种蕴藏在地层内的可燃气体,主要成分烷烃,其中甲烷占绝大多数,另有少量的乙烷、丙烷和丁烷。此外一般还含有硫化氢、二氧化碳、氮、水气及微量的惰性气体,如氦和氩等。它是一种无色气体,但有气味。天然气易燃,燃烧后无烟无灰,是较为清洁的燃料。天然气还可以制成合成氨、酒精、合成纤维等。

4. particulate matter（PM）（颗粒物）：科学家用PM表示每立方米空气中某种颗粒的含量（例如PM2.5,PM10）,这个值越高,就代表空气污染越严重。

5. polyaromatic hydrocarbon（PAHs）（多环芳烃）：是指具有两个或两个以上苯环的一类有机化合物。多环芳烃是分子中含有两个以上苯环的碳氢化合物,包括萘、蒽、菲、芘等150余种化合物。有些多环芳烃还含有氮、硫和环戊烷,常见的、具有致癌作用的多环芳烃多为四到六环的稠环化合物。国际癌症研究中心（IARC）列出了94种对实验动物致癌的化合物。其中15种属于多环芳烃,由于苯并(a)芘是第一个被发现的环境化学致癌物,而且致癌性很强,故常以苯并(a)芘作为多环芳烃的代表,它占全部致癌性多环芳烃的1%～20%。

Section C　Exercises

I. Translate the following words or phrases into Chinese.

1. less emission
2. documentary
3. air pollutant
4. lung function decrease
5. ULEZ
6. absorb
7. corrode
8. outcome

II. Translate the following words or phrases into English.

1. 海洋酸化
2. 矿物燃料燃烧
3. pH 值
4. 海洋生物
5. 呼吁
6. 减少碳酸根离子的有效性
7. 可怕的结果
8. 外壳和骨架的生长

III. Role play.

A is a student majoring in Environment Engineering, and B is a researcher who has done lots of study on marine science. A tries to ask B about some professional questions on threats that marine creatures are facing. Try to use the words and phrases you have learned to ask and answer questions.

Section D Related Words and Phrases

1.	pollution	污染
2.	poison	毒物
3.	ocean current	洋流
4.	maritime transport	海运
5.	landslide	山崩,地滑,崩塌
6.	compost	堆肥
7.	atmosphere	大气
8.	alga	藻,海藻(常用复数,algae)
9.	acid rain	酸雨
10.	water treatment	水处理
11.	water pollution	水污染
12.	pollution source	污染源
13.	oceanography	海洋学
14.	environmental law	环境法
15.	desertification	沙漠化,土壤贫瘠
16.	waste recovery	废物回收
17.	waste disposal	废物处置
18.	urban water supply	城市供水
19.	trans-frontier pollution	越境污染
20.	toxic substance	有毒物质
21.	thermal sea power	海洋热能
22.	soil erosion	土壤侵蚀
23.	soil degradation	土壤退化
24.	soil capability	土壤潜力
25.	sanitation	环境卫生

Section E Useful Expressions and Sentences

1. Many environmental problems could be decreased or even eliminated based on modern technology.

   许多环境问题可以运用现代技术减少甚至是消除。

2. The environmental technology is adopted to solve the pollution problems of water, air and environment currently.

   环境控制技术目前适用于水、空气和环境污染问题。

3. What is interaction system?

   什么是互动系统?

4. Many environmental problems involve water, air and land systems.

   许多环境问题同时涉及水、空气和土壤。

5. The safe supply of water and disposal of wastes should be put under consideration.

   应该考虑水的安全供应和废物的处理。

6. The implementation of environmental law faces difficulties.

   环境法的实施有难度。

7. Waste recycling technology has not yet been widely adopted.

   废物回收技术在我国还没有得到广泛的使用。

8. You should catalyze the wastes.

   你应该给垃圾分类。

9. Normally, there are four basic types of measurements.

   测量通常有四种基本形式。

10. The addition of harmful chemicals into air is called primary air pollution.

    初级空气污染是指有害的化学物质直接进入空气中。

11. The role of carbon dioxide in the global heat balance is well-known.

    二氧化碳在全球热量平衡中的作用是公认的。

12. Human activities affect the global warming to a larger extent.

    人类活动在很大程度上影响全球气候变暖。

13. Less emission of CO_2 has a positive effect on global climate.

    减少二氧化碳的排放对全球气候有积极的影响。

14. Long-term exposure to atmosphere destroys plants.

    长期暴露在大气中的植物受到破坏。

15. Do you know the Europe's 6-star emission standard?

    你知道欧洲六星排放标准吗?

16. Data is used to establish air quality standard.

    数据用来建立空气质量标准。

17. His company was charged $2 million for excess emissions.

    他的公司因为超标排放被罚200万美元。

18. Newly-born babies should not be exposed to polluted air.

    新生儿不应该暴露在被污染的大气中。

19. Air pollution may lead to eye or nose irritation or difficult breathing.

    大气污染可能导致眼睛或鼻子的不适，或者呼吸困难。

20. Particles in the atmosphere reduce visibility.

    空气中的颗粒物降低能见度。

Topic 14 Chemical Engineering

Section A Dialogues

 Dialogue 1

Grace：*Customer*   *Nancy*：**Salesgirl**

Grace： I need a perfume. Can you help me?

Nancy： Sure. Which type do you prefer?

Grace： Eh, actually, I've never worn perfume before. I'm not sure which type is the best for me. What do you have?

Nancy： We have a variety of perfumes with different **fragrances**：**floral**, **fruity**, **woody**, **greens**, **oriental** and so on. You can choose different ones according to the occasions, weather and personality.

Grace： I want to choose a proper one for my date this weekend. Which perfume is suitable?

Nancy： Well, in that case, the floral perfumes may be a good choice for you. They have the fragrance of flowers. They contain **extracts** of **jasmine**, **lavender**, rose, etc. Their scents can evoke a sense of innocence and romance. We have Clinique Happy in Bloom, Vanitas, Petales, Lily for this category.

Grace： Do you have any **fragrance blotters** for them?

Nancy： Of course. But it will not smell exactly the same way on your body as it does on paper. We have samples. You can spray a small amount onto the inside of your wrist and wait ten minutes before smelling it. This allows the full range of the fragrance to emerge, giving you a better idea of whether or not the **scent** appeals to you.

Grace： I like the fragrance of Petales. I think it is the exact one I need. Well, can you tell me how to wear a perfume? You know, I've never used it before.

Nancy: OK. Have a bath and apply a **lotion** before applying your perfume since fragrances last longer on clean, moist skin.

Grace: That's good. And where should I spray?

Nancy: Spray on your pulse points behind your ears, on your chest, inside your elbows, and behind your knees. Because blood flows the strongest and the skin is the warmest there. And you should spray from a distance of five or six inches.

Grace. OK. Is there anything else I should keep in mind?

Nancy: Perfumes can also potentially **stain** or discolor certain **fabrics**, so be cautious when applying it when you're dressed. What's more, to make the fragrance last longer, you should store the bottle in a cool and dry place.

Grace: I see. Thank you so much for your detailed suggestions.

 Vocabulary

salesgirl	/ˈseɪlzɡɜːl/	n.	女售货员
fragrance	/ˈfreɪɡrəns/	n.	香味
floral	/ˈflɔːrəl/	adj.	花的
fruity	/ˈfruːti/	adj.	有果味的,水果的
woody	/ˈwʊdi/	adj.	木质的,木本的
green	/ɡriːn/	adj.	绿香调系的
oriental	/ˌɔːriˈentl/	adj.	东方的
extract	/ˈekstrækt/	n.	提取物,萃取物
jasmine	/ˈdʒæzmɪn/	n.	茉莉
lavender	/ˈlævəndə(r)/	n.	薰衣草
scent	/sent/	n.	气味
lotion	/ˈləʊʃn/	n.	洗剂,润肤乳
stain	/steɪn/	v.	污染
fabric	/ˈfæbrɪk/	n.	织物,织品,布
fragrance blotter			试香卡

Dialogue 2

Michael: Customer   Jimmy: Sales manager

Michael: Do you have any **household water filters**? I'm looking for a water filter for my family.

Jimmy: Yes. We have many types for you to choose from. Do you have any preference?

Michael: I'd like to have a **self-cleaning** one.

Jimmy: Sure. I think this one is a good choice for you. It works by the **ultrafiltration** technology which is the most popular technology for a water filter.

Michael: What makes that technology superior?

Jimmy: With this technology, water is forced by pressure from a salt **solution** through the **membrane** into fresh water. It uses a ultrafiltration membrane to remove larger **particles** from drinking water, such as **rust**, sand, and some **macromolecular organic components** to ensure water is purer and fresher with better taste after being purified. What's more, it has two spare **filter cartridges**.

Michael: That's good. What's the filter material? I've heard that **KDF55** is widely used in water filtration. Is it applied in this water filter?

Jimmy: Yes, of course. KDF55 can effectively remove heavy metals, **residual chlorine**, **sulfured hydrogen**, control **bacteria** and **scales**.

Michael: I see. What's the **treatment amounts** of this water filter? And how long is the **warranty**?

Jimmy: It can treat 37 tons of water, and we offer you a lifetime warranty.

Michael: Is it easy to **install** and maintain? I'm pretty fearful of such technical things.

Jimmy: Don't worry. We offer door-to-door services. Whenever you need help, call us. The phone number is in the user's manual.

Michael: That's terrific.

 Vocabulary

self-cleaning	/selfˈkliːnɪŋ/	adj.	自洁式的,自动清洗的
ultrafiltration	/ˌʌltrəfɪlˈtreɪʃn/	n.	(化学)超滤
solution	/səˈluːʃn/	n.	溶液,溶剂
membrane	/ˈmembreɪn/	n.	薄膜
particle	/ˈpɑːtɪkl/	n.	微粒

rust	/rʌst/	n.	铁锈
bacteria	/bækˈtɪərɪə/	n.	细菌
scale	/skeɪl/	n.	水垢,水锈
warranty	/ˈwɒrənti/	n.	保证,担保
install	/ɪnˈstɔːl/	v.	安装
household water filter			家用净水器
macromolecular organic component			大分子有机物
filter cartridge			滤芯
KDF55			高纯度铜锌合金55
residual chlorine			余氯
sulfured hydrogen			硫化氢
treatment amount			处理水量

Section B　Notes

1. fragrance blotter(试香卡)：闻香纸或者试香物。纸条上吸香味,可供香水师等人试闻香味。试纸一般是质地厚而结实的纸,香味会很好地保留在上面,即使回到家中也能清楚地辨认出香气的类型。

2. ultrafiltration technology(超滤技术)：通过过滤膜表面的微孔结构对物质进行选择性分离。当液体混合物在一定压力下流经膜表面时,小分子溶质透过膜(称为超滤液),而大分子物质则被截留,使原液中大分子浓度逐渐提高(称为浓缩液),从而实现大、小分子分离、浓缩、净化的目的。电泳漆经过超滤膜过滤,高分子树脂分子和色浆被截留,水分和小分子物质则透过分离膜,从而达到净化电泳漆、脱去水分的功效。

3. KDF55(高纯度铜锌合金55)：KDF55是一种高纯度的铜锌合金。它利用铜和锌在水中的氧化还原反应,产生电解质的环境,使细菌不能增长。它被作为净水器中使用的滤料,能抑制细菌,去除重金属(如铅、汞、铜、铁等)、氯、硫化氢,还能防止硬垢的产生。

Section C　Exercises

Ⅰ. **Translate the following words or phrases into Chinese.**

1. membrane
2. floral
3. lavender
4. fabric
5. scale
6. chlorine
7. zinc
8. lotion

II. Translate the following words or phrases into English.

1. 保证，担保
2. 提取物，萃取物
3. 试香卡
4. 家用净水器
5. 超滤技术
6. 高纯度铜锌合金 55
7. 滤芯
8. 绿香调系的

III. Role play.

A is a seller of perfumes, and B is a customer who wants to buy a perfume and knows little about perfumes. Try to use the words and phrases you have learned to ask and answer questions.

Section D Related Words and Phrases

1. distillation		蒸馏
2. uptake		提取，吸收
3. hydrate		（使）水合，（使）成水合物
4. feeder		给水器，进料器
5. osmosis		渗透
6. permeate		渗透，渗水
7. desalination		脱盐（作用）
8. precipitate		沉淀物，沉淀
9. salinity		盐度，盐浓度
10. finished water		成品水
11. sandalwood		檀香，檀香木
12. patchouli		广藿香，天竺薄荷
13. vanilla		香草
14. lily		百合

15. essential oil	精油
16. nutrient	滋养的,营养品
17. antiseptic	杀菌剂,防腐剂
18. fungal(＝fungous)	真菌的
19. peppermint	薄荷,薄荷油,薄荷糖
20. rosemary	迷迭香
21. cosmetics	化妆品,美容剂
22. cotton pad	化妆棉
23. Q-tip	Q牌棉签
24. lash curler	睫毛夹
25. biodegradable	能进行生物降解的

Section E Useful Expressions and Sentences

1. What are the benefits of essential oils?
   精油有什么好处?

2. Essential oils may soothe inflammation, act as an antiseptic, help dull pain and stimulate digestion.
   精油能缓解炎症,起到抗菌剂的作用,帮助缓解疼痛,促进消化。

3. This perfume may not suit your personality.
   这款香水可能不适合您的个性。

4. Perfumes have three notes of fragrance: the top, middle, and base.
   香水的香味分三个阶段:前味、中味和后味。

5. I prefer the scent of gardenia.
   我喜欢栀子花的香味。

6. Do you have any perfume with the fragrance of lavender?
   你们有薰衣草香味的香水吗?

7. Do you have any perfume for men? I want to buy a perfume for my boyfriend.
   你们有男士香水吗? 我想给我男朋友买一瓶。

8. We have some types of cologne for men.
   我们有几款男士古龙水。

9. Some people may be allergic to perfumes.
   有些人可能对香水过敏。

10. The scent of your perfume should only be as strong as a single flower and not

overpowering.

你的香水味道不能太强烈，要闻起来像一枝花的味道那么淡雅。

11. We have many different types of perfumes for you to choose from.

    我们有多款香水供您选择。

12. You can choose your perfume for different weather, for example, floral for gloomy and cloudy weather, and woody for snowy days.

    您可以根据不同天气选择不同香水，如阴天用花香系的香水，下雪天用木质系的香水。

13. What kind of membrane does this water filter have?

    这款净水器用什么类型的滤膜？

14. What are the main functions of this water filter?

    这款净水器的主要功能有哪些？

15. This water filter is applicable for family and hotel use.

    这款净水器可以家用，也可以用于旅馆。

16. The capacity of this water filter is large enough for a family of four.

    这款净水器的容量足够一个四口之家使用了。

17. The membrane of this filter can help to achieve a salt rejection rate of 97%.

    这款净水器的滤膜可使其脱盐率达97%。

18. You can drink the purified water directly, or if you like, you can boil it.

    您可以直接生饮净化后的水，如果喜欢也可以烧开喝。

19. With pesticide and fertilizer usage, many rural water sources are polluted and pollutants have surpassed national standards dramatically.

    随着农药和化肥的使用，许多农村水源被污染，污染物含量已严重超过国家标准。

20. Pesticide residues can be removed by this water purifier.

    使用这款净水器能去除农药残留物。

科技英语知识

科技英语的句法特点

科技英语文本基于其用词专业、语义客观、结构严密等文体特点，在句法上也有着自身的特点和规律。下面简要介绍科技英语文本最主要的 3 个句法特点。

1. 常使用无人称句

科技文本常用于阐述科学事实、实验结果，或是对某些仪器设备的结构和操作进行说明。为了体现其客观严谨，科技文本较其他文本使用第一人称、第二人称的频率较少，多使用无人称句，或是用 it 作形式主语。例如：

Computers may be classified as analog and digital.

计算机可分为模拟计算机和数字计算机两种。

In water sound travels nearly five times as fast as in air.

声音在水中的传播速度几乎是在空气中传播速度的 5 倍。

It seems that these two branches of science are mutually dependent and interacting.

看来这两个科学分支是相互依存、相互作用的。

2. 常使用被动句

科技文本常以客观陈述为主，说明某些科学现象或客观规律，因此，在科技英语中，被动句的使用非常普遍。例如：

When the radiant energy of the sun falls on the earth, it is changed into heat energy, and the earth is warmed.

太阳的辐射能到达地球后就转化为热能，从而使大地暖和起来。

Heat and light are given off by the chemical reaction.

这种化学反应能发出热和光。

It is universally known that the world is made of matter.

人人都知道世界是由物质构成的。

3. 常使用长句

在阐述一些科学事实，或解释科学术语时，科技英语文本常大量使用从句、动词非限定结构、分词短语等，这导致科技英语中句子长，结构复杂。例如：

It is because of the close association in most people's minds of tools with man that special attention has always been focused upon any animal able to use an object as a tool, but it is important to realize that this ability, on its own, does not necessarily indicate any special intelligence in the creature concerned.

　　由于在大多数人头脑中工具与人类的密切关系，人类才特别关注可以把物体当工具使用的任何一种动物，但值得注意的是，这种能力就其自身而言，并不表明这种动物有什么特别的智慧。

　　Such students will have acquired a set of engineering tools <u>consisting</u> essentially of mathematics and one or more computer language and the language of engineering graphics, and the ability to use the English language to express themselves in both oral and written forms, and will also have studied a number of basic engineering sciences, <u>including</u> engineering machines, materials and processes, and thermal fluids.

　　这样的学生将能获得一套工程技术技能、英语表达能力和许多基础工程学知识。工程技术技能主要包括数学、一种或数种计算机语言及工程制图语言。英语表达能力指用口头及书面英语两种形式表达自己。基础工程学知识包括工程机械学、材料和工艺学及热流体学。

Unit 5

Economy Management

Topic 15 Management

Section A Dialogues

 Dialogue 1

A: *General manager*　　B: *Secretary*　　C: *Manager of the Production Department*

A: Let's have a look at the current department projects. For the Finance Department, I believe they are changing the **accounting** system.

B: Yes, that's right. We're having some problems with the old system so they're looking into a new one.

A: Fine. Let's move on to the Marketing Department. Are they working on any special projects?

B: Not really, but they're planning an advertising campaign for our new product.

A: Good. I look forward to seeing it. What about the Production Department?

B: Well, as you know, they are **installing** the new automatic **assembly line**.

A: Of course. They are pretty busy. And the Personnel Department?

B: They are trying to recruit new graduates at the moment.

A: How is that going?

B: Fine.

A: How about the Management Service Department?

B: It seems they are running a series of quality-training **seminars** next month.

A: Right, that just about covers it. By the way, how is the new program going?

C: Great! We're moving right along that new line.

A: Are we going to be able to apply for a **patent** soon?

C: I hope so. I'm having fresh drawings prepared. We're still testing the product.

A: And what were the market research findings?

C: Well, it looks as if there's a fair market at the moment.

A: We'll have to run a good advertising campaign.

C: That's for sure.

A: It will certainly be to our advantage to have the patent on it as well.

C: Of course, we must be thorough. We must finish complete testing before we begin to market it.

A: Sure. We want it to be a success.

C: Has the price been worked out yet?

A: Not yet. We must move carefully.

 Vocabulary

accounting	/əˈkaʊntɪŋ/	n.	会计,会计学
install	/ɪnˈstɔːl/	v.	安装
seminar	/ˈsemɪnɑː/	n.	研讨会,研讨班
patent	/ˈpætnt/	n.	专利权,专利品,执照
assembly line			装配线,[工经] 流水作业线

 Dialogue 2

A: *Manager of the Human Resources Department*　　B: *General manager*

C: *Supervisor of the Training Center*

Scene 1

A: Since we have so many excellent technicians, I want to give them more than fair wages.

B: Will this enable us to be the best employer in this area?

A: Perhaps not. But it will certainly attract many technicians who are in search of a higher pay and a better employer.

B: Yes, some companies pay competitive wages. But generally speaking, high salaries stop people from moving on.

A: You mean, instead of overpaying, we should simply pay well to get the technician we need?

B: That's the point. The wage policy enables us to control the major part of the operation and to save money at the same time.

A: Then do you mean overtime work?

B: Right. Partly through overtime work, partly through other means.

A: I see. But more often than not, it's not the employer but the workers who control overtime.

B: There must be a solution to this problem.

A: Coming back to the power of salary, don't you think that high salaries are the key factor in **motivating** the staff?

B: It's really a complex issue. Higher salaries may encourage us to produce more, but I'm not sure whether it will make us more competitive.

A: So let's work out a better policy and go over the details.

Scene 2

C: Shall we discuss the training programs in detail?

A: OK. According to our agreement, we'll send our sales people to your center to receive technical training. They will learn to operate the latest models and the **software** you've developed.

C: No problem. We are very glad to do that.

A: How about the user training we discussed last time?

C: Oh, yes, I almost forgot about it.

A: Many of the users don't know how to use our operating system properly. So we hope you'll provide regular training classes for our users.

C: OK. We'll send you the latest schedule for the user-training classes.

A: Thank you. We also want the **interns** of our company to use the equipment at this center for their research.

C: No problem. It will be good for their future careers.

A: Yes. They need this kind of practice in advance.

C: It will also help expand your influence in China.

A: That's the point. It's **mutually** beneficial, isn't it?

 Vocabulary

motivate	/ˈməʊtɪveɪt/	v.	刺激,使有动机,激发……的积极性
software	/ˈsɒftweə(r)/	n.	软件
intern	/ˈɪntɜːn/	n.	实习生
mutually	/ˈmjuːtʃuəli/	adv.	共同地,相互地,彼此

Section B　Notes

1. advertising campaign(广告宣传活动)：指在某一特定市场上为实现某一重大目标所集中进行的大规模的广告活动，是广告决战思想的一种体现，是企业之间进行市场竞争的策略之一。广告是企业和消费者、政府和公众、广告主和受众之间沟通的桥梁，是前者向后者传播信息的重要途径。广告宣传方式有很多，如媒体广告，包括电视、报纸、杂志、网络等；平面广告使用KT板、户外招牌等；立体广告使用展示活动等；还有如发宣传单或海报、短信代发、赠送礼品、促销等。不同的产品会使用不同的广告宣传。

2. assembly line(装配线)：是人和机器的有效组合，最充分体现设备的灵活性，它将输送系统、随行夹具和在线专机、检测设备有机地组合，以满足多品种产品的装配要求。装配流水线的传输方式可以是同步传输(强制式)，也可以是非同步传输(柔性式)，根据配置的选择，实现手工装配或半自动装配。装配线在企业的批量生产中不可或缺。

Section C　Exercises

I. Translate the following words or phrases into Chinese.

1. Finance Department
2. Human Resources Department
3. seminar
4. patent
5. wage
6. assembly line
7. advertising campaign
8. operating system

II. Translate the following words or phrases into English.

1. 市场部
2. 生产部
3. 优势
4. 技术人员
5. 软件
6. 加班
7. 常规训练
8. 互惠互利

III. Role play.

If A is a general manager, and B is a sales manager. A and B are talking about the product marketing. Try to use the words and phrases you have learned to create the dialogue.

"Well, there's nowhere to go but up."

Section D Related Words and Phrases

1.	the Marketing Theory of 4Cs	4C 营销理论
2.	the Marketing Theory of 4Rs	4R 营销理论
3.	the Marketing Theory of 4Ps	4P 营销理论
4.	cross marketing	交叉营销
5.	knowledge marketing	知识营销
6.	experience marketing	体验营销
7.	relationship marketing	关系营销
8.	the co-marketing solution	合作营销
9.	management by objectives (MBO)	目标管理
10.	open management	开明管理
11.	crisis management	危机管理
12.	managing for performance	绩效管理
13.	logistics management	物流管理
14.	time management	时间管理
15.	supply chain management (SCM)	供应链管理
16.	customer relationship management (CRM)	客户关系管理
17.	process of quality management	过程质量管理法
18.	principle of 7S	7S 模型
19.	ABC analysis	ABC 分析法
20.	SWOT analysis	SWOT 分析
21.	in-time inventory	零库存
22.	constituency share	顾客份额
23.	dynamic salary	动态薪酬
24.	management buy-out	管理层收购
25.	employee stock ownership plan (ESOP)	员工持股计划

Section E Useful Expressions and Sentences

1. We're having some problems with the old system so they're looking into a new one.
   我们的旧系统存在一些问题，所以他们正在调查新系统。
2. We're moving right along that new line.

我们正开发新的生产线。

3. But generally speaking, high salaries stop people from moving on.

   但总的说来,高薪会让人止步不前。

4. There must be a solution to this problem.

   一定有办法来解决这个问题。

5. Coming back to the power of salary, don't you think that high salaries are the key factor in motivating the staff?

   回到薪水影响力的问题上来,你不认为高薪是激励员工的重要因素吗?

6. Shall we discuss the training programs in detail?

   我们讨论一下培训项目的细节好吗?

7. I think we can draw up a tentative plan now.

   我认为现在可以草拟一个临时方案。

8. If he wants to make any changes, minor alternations can be made.

   如果他有什么意见的话,我们还可以对计划稍加修改。

9. Is there any way of ensuring we'll have enough time for our talks?

   我们是否能保证有充足的时间来谈判?

10. We'd have to compare notes on what we've discussed during the day.

    我们想研究讨论一下白天谈判的情况。

11. That'll put us both in the picture.

    这样双方都能了解全面的情况。

12. Then we'd have some ideas of what you'll be needing.

    那么我们就会心中有点儿数,知道你们需要什么了。

13. I'm afraid that won't be possible, much as we'd like to.

    尽管我们很想这样做,但恐怕不行了。

14. We've got to report back to the head office.

    我们还要回去向总部汇报情况呢。

15. Thank you for your cooperation.

    谢谢你们的合作。

16. If you have any questions on the details, feel free to ask.

    如果对某些细节有意见的话,请提出来。

17. I can see you have put a lot of time into this plan.

    看得出来,你在这个计划上花了不少精力。

18. I can assure you of our close cooperation.

    我保证通力合作。

19. They've met with great favor home and abroad.

这些产品在国内外很受欢迎。

20. All these articles are best-sellers.

    所有这些产品都是我们的畅销货。

21. I would like to present our comments in the following order.

    我希望能依照以下的顺序提出我们的看法。

22. When I present my views on the competitive products, I will refer to the patent situation.

    专利的情况会在说明竞争产品时一并提出。

23. Please proceed with your presentation.

    请开始你的汇报。

24. Yes, we have done a little. But we have just started and have nothing to show you.

    是的,我们做了一些,但因为我们才刚起步,并没有任何资料可以提供给你们。

25. By the way, before leaving this subject, I would like to add a few comments.

    在结束这个问题之前顺便一提,我希望能再提出一些看法。

26. Would it be too much to ask you to respond to my question by tomorrow?

    可以请你在明天之前回复吗?

27. I would really appreciate you persuading your management.

    如果你能说服经营团队,我会很感激。

28. Maybe we should hold off until we have covered Item B on our agenda.

    也许我们应该先谈论完 B 项议题。

29. If you insist, I will comply with your request.

    如果你坚持,我们会遵照你的要求。

30. There should always be exceptions to the rule.

    凡事总有例外。

Topic 16 Finance and Economics

Section A Dialogues

Dialogue 1

Jane: **Taxpayer**   Sam: Tax official

Jane: Good morning. My company is a foreign investment **enterprise**. We are **permitted** to **engage in** the development of **real estate** and the sale of the **constructive material**. Could you tell me how to **register** with the **tax authorities**?

Sam: Good morning. I'd like to tell you that your businesses are subject to **business tax** and **value added tax**. So you should register with the **national and regional tax authorities** respectively.

Jane: What is the difference between the two tax authorities?

Sam: The main difference is that the two tax authorities **administers** are intended for different types of tax.

Jane: I see. What is the time requirement for the **tax registration**?

Sam: The tax registration is **due** within 30 days after you have received the **business certificate.**

Jane: What should we do in the process of registration?

Sam: Fill in the **application form** there, and present the prescribed materials according to different kind of enterprise.

Jane: Is the **copy** all right?

Sam: Yes, it is.

Jane: How long will it take for my company to receive the certificate of the registration?

Sam: About 30 days after we have received the above **prescribed** documents. As soon as your application is **approved**, I will personally notify you.

Jane: What is the charge of the registration?

Sam: RMB 80.

Jane: By the way, could you tell me your telephone number and working hours?

Sam: Our telephone number is 68945790, and the **working hours** are from 8:30 to 12:00 and from 14:00 to 17:30.

Jane: Thank you.
Sam: You are welcome.

Vocabulary

taxpayer	/ˈtækspeɪə(r)/	n.	纳税人
enterprise	/ˈentəpraɪz/	n.	公司,企业
permit	/pəˈmɪt/	v.	允许
real estate	/ˈriːəl ɪˈsteɪt/	n.	房地产,不动产
register	/ˈredʒɪstə(r)/	v.	登记,记录,给……注册
administer	/ədˈmɪnɪstə(r)/	v.	掌管,料理……的事务
due	/djuː/	adj.	预定应到的,预定的
copy	/ˈkɒpɪ/	n.	复印件
prescribe	/prɪˈskraɪb/	v.	规定,指定
approve	/əˈpruːv/	v.	批准,核准
engage in			从事,参加
constructive material			建材
tax authority			税务登记,税务机关
business tax			营业税
value added tax			增值税
national tax authorities			国家税务机关(国税局)
regional tax authorities			地方税务机关(地税局)
tax registration			税务登记
business certificate			营业执照
application form			申请表
working hour			工作时间

Dialogue 2

Jane: Freshman majoring in Economics   Lin: Jane's roommate and classmate

Jane: Wow! You are shopping online again!
Lin: Why not? They are all offering such attractive **discounts**! Tomorrow is Singles' Day! Stores and e-commerce sites are offering huge sales.

Jane: Oh! China's Singles' Day! The "holiday" has become into a **consumerism** festival.

Lin: I think the original idea is to try and get people who are single and bored at home in cold weather, November, to start shopping online. But then it spreads out to everybody because the deals are too good.

Jane: Alibaba said last November 11 had **racked up** more than $9 billion in sales. That beats Alibaba's previous record of $5.9 billion. In comparison, American shoppers spent just $1.2 billion during last year's Black Friday.

Lin: JD.com said sales in the first 10 hours of Singles' Day were 2.4 times last year's **volume**, and many small- and mid-sized **retailers** say up to 15 to 20 percent of their **annual revenue** comes from sales on this one day of the year.

Jane: That is crazy!

Lin: Many buyers such as me will **stock up** on items for homes, just small stuff, like a blender, home **appliances**. You can buy anything online; it's very convenient.

Jane: That's true! E-commerce offers convenient **delivery** and a safe payment system for online buying. E-commerce sites have changed people's shopping habits in China.

Lin: Singles' Day and e-commerce sites indeed impact China's economy. The explosion of consumer spending comes at a time when China's economy is slowing. The economy grew at 7.3 percent in the third **quarter** last year; that's the slowest pace since the economic **recession** in 2009. China's President Xi Jinping has promised deep and comprehensive reforms of China's economy with a shift towards **domestic** spending as a driver of future economic growth.

Jane: Aha! Alibaba and its 25,000 **merchants** will **contribute to** that transformation.

Lin: He did say that "internal demand is much needed and Alibaba is fortunate enough to be able to **tap** this demand".

Jane: Well, he is really somebody! Last year Alibaba **posted** the largest initial public offering(IPO) at $25 billion in America, with its value resting on the **potential** of Chinese consumer demand.

Vocabulary

discount	/ˈdɪskaʊnt/	n.	折扣
consumerism	/kənˈsjuːmərɪzəm/	n.	消费主义
volume	/ˈvɒljuːm/	n.	量,额
retailer	/ˈriːteɪlə(r)/	n.	零售商

appliance	/əˈplaɪəns/	n.	器具，器械
delivery	/dɪˈlɪvəri/	a.	投递，分送，送交
quarter	/ˈkwɔːtə(r)/	n.	四分之一
recession	/rɪˈseʃn/	n.	（经济的）衰退
domestic	/dəˈmestɪk/	adj.	国内的
merchant	/ˈmɜːtʃənt/	n.	商人，店主
tap	/tæp/	v.	敲击
post	/pəʊst/	v.	宣布，公布
potential	/pəˈtenʃl/	adj.	潜在的
rack up			累积，聚集
annual revenue			年收入
stock up			贮备，备足
contribute to			是……的原因之一

➡ Section B　Notes

1. Black Friday（黑色星期五）：是美国感恩节过后的第一个星期五，也是传统购物季的开始之日。黑色星期五那天的交通十分拥挤，商铺都很早开门，却很晚关门。在黑色星期五当天，很多人都去购物一整天，因为商家在那天大让利。

2. JD.com（京东商城）：中国最大的自营式电商企业，2013年，活跃用户数达到4740万人，完成订单量达到3233亿份。2010年，京东跃升为中国首家规模超过百亿的网络零售企业。京东创始人刘强东担任京东集团CEO。2014年5月22日，京东在纳斯达克挂牌，股票代码为JD，是成为仅次于阿里巴巴、腾讯、百度的中国第四大互联网上市公司。

3. Alibaba（阿里巴巴）：Alibaba Corporation，中国最大的网络公司和世界第二大网络公司，由马云在1999年一手创立企业对企业的网上贸易市场平台。2003年5月，马云投资1亿元人民币建立个人网上贸易市场平台——淘宝网。2004年10月，阿里巴巴投资成立支付宝公司，面向中国电子商务市场推出基于中介的安全交易服务。阿里巴巴在香港成立公司总部，在杭州成立中国总部，在海外设立美国硅谷、伦敦等分支机构，合资企业3家，并在中国超过40个城市设有销售中心。2014年2月10日，阿里巴巴对高德公司股票进行全面收购。2014年9月19日，阿里巴巴登录纽交所，以每股美国存托股68美元的发行价，成为美国融资额最大的IPO（initial public offerings），证券代码为BABA。

4. initial public offerings（首次公开募股）：简称IPO，指股份公司首次向社会公众公开招股。

5. recession（经济衰退）：按照美国的标准，当经济中总产出、收入和就业连续6个月到一年出现明显下降,经济中很多部门出现普遍收缩,这种经济下降就称为衰退。更严重的持续的经济低迷称为萧条。毁灭性的经济衰退则被称为经济崩溃。凯恩斯认为对商品总需求的减少是经济衰退的主要原因。经济衰退可能会导致多项经济指标同时出现下滑,比如就业、投资和公司盈利,其他伴随现象还包括下跌的物价(通货紧缩)。当然,如果经济处于滞胀(stagflation)的状态下,物价也可能快速上涨。经济衰退表现为普遍性的经济活力下降,以及随之产生的大量工人失业。经济衰退与过量商品存货、消费量的下降(可能由于对未来失去信心)、技术创新和新资本积累的缺乏及股市的随机性有关。美国历史上最糟糕的经济衰退出现在20世纪30年代,当时的失业率大约是25%。

Section C Exercises

Ⅰ. Translate the following words or phrases into Chinese.

1. small- and mid-sized retailer
2. annual revenue
3. home appliance
4. the economic recession
5. internal demand
6. contribute to
7. shopping habit
8. IPO

Ⅱ. Translate the following words or phrases into English.

1. 网购
2. 潜在需求
3. 拉动内需
4. 电子商务网站
5. 商户
6. 贮备,备足
7. 黑色星期五
8. 大人物

Ⅲ. Role play.

A is Terry who wants to cash his traveler check in a bank, and B is Lily, a bank clerk. Try to use the words and phrases you have learned to make a dialogue between A and B.

Section D Related Words and Phrases

1. balance sheet — 资产负债表,决算表
2. income and expenditure/receipt and expenditure/output and input — 支出和收入
3. assets — 资产
4. liabilities — 债务,负债
5. debit — 借方,借记,借入
6. turnover/volume of business — 营业额,成交量
7. cash on hand — 留存现金,库存现金
8. deficit — 赤字,逆差,亏损
9. individual income tax — 个人所得税
10. tax avoidance — 逃税
11. current assets — 流动资产
12. short-term investment — 短期投资
13. stock — 股票
14. corporate bonds — 债券
15. all-ordinaries index — 所有普通股指数
16. asking price — 讨价,索价,询价
17. bear market — 熊市
18. bidding price — 卖价,出价
19. bull market — 牛市
20. call option — 认购期权
21. capital gain — 资本增值
22. capital market — 资本市场
23. collateral — 担保品
24. diversification — 分散风险,多样化经营
25. duration — 持续,持久,持续期间

Section E Useful Expressions and Sentences

1. Are you going to deposit the cash in the bank?
   你要去银行存现金吗?

2. After hard negotiation, the bank agreed to loan us a 500,000 *yuan* short-term credit at last.
   经过艰苦的谈判,我们终于同银行谈妥了一笔50万元的短期贷款。

3. These are the account reconciliation for our ledgers for last month.
   这些是我们上个月总账的对账报告。

4. A cyclic economy will be achieved by coupling maximum waste prevention with material recycling.
   节约各类能源和资源,努力发展循环经济。

5. Unlike traditional economy, cyclic economy advocates a model of development on the basis of constant and circulatory use of resources.
   与传统经济不同的是,循环经济倡导发展基于持续、合理地利用能源的新模式。

6. Hey, son, are you insured?
   嗨,儿子,你买保险了吗?

7. Can I change foreign currency here?
   我可以在这里兑换外币吗?

8. Could you tell me my account balance? My account number is …
   你可以告诉我的账户还有多少余额吗? 我的账号是……

9. I want to take out a loan for school. What kind of interest rate do you offer?
   我想办理助学贷款。你们的利率是多少?

10. There are data, reports and discussion forums to educate people on how to invest.
    网上有数据、报告和论坛教人们如何投资。

11. The stock market just took a huge plunge and we've lost a lot of money!
    股票市场刚刚暴跌,我们已经损失了很多钱。

12. There are many factors that weigh in, but NASDAQ is down 200 points, the Dow-Jones indicator also suffered! Our portfolio is worth half of what it was worth a week ago.
    有很多因素起作用,但是,纳斯达克下降了200点,道-琼斯指数也下跌了很多,我们的投资市值只有一周前的一半。

13. You still have some high yield trash bonds and government bonds that will give us enough liquidity to cut our losses and reinvest in emerging markets.

你还有很多高收益的债券和政府债券，它们可以流通，从而弥补我们的损失，并重新投资市场。

14. Governments in the past created distrust among banks and financial institutions, so now people prefer to have money hidden in a jar to a piggy bank.

    过去，政府让银行和金融机构之间互不信任，所以现在，人们更愿意将钱藏到罐子里，而不是存到贪心的银行里。

15. Please tell me what the annual interest rate is.

    请告诉我年利率是多少。

16. Five twenties and ten singles, please.

    请给我 5 张 20 元和 10 张 1 元的。

17. I need 300 dollars in 100-dollar cheques.

    我要 300 美元的支票，票面价值为 100 美元。

18. I hope you'll give me ten traveler's cheques of 100 dollars each.

    我希望你给我 10 张面额为 100 美元的旅行支票。

19. Press the buttons on this machine, and enter your four digit pin numbers.

    按这台机器上的按钮，输入 4 位阿拉伯数字的密码。

20. I'd rather open a current account.

    我想开一个活期存款账号。

Topic 17 Logistics

Section A Dialogues

Dialogue 1

Jane: *Busy manager in charge of the delivery of all the goods to a fair*

Sam: *Worker in a **freight forwarder***

Jane: Could you transport our items on display, **the Canton Fair**?

Sam: Sure!

Jane: I would like you to transport the displayed items directly from our **warehouse** to the **exhibition hall**, and transport them back to our company after the exhibition.

Sam: No problem.

Jane: When could the items be delivered to the fair?

Sam: Well, usually, two days before the exhibition.

Jane: The exhibition is from October 10th to 15th, and we are asked to have them on 9th October.

Sam: Then, we will deliver them on 6th. Considering the **transportation** of road and rail, you must arrange the delivery in advance.

Jane: Of course. Thank you.

Sam: You are welcome. What else can I do for you?

Jane: Oh … Do you have any large cases capable to use for the show?

Sam: Let me see … We might have one that is 5 × 4 × 6.

Jane: That is great! I need to take this 250-pound case for the fair.

Sam: When do you need it?

Jane: I will need it in Guangzhou within two weeks. As this is the first time that we will take part in this fair, I want to be sure that they will arrive on time.

Sam: You have my word.

Jane: This is going to mean a lot to our company. I need a **guarantee** that it will be there.

Sam: Your satisfaction will be guaranteed. You will sign a contract later.

Jane: Good.

Sam: Now let's talk about the charge …

 Vocabulary

warehouse	/ˈweəhaʊs/	n.	仓库
transportation	/ˌtrænspɔːˈteɪʃn/	n.	交通
guarantee	/ˌɡærənˈtiː/	n.	保证
freight forwarder			货运代理商
the Canton Fair			广交会
exhibition hall			展览厅

 Dialogue 2

Jane: Customer   Lin: Sales manager

Jane: Your **cloisonné** vases are very charming! I want to order some, but the price is higher than I expected.

Unit 5 Economy Management

Lin: What model and how many do you want?

Jane: 80, Model CHZ01.

Lin: 80 dollars each, CIF New York.

Jane: I think your price is still high. This price would be difficult for market sales.

Lin: You know they're completely hand-made.

Jane: I must say your products are really **enchanting**. We are aware of the advantages of the goods. Honestly, there are too many products in the market, and we are new in there, we should have a **competitive** price.

Lin: I'm confident with this product in your market.

Jane: Well, I hope this **initial order** could help us to develop our market.

Lin: Then, the best I can do is 75 dollars. That's our bottom line.

Jane: Maybe. Let's talk about the **payment** terms first.

Lin: OK. Our usual practice is to be paid by **irrevocable** L/C at sight.

Jane: Oh, payment by L/C is rather inconvenient for us. It will add to our cost and undoubtedly tie up our **liquid funds**. We hope you could extend us easier payment terms as an exception, say T/T?

Lin: If that's the case, we could only accept T/T in advance. I hope you can understand our position. This can give us a **guarantee**.

Jane: OK. And I want to make sure whether the insurance covers **breakage**.

Lin: Yes. We will cover insurance with PICC for 110% of the **invoice** value against All Risks.

Jane: Good. And about the packing … I'm afraid the **cardboard boxes** are not strong enough for such a heavy load.

Lin: Well, we have taken every possible **precaution** to make sure of safe transportation of our products. Now shall I make out the **sales contract** for you?

Jane: Fine.

 Vocabulary

cloisonné	/klwɑːˈzɒneɪ/	n.	景泰蓝瓷器
enchanting	/ɪnˈtʃɑːntɪŋ/	adj.	令人着迷的,迷人的
competitive	/kəmˈpetətɪv/	adj.	有竞争力的
payment	/ˈpeɪmənt/	n.	支付,付款
irrevocable	/ɪˈrevəkəbl/	adj.	不可撤销的,最终的

119

guarantee	/ˌgærənˈtiː/	n.	保障
breakage	/ˈbreɪkɪdʒ/	n.	破碎费,赔偿损失费
invoice	/ˈɪnvɔɪs/	n.	发票
precaution	/prɪˈkɔːʃn/	n.	预防措施,预防
initial order			首次订单
liquid fund			流动资金
cardboard box			纸箱
sales contract			买卖/销售合同

Section B Notes

1. the Canton Fair(广交会):中国进出口商品交易会(China Import and Export Fair),又称广交会,创办于1957年春季,每年春秋两季在广州举办,迄今已有60年历史,是中国目前历史最长、层次最高、规模最大、商品种类最全、到会采购商最多、分布国别地区最广、成交效果最好、信誉最佳的综合性国际贸易盛会。

2. letter of credit(信用证):是指证银行应申请人的要求,并按其指示向第三方开立的载有一定金额的,在一定的期限内凭符合规定的单据付款的书面保证文件。信用证是国际贸易中最主要、最常用的支付方式。只要卖方提交了与信用证规定的完全相符的单据,银行保证付款。在信用证支付方式下,出口商在出运货物后,向付款行开出汇票并将全套单据交给议付行。付款行收到单据后即审单,如果单证相符的话,付款行付款,然后通知开证申请人付款赎单。开证申请人审核无误后必须按约定的方式付款。以开证行所负的责任为标准可以分为不可撤销信用证(irrevocable L/C)、可撤销信用证(revocable L/C)。不可撤销信用证(irrevocable L/C)指信用证一经开出,在有效期内,未经受益人及有关当事人的同意,开证行不能片面修改和撤销,只要受益人提供的单据符合信用证规定,开证行必须履行付款义务。irrevocable L/C at sight(即期不可撤销信用证),见单付款,是开证人被开证行提示的时候就是见单的时候,也是该付款的时候。

3. T/T = telegraphic transfer(电汇):汇付方式的一种。电汇是汇出行应汇款人的申请,拍发加押电报或电传(tested cable/telex),或者通过SWIFT给国外汇入行(也称解付行),指示其解付一定金额给收款人的一种汇款结算方式。其他汇付方式还包括信汇mail transfer (M/T)、票汇demand daft (D/D)、信用letter of credit (L/C)。T/T in advance:预先电汇现金。

4. T/T与L/C的区别:(1)在T/T方式下,进口商不需向银行申请开发信用证,有关于信用证部分的流程都可省去。(2)出口商在办完报关等手续后,不再采用押汇方式向银行交付单据,而是在单据列表页面中直接将单据送进口商。(3)进口商收到单据可直接办理相关手续,可销货收回资金后再付款给出口商。(4)进口商付款后,银行才能通知出口商结汇。

5. SWIFT:电汇汇款的方式之一。SWIFT 又称为"环球同业银行金融电讯协会"(Society for Worldwide Interbank Financial Telecommunication),是国际银行同业间的合作组织,成立于1973年。

6. sales contract(买卖/销售合同):买卖双方经过多次协商达成一致意见后,须签订销售合同(销售确认书)。这是对双方均有约束力的正式书面文件,由双方签字方可生效,一般称为 sales contract 或 sales confirmation,缩写为 S/C。

7. CIF:CIF 由 cost,insurance 和 freight 三个实词的第一个字母大写组成,中文意思为"成本加保险费加运费",指当货物在装运港越过船舷(实际为装运船舱内)时,卖方即完成交货。货物自装运港到目的港的运费、保险费等由卖方支付,但货物装船后发生的损坏及丢失的风险由买方承担。该术语仅适用于海运和内河运输。CIF 一般指定目的港,比如 CIF New York,目的港纽约。

8. PICC:The People's Insurance Company of China,中国人民保险公司。

Section C Exercises

Ⅰ. **Translate the following words or phrases into Chinese.**

1. hand-made
2. bottom line
3. payment term
4. in advance
5. liquid fund
6. arrive on time
7. exhibition hall
8. sales contract

Ⅱ. **Translate the following words or phrases into English.**

1. 不可撤销信用证
2. 货运代理商
3. 签合同
4. 保险金额
5. 广交会
6. 投保
7. 预防措施
8. 超出预期

Ⅲ. **Role play.**

A is a student reporter in Lushan College. He/She wants to interview one of the managers of the Wheat Commune in this college about the detailed plans of the luggage delivery for the graduates. B is the manager. Try to use the words and phrases you have learned to ask and answer questions.

Section D Related Words and Phrases

1.	FOB(free on board)	离岸价格
2.	CIF(cost, insurance and freight)	成本、保险加海运费
3.	CIP(carriage and insurance paid to)	运费、保险费付至目的地
4.	CPT(carriage paid to)	运费付至目的地
5.	CTNR(container)	柜子
6.	CY/CY	整柜交货(起点/终点)
7.	D/A(document against acceptance)	承兑交单
8.	D/O(delivery order)	提货单
9.	D/P(document against payment)	付款交单
10.	DAF(delivered at frontier)	边境交货
11.	DDC(destination delivery charge)	目的港码头费
12.	DDP(delivered duty paid)	完税后交货
13.	shipment	装运
14.	FPA(free from particular average)	平安险
15.	WPA(with particular average)	水渍险
16.	All Risks	一切险
17.	prompt delivery	即期装运,即期交货
18.	transshipment	转运
19.	port of loading	装运港
20.	port of discharge	卸货港
21.	port of destination	目的港
22.	FCL(full container load)	整箱货
23.	LCL(less than container load)	拼箱货
24.	wooden case	木箱
25.	payment in advance	预付(货款)

Section E Useful Expressions and Sentences

1. We've covered insurance on these goods for 10% above the invoice value against All Risks.

   我们已经将这些货物按发票金额加 10% 投保综合险。

2. How do you prefer the goods to be dispatched, by rail or by sea?

   你方将怎样发运货物,铁路还是海运?

3. We have insured the shipment against WPA at the rate of 0.3% for the sum of USD300,000 with PICC.

   我们已为这批货物向中国人民保险公司投保水渍险,保险费率为0.3%,投保额为 30 万美元。

4. We pack the goods in light containers in order to pay less freight.

   我们用轻盈包装箱装货,以便少付些运费。

5. an initial payment of USD500 and ten installments of USD200

   500 美元的首期付款加 10 次 200 美元的分期付款

6. Please pack the vases a dozen to a wooden case and 100 to a 20' FCL.

   请将一打花瓶装一个木箱,100 个木箱装一个 20 英尺集装箱。

7. Please mark the bags according to the drawing given.

   请按照所给的图样给这些袋子进行标识。

8. With regard to the packing for tea, we'd like to give you our requirements as follows.

   关于茶叶的包装问题,我方想提一些要求。

9. As your order covers such a large quantity, we are not in a position to promise immediate shipment. But we will let you know when our supply condition improves.

   因贵方订单数量较大,我们无法保证立刻装运。一旦供应状况好转,我们将立刻告知。

10. Our buyers are in urgent need of the goods. Could you manage to expedite the shipment?

    我们买主急需这批货,你方能否尽快装运?

11. We regret our delay in shipping.

    很遗憾,我们延误发货了。

12. The company has experienced a serious difficulty in financing and payments are delayed.

    该公司遇到严重的财务困难,故延误付款。

13. The time of shipment is approaching, but we have not yet received your L/C.

Please do your utmost to expedite its establishment so that we may effect shipment before the end of this month.

装运期已临近,但我们还未收到相关信用证,请尽最大努力开立信用证以便我方在月底前发货。

14. Logistics operation and management include packaging, warehousing, material handling, inventory control, transport, forecasting, strategic planning, customer service, etc.

    物流操作和管理包括包装、仓储、物料搬运、库存控制、运输、预测、战略计划和客户服务等方面。

15. A container terminal connects sea and land, transferring containers to and from ships. It is capable of handling containers more quickly, economically, accurately and in greater volumes than conventional ports.

    集装箱码头连接陆运和海运,经船上装运集装箱。在装卸搬运上,集装箱码头比普通杂货码头更快、更经济、更准确,吞吐量更大。

16. Information is the key to the success of logistics.

    信息是物流成功的关键。

17. Warehousing is not a new business, but it has gained new functions in modern logistics.

    仓储不是新的行业,但在现代物流中有了新的功能。

18. Inventory control can effectively reduce logistics cost.

    库存控制能有效地降低物流成本。

19. Due to improper packing, the goods are terribly damaged.

    由于包装不善,货物严重受损。

20. Things like plastic, steel and glass can be recycled to reduce production cost so that natural resources are saved.

    塑料、钢铁和玻璃这样的物品能回收利用以降低生产成本,节约自然资源。

Unit 5　Economy Management

Topic 18　Marketing Management

Section A　Dialogues

Dialogue 1

Sarah: DJ of English for Marketing Learning
*Roger: Special guest, manager of the **Marketing Department** in a company*

Sarah: Good morning, everyone. Welcome to our program. Today, our special guest is Roger, the manager of the Marketing Department. Hello, Roger. Thank you for coming.

Roger: Good morning, Sarah. It's my pleasure to be here.

Sarah: So today our topic is the **concept** of marketing. Most people think of marketing only as selling and advertising. What's your understanding, Roger?

Roger: I can tell you that selling and **advertising** are only **the tip of the marketing iceberg**. Although they are important, they are only two of many marketing functions and often not the most important ones.

Sarah: In this case, what is marketing?

Roger: Briefly, marketing is getting the right goods and services to the right people at the right time, at the right place and price, with the right communication.

Sarah: Normally, we think a market is a place where buyers and sellers gather to **exchange** their goods and services.

Roger: That's right. But more importantly, a market is the set of actual and **potential** buyers (customers) of a product or service. These buyers (customers) share a particular need or want that can be **satisfied** through exchanges and relationships.

Sarah: From your explanation, I notice these key words: customers' needs, wants and demands. So is the saying "The customer is king" correct in marketing?

Roger: Ah, almost right! All markets ultimately are people. Even when we say a **firm** bought a Lenovo computer, we mean one or several people in the firm decided to buy it.

Sarah: Thank you for your **vivid illustration**, Roger. I have a better understanding of what marketing is now. Can you make a brief summary of the concept of marketing?

Roger: Essentially, marketing is the process of creating or **directing** an organization to be successful in selling a product or service that people not only desire, but **are willing to** buy.

Sarah: Thank you for your patient explanation, Roger. We hope you can come to our program next time.

 Vocabulary

concept	/ˈkɒnsept/	n.	概念
advertising	/ˈædvətaɪzɪŋ/	n.	广告
iceberg	/ˈaɪsbɜːɡ/	n.	冰山
exchange	/ɪksˈtʃeɪndʒ/	n.	交换, 交易
potential	/pəˈtenʃl/	adj.	潜在的
satisfy	/ˈsætɪsfaɪ/	v.	使满意
firm	/fɜːm/	n.	公司
vivid	/ˈvɪvɪd/	adj.	生动的
illustration	/ɪləˈstreɪʃn/	n.	说明, 阐释
direct	/daɪˈrekt/	v.	导向, 指向
Marketing Department			市场部, 营销部
the tip of the marketing iceberg			市场营销的冰山一角
be willing to ...			愿意……, 乐意……

 Dialogue 2

Jenny and Elias are business partners. Now they are talking about running a new **branch office**.

Jenny: What do you think we need to do to get our new branch office running well?

Elias: First, I'd make sure that we have a good, local, **corporate** lawyer. He or she will know all the local **laws and regulations**.

Jenny: That's very important. A friend recommended a good law firm to me. We'll need someone to hire **staff**.

Elias: I think that we should send one of our HR people to do that. I don't think we should use an **agency**, because they won't **be familiar with** the type of people we employ. By the way, have we decided on the location of the branch?

Unit 5 Economy Management

Jenny: Yes, we have. We chose the **location** in the northeast of the city, not too far from the airport and **on the edge of** the CBD.

Elias: Why didn't we choose an office in the CBD?

Jenny: The offices there are too expensive. Have we **negotiated** any **contracts** yet?

Elias: Yes. We've signed two contracts with companies since we already did **market research** in this country. We hope to sign another three this month.

Jenny: Great! When will the branch open?

Elias: Hopefully next month. Everything is a little **rushed**. We should be able to **set up** our new branch and **expand** our business quickly.

Jenny: Has an advertising **campaign** been prepared?

Elias: Yes, it has. We're going to **target** the business community through business magazines.

Jenny: OK. I made plenty of business contacts on my last visit through the **embassy**. We should be able to get plenty of customers.

Vocabulary

corporate	/ˈkɔːpərət/	adj.	公司的,法人的
staff	/stɑːf/	n.	职员
agency	/ˈeɪdʒənsi/	n.	代理,中介
location	/ləʊˈkeɪʃn/	n.	位置
negotiate	/nɪˈgəʊʃieɪt/	v.	谈判,商议
contract	/ˈkɒntrækt/	n.	合同
rushed	/rʌʃt/	adj.	匆忙的
expand	/ɪkˈspænd/	v.	扩大,扩张
campaign	/kæmˈpeɪn/	n.	运动,活动
target	/ˈtɑːgɪt/	v.	把……作为目标
embassy	/ˈembəsi/	n.	大使馆
branch office			分公司,分店
laws and regulations			法律法规
be familiar with			熟悉
on the edge of			在……的边缘
market research			市场调研
set up			建立

Section B　Notes

1. Marketing Department：市场部，营销部。它是一个企业的经济命脉，营销部业绩的好坏直接影响企业收入的高低。一般来说，营销部负责人的要求比较高，要有较好的沟通能力、市场开发和分析能力、管理能力、应变能力，责任心强，有号召力，熟悉营销模式，具有业务开拓渠道、良好的营销管理策略及经验。

2. HR(human resources)：人力资源。戴维·尤里奇(Dave Ulrich)被奉为人力资源管理的开创者，他最早提出了HR(人力资源)这一概念。HR目标是让企业更好地进行人力资源的发展和规划，系统重点是实现人力资源部门在员工素质管理、薪酬管理、绩效考核等方面的需求。

3. CBD(central business district)：中央商务区，指一个国家或大城市里主要商业活动进行的地区，这些区域同时也是市中心。其概念最早产生于1923年的美国，当时定义为"商业汇聚之处"。随后，CBD的内容不断发展丰富，成为一个城市、一个区域乃至一个国家的经济发展中枢。一般而言，CBD高度集中了城市的经济、科技和文化力量，作为城市的核心，应具备金融、贸易、服务、展览、咨询等多种功能，并配以完善的市政交通与通信条件。

Section C　Exercises

I. Translate the following words or phrases into Chinese.

1. exchange
2. satisfy
3. direct
4. agency
5. negotiate
6. the tip of the marketing iceberg
7. branch office
8. market research

II. Translate the following words or phrases into English.

1. 广告
2. 公司
3. 法人的
4. 合同
5. 扩大
6. 把……作为目标
7. 法律法规
8. 广告宣传活动

III. Role play.

Suppose A and B are business partners. They want to run a new branch office in another country. What should they do to run the new branch office successfully? Try to use the words and phrases you have learned to make a dialogue.

Section D Related Words and Phrases

1. need — 需要
2. want — 欲望
3. demand — 需求
4. relationship marketing — 关系营销
5. marketing network — 营销网
6. brand strategy — 品牌策略
7. pricing strategy — 定价策略
8. public relation — 公共关系
9. buying role — 购买者角色
10. purchasing power — 购买力
11. seller's market — 卖方市场
12. buying behavior — 购买行为
13. product strategy — 产品策略
14. consumer market — 消费者市场
15. distribution channel — 分销渠道
16. customer satisfaction — 顾客满意度
17. total customer value — 顾客总成本
18. marketing environment — 营销环境
19. follow-up survey — 跟踪调查

20. marketing director　　　　　营销总监
21. wholesale　　　　　　　　　批发
22. transaction　　　　　　　　　交易
23. overseas market　　　　　　海外市场
24. falling market　　　　　　　下滑市场
25. market situation　　　　　　市场行情

Section E　Useful Expressions and Sentences

1. In marketing, market is defined as people with the desire and with the ability to buy a specific product.
   在营销学中,市场是指对某种产品有购买欲望和购买力的人群。

2. Selling and advertising are only the tip of the marketing iceberg.
   销售和广告仅仅是市场营销中的冰山一角。

3. The concepts of exchange and relationship lead to the concept of a market.
   交换和关系的概念引发市场概念的产生。

4. Today's customer faces a vast array of product and brand choices, as well as price and suppliers.
   如今的消费者要面对大量的产品、品牌、价格和厂商。

5. A new-product strategy is part of the organization's overall marketing strategy.
   某一新产品的策略是一个公司总体市场策略的一部分。

6. Customer satisfaction with a purchase depends on the product's performance relative to a buyer's expectation.
   相对于购买者的期望值来说,顾客的满意度更依赖于产品的性能。

7. Lenovo cooperates effectively with distributors through the distribution system.
   联想公司通过分销模式有效地和经销商合作。

8. Lenovo develops rapidly and has a large proportion of the market.
   联想公司发展很快,并且在市场上占有很大的份额。

9. There are both costs and benefits to conduct marketing research.
   进行市场调研既有成本也有效益。

10. Will the payoff or rate of return be worth the investment?
    从盈利或者回报率来说,此项投资值得吗?

11. How is Egyptian market going so far?
    目前埃及市场的情况怎么样?

12. We brought the products to the market two months ago.

    我们的产品两个月前刚投放市场。

13. This kind of product will be popular in the market or good demanding.

    这类产品在那里有市场需求。

14. The market situation is much better than we expected.

    市场行情比我们预计得要好。

15. We cannot forecast the future market in this area.

    我们无法确定这些地区未来的市场行情。

16. Our product is really competitive in the global market.

    我们的产品在国际市场上很有竞争力。

17. Understanding the buying behavior of the target market is the main task of marketing managers.

    了解目标市场的购买行为是营销经理的主要任务。

18. Customers also may tell their family, friends and acquaintances about their experiences with buying and using products.

    消费者还会将购买和使用产品的经历和体会告知家人、朋友和熟人。

19. This industry still has big potential.

    这个行业还有一个很大的市场。

20. There is still a big gap for 2 years in the market.

    今明两年市场还有较大空缺。

Topic 19　Tourism

Section A　*Dialogues*

Dialogue 1

Tony：Travel agency clerk　　Betty：Customer

Tony：Good morning. What can I do for you?

Betty：Yes. I'd like some information about the European tour.

Tony：My pleasure. We have many **tour packages**, which last from ten days to two weeks. The ten-day trip is very popular.

Betty: I would be interested in the ten-day trip. How much would it cost?

Tony: The price is RMB 9,999 for each person.

Betty: Well, I see. What does the package include?

Tony: It includes **return flights**, nine-night hotel with breakfast.

Betty: That sounds reasonable. How about the children? My son is only 7 years old. He can share a bed with me. Will it be cheaper?

Tony: Sorry, even if you don't require any extra beds, the price will be the same as an adult's. And when would you like to go?

Betty: Perhaps around National Day.

Tony: We have one ten-day trip that is still available. It will depart from Beijing on September 30. Is that OK?

Betty: OK. It would be perfect for me, because I don't need to work that day. Let me think it over. I'll call you back to **make a reservation** soon.

Tony: OK. You'd better make a decision quickly; otherwise this spot may be taken by someone else. On **National Day**, so many people want to go abroad, especially to Europe.

Betty: I'll decide as soon as possible. May I have your **business card**?

Tony: Of course. Here you are. You can dial the telephone number on it.

Betty: Thanks. Do you have any **brochures** about the European tours?

Tony: If you want to get more information, you can get the **guidebooks** in different languages on the information desk.

Betty: Thank you. See you.

Tony: See you.

Vocabulary

brochure	/ˈbrəʊʃə(r)/	n.	手册,小册子
guidebook	/ˈɡaɪdbʊk/	n.	指南
tour package			旅行套餐
return flight			往返航班
make a reservation			预订
National Day			国庆节
business card			名片

Dialogue 2

Mary: Receptionist   John: Tourist

Mary: Good evening, sir. May I help you?
John: Good evening. I'd like to **check in**, please.
Mary: Have you got the reservation, sir?
John: Yes. I made a reservation for four nights on the day before yesterday.
Mary: May I have your name, please?
John: Sure. John Smith.
Mary: Just a moment, please. Yes, we have it. One **single room**, four nights.
John: But I prefer a **double room** with a **private bathroom** now, if possible.
Mary: It is the peak season at this moment. I'll check if we have it or not. (*One minute later*) Sorry, we don't have it.
John: Is there anyone who will check out tomorrow?
Mary: Wait a moment, please. Yes, two customers will **check out** tomorrow morning. It's a double room with a private bathroom.
John: OK, I'm taking the single room for tonight. Please arrange the double room for me once the guests leave.
Mary: How long do you intend to stay? Just four nights?
John: Probably longer.
Mary: Here is your card. The **porter** will take your cases up to your room.
John: Thank you. By the way, I'd like to be called at 7 tomorrow morning.
Mary: No problem. Would you like your breakfast served in your room?
John: Yes, just for tomorrow's breakfast with one *China Daily* for me, please.
Mary: Certainly.
John: By the way, is **the Forbidden City** far from here?
Mary: It takes about 20 minutes by bus in **rush hour**.
John: Are there many people at the Forbidden City every day?
Mary: It should be. The Forbidden City used to be the **imperial** palace of the Ming and Qing **Dynasties**, and it is really **magnificent**. So it attracts lots of tourists every day.
John: Thank you.
Mary: My pleasure.

Vocabulary

porter	/ˈpɔːtə(r)/	n.	服务员，行李搬运工
imperial	/ɪmˈpɪəriəl/	adj.	皇帝的
dynasty	/ˈdɪnəsti/	n.	王朝，朝代
magnificent	/mægˈnɪfɪsnt/	adj.	宏伟的，壮丽的
check in			报到，登记入住
single room			单人间
double room			双人间
private bathroom			独立卫生间
check out			退房，结账离开
China Daily			《中国日报》
the Forbidden City			紫禁城
rush hour			上下班高峰期

Section B Notes

1. travel agency（旅行社）：世界旅游组织给出的定义为：零售代理机构向公众提供关于可能的旅行、居住和相关服务，包括服务酬金和条件的信息。旅行组织者或制作批发商或批发商在旅游需求提出前，以组织交通运输，预订不同的住宿和提出所有其他服务为旅行和旅居做准备的行业机构。我国《旅行社管理条例》中指出，旅行社是指以营利为目的、从事旅游业务的企业。其中，旅游业务是指为旅游者代办出境、入境和签证手续，招徕、接待旅游者，为旅游者安排食宿等有偿服务的经营活动。旅行社的营运项目通常包括各种交通运输票券（例如机票、巴士票与船票）、套装行程、旅行保险、旅行书籍等的销售，以及国际旅行所需的证照（例如护照、签证）的咨询、代办。从旅行社衍生的职业有领队、导游、票务员、签证专员、计调员（旅游操作）等。经营旅行社必须持有当局签发的有效牌照，并且必须是某指定旅行社商会的会员才能经营旅行团，进行带团旅行。

2. package tour（包价旅游）：是指旅游者在旅游活动中开始前即将全部或部分旅游费用预付给旅行社，由旅行社根据同旅游者签订的合同，相应地为旅游者安排旅游途中的吃、住、行、游、购、娱等活动。又可分为团体包价旅游、半包价旅游、小包价旅游和零包价旅游。

3. the Forbidden City（紫禁城）：是中国明、清两代24个皇帝的皇宫。明朝第三位皇帝朱棣迁都北京，开始营造紫禁城宫殿，至明永乐十八年（1420年）落成。依照中国古代星象学，紫微垣位于中天，乃天帝所居，天人对应，所以，皇帝的居所又称紫禁城。

Unit 5 Economy Management

Section C Exercises

I. Translate the following words or phrases into Chinese.

1. brochure
2. porter
3. imperial
4. magnificent
5. check in
6. package tour
7. return flight
8. check out

II. Translate the following words or phrases into English.

1. 指南
2. 朝代
3. 名片
4. 预订
5. 单人间
6. 独立卫生间
7. 紫禁城
8. 上下班高峰期

III. Role play.

A is a travel agency clerk, and B is a customer who wants to get some information about the US tour. Try to use the words and phrases you have learned to ask and answer questions.

Section D Related Words and Phrases

1. travel agency — 旅行社
2. tour arrangement — 旅行安排
3. airline company — 航空公司
4. ticket office — 购票处
5. single ticket — 单程票
6. return ticket — 往返票
7. economy class — 经济舱
8. business class — 商务舱
9. first class — 头等舱
10. luggage tag — 行李牌
11. departure lounge — 候机室
12. check-in — 登机手续办理
13. boarding pass/card — 登机牌
14. departure gate — 登机口
15. luggage claim — 行李领取处
16. duty-free shop — 免税店
17. currency exchange — 货币兑换处
18. visa — 签证
19. customs — 海关
20. passport — 护照
21. goods to declare — 报关物品
22. tour brochure — 旅游小册子
23. local guide — 地陪,地方导游
24. place of interest — 风景名胜
25. China National Tourism Administration — 中国国家旅游局

Section E Useful Expressions and Sentences

1. What is the lowest airfare (most economic flights) to Paris?
   到巴黎最便宜的票价是多少?
2. Can you reserve me two seats to Hong Kong, non-stop, please?

请你帮我订两张直飞香港的机票。

3. I'd like to reserve a flight to Tokyo for the first of October.
   我想预订10月1日飞往东京的航班。

4. Can I get a ticket for the sight-seeing bus here?
   是否可在此购买观光巴士券?

5. Where is the metro station near here?
   最近的地铁站在哪里?

6. Your flight has been delayed one hour.
   你的航班已经延后1个小时。

7. Could you show me where my seat is?
   请告诉我,我的座位在哪里?

8. How long does it take to fly from A to B?
   从A到B的飞行时间要多久?

9. May I see your passport, please?
   请把你的护照给我看一下,好吗?

10. Anything to declare?
    有什么东西要申报吗?

11. One-way trip or round trip?
    单程还是来回?

12. When do I have to check in?
    何时办理乘机手续?

13. May I have your flight number, please?
    请问您的航班号码是多少?

14. Please arrive at the airport two hours before departure.
    请在起飞前两小时到达机场。

15. Do you any vacant (spare) room in the hotel?
    旅馆里有空余房间吗?

16. I'd like to book a double room for Tuesday next week.
    我想订一间下周二的双人房间。

17. Is hot water always available?
    随时都有热水供应吗?

18. I'll take this room.
    我要订这间房。

19. Could you store my valuables?
    是否可代为保管贵重物品?

20. How long do you intend to stay in this hotel?
    您准备在这家旅馆住多久?

科技英语知识

科技英语的篇章特点

科技英语篇章崇尚严谨周密,概念准确,逻辑性强,行文简练,重点突出,句式严整,少有变化。

科技英语的篇章结构有以下几个明显的特点。

1. 语篇的格式化

各类论文、实验报告、测试报告格式固定,国际贸易中的合同、订单、函电等也采用国际通用格式,各类产品的说明书格式也十分相似。

2. 语篇逻辑紧密,系统性强

科技英语的语篇注重词汇衔接和逻辑连接。语篇中句子和句子之间、段落和段落之间、部分与部分之间联系紧密,连贯性优于其他种类文体。

在词汇衔接方面,科技英语文体采用词汇的重复出现来避免语言在传递过程中产生歧义,使读者易于正确地理解作者所要论述的客观事实或复杂的认识过程,体现了科技英语的准确性。如:

Many stories about the spread of <u>AIDS</u> are false. You cannot get <u>AIDS</u> working or attending with someone who has the disease. You cannot get it by touching drinking glasses or other objects used by such persons.

科技英语的语篇通过逻辑连接手段的运用,使读者可以了解句子的语义联系,甚至可经前句从逻辑上预见后续句的语义,体现了科技英语的逻辑推理性和严密性。如:

Microsurgery is helping to solve all kinds of medical problems that had been thought hopeless. For example, doctors can use the technique to restore blood flow to the brain to prevent strokes. <u>And</u> they can reopen parts of the reproductive system <u>so</u> some men and women who are not fertile can have children. Eye and ear doctors have used the techniques of microsurgery since the 1920s. <u>But</u> it was not until the early 1970s that doctors began to develop a better understanding of the possibilities of microsurgery.

3. 语篇段落规范

科技英语语篇段落一般在段首均有一个概括该段内容的主题句,并能暗示该段落的展开方式,使读者快速了解段意,并给读者提供更多信息。主题句之后的扩展句与主题句紧密相连,结尾部分还有一个总结句,与主题句呼应,加深读者印象。

科技英语篇章一般由导言、正文和结论或结束语三部分组成。科技英语文体往往也借用其他文体(如文学文体)的词语或句式和其他的修辞手段,以增加语言表达效果。总之,清晰、准确、精练、严密是科技英语篇章的文体特点。

Unit 6

Art

Topic 20 Industrial Design

Section A Dialogues

 Dialogue 1

Linda: **Representative** *of* **Phoenix Bike Company**

Clark: *Representative from an American company*

Clark: Good afternoon. My name is Mr. Clark. I'm from the U. S., and here is my card.

Linda: Thanks. Nice to meet you, Mr. Clark. I'm Linda, the representative of Phoenix Bike Company. This is my card.

Clark: Thank you. Nice to meet you, too, Miss Linda. This is my first time to travel to China to attend the **exhibition**, and I'm interested in your products. Can you make a **brief** introduction of your latest bike?

Linda: Sure. This is our company's new bike. It is in the middle of our exhibition hall.

Clark: Oh, yes. I have just seen it this morning. I find that bike very beautiful in design.

Linda: Yes. The new type of the bike designed by our **engineers** is **ingenious** and practical. This bike can be **folded** in half and is handy to carry around, especially **convenient** during traffic jams or travel. And the tire is **characteristic** of **nonskid** stops on wet roads.

Clark: Yes. What are the **specifications**?

Linda: If I may refer you to Page 6 of the brochure, you'll find all the specifications there.

Clark: Great.

Linda: Because of its precise **mechanical structure**, this bike has few **breakdowns** and is very easy to **maintain**. This type of bike has met with great favor overseas and is always in great **demand**.

Clark: Oh, I see. Thank you very much, Miss Linda. I will contact you soon when I need further information about your products.

Linda: Sure. I hope we shall be hearing from you very shortly.

Clark: I expect you will, Miss Linda.

 Vocabulary

representative	/ˌreprɪˈzentətɪv/	n.	代表
exhibition	/ˌeksɪˈbɪʃn/	n.	展览会
brief	/briːf/	adj.	简洁的,简短的
engineer	/ˌendʒɪˈnɪə(r)/	n.	工程师
ingenious	/ɪnˈdʒiːniəs/	adj.	精巧的,新颖独特的
fold	/fəʊld/	v.	折叠,合拢
convenient	/kənˈviːniənt/	adj.	便捷的,方便的
characteristic	/ˌkærəktəˈrɪstɪk/	n.	特征,特性
nonskid	/nɒnˈskɪd/	adj.	(轮胎等)不滑的
specification	/ˌspesɪfɪˈkeɪʃn/	n.	规格,详述
breakdown	/ˈbreɪkdaʊn/	n.	故障,崩溃
maintain	/meɪnˈteɪn/	v.	维持,维修
demand	/dɪˈmɑːnd/	n.	需求
Phoenix Bike Company			凤凰自行车公司
mechanical structure			机械结构

 Dialogue 2

Alice: Salesgirl   Frank: Salesman

Alice: Good morning, Frank. Glad to see you!

Frank: Good morning, Alice. Glad to see you! I came here to introduce our newly designed **suitcase**. Have a look, please!

Alice: Mmm ... the suitcase is very beautiful.

Frank: Yes. This suitcase is of **superb** quality as well as the typical **artistic beauty**. The suitcase has a **durable** and easy-to-clean surface. Compared with other suitcases, our

Unit 6 Art

product uses **light composite materials** with **dynamic design** which makes it more efficient, economical and practical for all walks of life.

Alice: That looks brilliant. What about the color of your products?

Frank: The suitcase's cover comes in various kinds of colors including **jet black**, pure white, space grey, bright silver, shiny red, gold and rose gold. All are the latest **fashion colors**. The products are magnificent and **tasteful** and have a long enjoyed great fame both at home and abroad. The products have met with a warm **reception** and quick sale in most European countries. There has been a steady demand in the market for this kind of suitcase.

Alice: Impressive! How much for each?

Frank: 45 dollars.

Alice: It seems a bit expensive. Can you give me a **discount**?

Frank: Well, the cost of **raw material**, you know, has gone up by 10% since last season. Our products are the best kind in Asia and we can very well compete against Japan in price. Our usual figure is around 5%. You are my important partner, and I can give you 8%, but that depends on the size of the order.

Alice: OK, I'll take 500 pieces. **Deliver** the goods here tomorrow.

Frank: No problem.

Vocabulary

suitcase	/ˈsuːtkeɪs/	n.	手提箱
superb	/suːˈpɜːb; sjuː-/	adj.	极好的,华丽的
durable	/ˈdjʊərəbl/	adj.	耐用的,持久的
tasteful	/ˈteɪstfl/	adj.	高雅的,有雅致的
reception	/rɪˈsepʃn/	n.	欢迎,反应,反响
discount	/ˈdɪskaʊnt/	n.	折扣
deliver	/dɪˈlɪvə(r)/	v.	递送,交付
artistic beauty			艺术美学
light composite material			轻型复合材料
dynamic design			动态设计
jet black			亮黑
fashion color			流行色
raw material			原材料

Section B Notes

1. dynamic design：动态设计，是指在动态作用下，以结构构件动力状态反应为依据的设计。

2. fashion color：流行色，即合乎时尚的色彩，是指某一时期逐渐盛行起来、受欢迎的色彩，具有新鲜、时髦、变化快的特点，也被称为时尚色彩。

Section C Exercises

Ⅰ. **Translate the following words or phrases into Chinese.**

1. ingenious
2. specification
3. mechanical structure
4. demand
5. superb quality
6. light composite material
7. dynamic design
8. meet with warm reception

Ⅱ. **Translate the following words or phrases into English.**

1. 工程师
2. 便捷的
3. 不打滑的
4. 耐用的
5. 折扣
6. 原材料
7. 稳定的需求量
8. 伙伴

Ⅲ. **Role play.**

Suppose A is a businessman, and B is a representative of one printer company. B is introducing a new designed printer to A. Try to use the words and phrases you have learned to ask and answer questions.

Unit 6 Art

Section D Related Words and Phrases

1. product design — 产品设计
2. brief introduction — 简要介绍
3. beautiful in design — 设计精美
4. engineer — 工程师
5. traffic jam — 交通堵塞
6. characteristic — 特点
7. specification — 规格
8. brochure — 手册
9. mechanical structure — 机械结构
10. breakdown — 损坏
11. maintain — 保养
12. demand — 需求
13. superb quality — 高质量
14. artistic beauty — 艺术美学
15. light composite material — 轻型复合材料
16. jet black — 亮黑
17. pure white — 纯白
18. space grey — 太空灰
19. bright silver — 亮银
20. shiny red — 亮红
21. rose gold — 玫瑰金
22. raw material — 原材料
23. figure — 指标
24. partner — 伙伴
25. order — 订单

Section E Useful Expressions and Sentences

1. I'm interested in your products.
   我对贵公司的产品很感兴趣。

2. Can you make a brief introduction of your latest bike?
   你能简要介绍一下你们的最新款自行车吗?

3. I find that bike very beautiful in design.
   我觉得那款自行车设计得非常精美。

4. The new type of the bike designed by our engineers is ingenious and practical.
   我公司工程师设计的新款自行车非常精巧、实用。

5. This bike can be folded in half and is handy to carry around, especially convenient during traffic jams or travel.
   这款自行车可以半折叠,方便携带,尤其在交通堵塞中或旅行时特别方便。

6. The tire of this bike is characteristic of nonskid stops on wet roads.
   这款自行车的轮胎具有在潮湿路面不打滑的特点。

7. What are the specifications?
   都有哪些规格呢?

8. If I may refer you to Page 6 of the brochure, you'll find all the specifications there.
   如果您看一下手册的第6页,就会在那儿找到所有的规格。

9. Because of its precise mechanical structure, this bike has few breakdowns and is very easy to maintain.
   这款自行车由于机械构造简洁,所以很少有故障,且易于保养。

10. This type of bike has met with great favor overseas and is always in great demand.
    这款自行车在国外很受欢迎,需求量一直很大。

11. I will contact you soon when I need further information about your products.
    如果我还须进一步了解你们的产品,我会联系您的。

12. I hope we shall be hearing from you very shortly.
    希望尽快听到您的消息。

13. I came here to introduce our newly designed suitcase.
    我来向您介绍我们的新手提箱。

14. This suitcase is of superb quality as well as the typical artistic beauty.
    这款手提箱品质优良,很具艺术美感。

15. The suitcase has a durable and easy-to-clean surface.
    这款手提箱的表面耐用并容易清洗。

16. Compared with other suitcases, our product uses light composite material with dynamic design which makes it more efficient, economical and practical for all walks of life.

    与其他手提箱相比,该产品使用了轻型复合材料和动态设计,使之适用于不同人群,更高效、经济和实用。

17. What about the color of your products?

    你们的产品有哪些颜色?

18. The suitcase's cover comes in various kinds of colors.

    这款手提箱有多种颜色。

19. The products are magnificent and tasteful and have a long enjoyed great fame both at home and abroad.

    这款产品精美、高雅,在国内外久享盛誉。

20. The products have met with a warm reception and quick sale in most European countries.

    该产品很受欢迎,在欧洲多国销量很快。

21. There has been a steady demand in the market for this kind of suitcase.

    这款手提箱在市场中一直保持稳定的需求量。

22. Can you give me a discount?

    你能给我一个折扣吗?

23. The cost of raw material has gone up by 10% since last season.

    原材料价格从上季度以来就上涨了10%。

24. Our products are the best kind in Asia and we can very well compete against Japan in price.

    我们的产品是亚洲最好的,在价格上完全可以跟日本竞争。

25. Our usual figure is around 5%.

    我们通常让利指标为5%。

26. You are my important partner, and I can give you 8%, but that depends on the size of the order.

    你是我重要的合作伙伴,我给你让利8%,但那还需要根据订货的多少来决定。

Topic 21　Environmental Art Design

Section A　Dialogues

Dialogue 1

David and Cindy: landscape designers of Green City Company

Cindy: Hi, David, where have you been these days?

David: I just came back from Suzhou, China.

Cindy: Suzhou. It makes me think of **classical** gardens.

David: Yeah. There are **abundant** Chinese gardens. I visited Zhuozheng Yuan.

Cindy: What does it mean?

David: It is the name of the garden, which can be translated as **Humble Administrator's Garden**. It is the largest and most **renowned** among Suzhou gardens.

Cindy: It must be very beautiful.

David: Right, very attractive. Both the **water features** and the natural **landscapes** are impressive.

Cindy: Water feature? Is it a **unique** characteristic of Chinese gardens?

David: Yes. There is a famous idiom about Chinese gardens: "No water, no landscape".

Cindy: Interesting. So, there must be bridges if there is water.

David: Yeah. I remember the **Small Flying Rainbow Bridge**. It's quite **exquisite**, with red **carved** wooden **guardrails**. The buildings in the garden are located around water.

Cindy: Water is really important to a garden. What about the landscape?

David: Its natural landscape includes small forests and hills. There are also man-made **pavilions**, halls and **parlors** in the garden.

Cindy: It's quite different from my small garden.

David: Of course. It covers about 52,000 square meters and yours is just a mini garden.

Cindy: I must go to visit the garden someday. Maybe I can get inspiration from it and make mine more elegant.

David: Great! I'm looking forward to seeing your mini Chinese garden.

Unit 6 Art

 Vocabulary

classical	/ˈklæsɪkl/	adj.	古典的,经典的,传统的,第一流的
abundant	/əˈbʌndənt/	adj.	大量的,充足的,丰富的,富有的
renowned	/rɪˈnaʊnd/	adj.	有名的,享有盛誉的,有声望的
landscape	/ˈlændskeɪp/	n.	风景,风景画
unique	/juˈniːk/	adj.	唯一的,独一无二的,独特的
exquisite	/ɪkˈskwɪzɪt/	adj.	精致的,细腻的,优美的
carved	/kɑːvd/	adj.	雕刻的
guardrail	/ˈɡɑːdreɪl/	n.	栏杆,护轨,护栏
pavilion	/pəˈvɪliən/	n.	亭,阁楼
parlor	/ˈpɑːlə(r)/	n.	客厅,起居室,(旅馆中的)休息室
Humble Administrator's Garden			拙政园
water feature			水景
Small Flying Rainbow Bridge			小飞虹

 Dialogue 2

Maggie: garden lover   Tina: Maggie's colleague

Maggie: Let's go shopping. Are you free tomorrow?

Tina: Sorry, I'm busy. It's time to plant my garden.

Maggie: Lucky you. I don't have a garden. What will you plant?

Tina: I usually plant some vegetables and some flowers.

Maggie: Wow, so it will be both **practical** and **ornamental**. Which vegetables are you going to plant?

Tina: I'm going to have a row of **carrots** and a row of **lettuce**. I already have the seeds. They're easy to grow. And, I always plant some tomatoes.

Maggie: Tomatoes fresh from the garden are delicious. What else will you plant?

Tina: Last year, we had a **cucumber patch**. They were good, but they **sprawled** everywhere. So, I'm not going to plant any this year.

Maggie: I see. Will you plant any peas or **peppers**? They're my favorites.

Tina: No, peas take too much work. And, my peppers always die.

Maggie: Oh, dear. What kinds of flowers are you going to plant?

Tina: I think I'll just pick up some flower trees or **perennial** flowers, because I'm too busy to take care of them.

Maggie: What about **cape jasmine** and **camellia**? They are lovely.

Tina: Good. I'll plant some. I'll also plant lily, rose and **narcissus**. It will be a perfect garden.

Maggie: Will you lay a **lawn** for Tom to place toys?

Tina: That's a good idea but it means more work. If you can help me, I'll think about it.

Maggie: OK. But you must help me design my garden next week. Where will you get the flowers?

Tina: There's a garden center in front of my local supermarket.

Maggie: I hope they all bloom for you. It sounds like a lot of work.

Tina: Yes. I must turn over the soil, dig holes, plant plants and sow seeds, and then water everything. But, that's just the beginning.

Maggie: Really? Is it hard to **tend** a garden? What else do you need to do?

Tina: I must **weed** the garden regularly, water it and **fertilize** it. I've got to watch out for **bugs**, too. Taking care of a garden is a lot of work.

Maggie: But the beauty is worth all the trouble.

Vocabulary

practical	/ˈpræktɪkl/	adj.	实践的,实际的,实用的
ornamental	/ˌɔːnəˈmentl/	adj.	装饰性的,装饰用的
carrot	/ˈkærət/	n.	胡萝卜
lettuce	/ˈletɪs/	n.	莴苣,生菜
cucumber	/ˈkjuːkʌmbə(r)/	n.	黄瓜
patch	/pætʃ/	n.	补丁,补片,斑点,小块
sprawl	/sprɔːl/	v.	蔓延,杂乱无序地拓展
pepper	/ˈpepə(r)/	n.	胡椒,辣椒,胡椒粉
perennial	/pəˈreniəl/	adj.	终年的,长久的,多年生的
cape jasmine	/keɪp ˈdʒæzmɪn/	n.	栀子
camellia	/kəˈmiːliə/	n.	山茶,山茶花
narcissus	/nɑːˈsɪsəs/	n.	水仙,水仙花
lawn	/lɔːn/	n.	草地,草坪
tend	/tend/	v.	照料,照顾,护理
weed	/wiːd/	n.	杂草,烟草

		v.	给……除杂草,除(草)
fertilize	/ˈfɜːtəlaɪz/	v.	使肥沃,使受孕,施肥
bug	/bʌg/	n.	昆虫,瑕疵,细菌

Section B　Notes

1. Humble Administrator's Garden:拙政园,位于江苏省苏州市,始建于明正德初年(16世纪初),江南古典园林的代表作品,由江南四大才子之一的文徵明历时17年设计建造而成。园内回廊起伏,水中倒影如画,景色绝佳,是江南古典园林的代表作品,与北京颐和园、承德避暑山庄、苏州留园一起被誉为中国四大名园。

2. Small Flying Rainbow Bridge:拙政园的小飞虹,是苏州园林中极为少见的廊桥。朱红色桥栏倒映水中,水波粼粼,宛若飞虹,故以为名。

3. perennial flowers:宿根花卉,指植株地下部分可以宿存于土壤中越冬,翌年春天地上部分又可萌发生长、开花结籽的花卉,如芍药、石竹类、蜀葵、天蓝绣球、玉簪类、鸢尾类等。

Section C　Exercises

Ⅰ. Translate the following words or phrases into Chinese.

1. pavilion　　　　　　2. cape jasmine
3. cucumber　　　　　 4. ornamental
5. guardrail　　　　　 6. bloom
7. landscape　　　　　 8. exquisite

Ⅱ. Translate the following words or phrases into English.

1. 宿根花卉　　　　　 2. 小飞虹
3. 施肥　　　　　　　 4. 水仙
5. 山茶　　　　　　　 6. 锄草
7. 古典园林　　　　　 8. 水景

Ⅲ. Role play.

Suppose A is a tour guide, and B is a traveler. A is introducing a Chinese garden for B. Try to use the words and phrases you have learned to ask and answer questions.

Section D Related Words and Phrases

1. indoor design — 室内设计
2. ceiling — 天花板
3. style — 风格
4. human-orientation — 以人为本
5. living room — 客厅
6. partition wall — 隔断
7. sofa — 沙发
8. lighting — 采光
9. natural style — 自然风格
10. archaic style — 复古风格
11. wallpaper — 墙纸
12. carpet — 地毯
13. curtain — 窗帘
14. Western modern style — 西洋现代风格
15. table lamp — 台灯
16. courtyard design — 庭院设计
17. Chinese-style garden — 中式园林
18. harmony — 和谐
19. simplicity — 简单
20. maintenance — 养护
21. woody plants — 木本植物
22. hidden scene — 藏景
23. scenic spot — 景点
24. shrub — 灌木
25. osmanthus tree — 桂花树

Section E Useful Expressions and Sentences

1. They were sitting on the lawn under a large beech tree.
   他们坐在一棵高大的山毛榉树下的草坪上。
2. The daffodil belongs to the genus Narcissus.
   黄水仙是水仙属植物。
3. Caspar was weeding the garden.
   卡斯珀正在给花园除杂草。
4. Jim gardened at the homes of friends on weekends.
   吉姆周末帮忙打理朋友家的花园。
5. No smoking in any indoor facilities.
   所有室内场所都不许吸烟。
6. They walked through the arch and into the cobbled courtyard.
   他们穿过拱门走进铺着鹅卵石的院子。
7. The interior walls were painted green.
   内墙漆成了绿色。
8. With its simple decoration, the main bedroom is a peaceful haven.
   主卧室装饰简单，像一处宁静的港湾。
9. Trees and bushes grew down to the water's edge.
   树和灌木丛一直长到了水边。
10. The terrain changed quickly from arable land to desert.
    那个地带很快就从耕地变成了沙漠。
11. The drainage system has collapsed because of too much rain.
    由于降雨过多，排水系统已经彻底瘫痪了。
12. We moved to Northamptonshire and a new landscape of hedges and fields.
    我们迁往北安普敦郡，置身于一派树篱和田野的新景致中。
13. Bedrooms have again been created by partitioning a single larger room.
    用隔断断开的方法，将一间大房间又隔出了几间卧室。
14. The whole room is bathed in soft lighting.
    整个房间沐浴在柔光之中。
15. A supportive house for eight to ten older people, each with his or her own room, provides privacy and a sense of community.
    一幢扶助性住宅可供8至10位老人居住，每个人都有自己单独的房间，在这里，他们既能独处，又有社区归属感。

16. The inn has a garden of semi-tropical vegetation.

    这家小旅馆里有一个亚热带植物园。

17. The symmetrical design of this church makes it very beautiful.

    对称性结构使这座教堂十分美丽。

18. There are many karst caves in Guilin.

    桂林有许多溶洞。

19. Natural style is the main style of British garden.

    英国园林主要以自然风格为主。

20. Winding roads with tall trees on both sides will make people feel that "The courtyard is deep".

    曲折小道配合高大树木让人产生"庭院深深"的感觉。

Topic 22　Dress and Costume

Section A　Dialogues

 Dialogue 1

Olivia：Customer

Salesgirl A：Good morning. Can I help you?

Olivia：　　I'm looking for some **infant clothes** for my baby.

Salesgirl A：Please follow me. Look, all of these clothes are 100% **cotton**.

Olivia：　　This **jumpsuit** looks lovely.

Salesgirl A：Yes. It's one of the best-sellers in our shop. The **fabric** is very soft. We have blue, yellow and pink.

Olivia：　　Blue is pretty. My boy will love it. But this one is a little bit short. Have you got any in Size 80?

Salesgirl A：Wait a moment, please. I'll check for you. Yeah, we've got some.

Olivia：　　How much is it?

Salesgirl A：125 *yuan*.

Olivia：　　Oh, that's shocking.

Salesgirl A：But, madam, look at the quality. It's the **first-rate** product. Baby's skin is very

sensitive. Our clothes are best for babies.

Olivia: Yes, this **brand** is quite famous. All right, I'll take this one. Could you please **wrap** it?

Salesgirl A: Certainly, madam.

Olivia: I also want to buy a dress and a **scarf** for myself. Where can I get them?

Salesgirl A: The women clothing and **knitted-wear counters** and **accessories** are on the third floor.

Olivia: Thank you.

(*Olivia goes upstairs.*)

Salesgirl B: Good morning. Have you been taken care of?

Olivia: No, not yet. I'm looking for a dress. I want something **stunning** to wear in a party.

Salesgirl B: I see. What about this blue dress?

Olivia: I like the style, but I don't think **polyester** is good enough. I prefer silk.

Salesgirl B: What about this **little black dress**(**LBD**)? It's Audrey Hepburn style. Such classic and **iconic** style will never be **out of fashion**.

Olivia: I like the wide **flare** and the smart design. The **workmanship** looks fine, too. OK, let me try it on.

Salesgirl B: What is your size?

Olivia: I used to wear Size M. But after I had my baby I am fatter.

Salesgirl B: Let me take your measurement. Your **bust measurement** is 42 inches, waist 28 inches, hips 45. Size L should fit you.

Olivia: OK. Where is the **dressing room**?

Salesgirl B: It's right there, behind that coffee-cream sofa.

(*Olivia tries on the dress.*)

Salesgirl B: It looks terrific on you.

Olivia: Do you think I need to buy a scarf to match it?

Salesgirl B: A white silk scarf goes with it. But a pearl necklace or a diamond necklace will make you look more fashionable and elegant at the party.

Olivia: Thank you for your suggestions. I'll take the dress.

 Vocabulary

| cotton | /ˈkɒtn/ | n. | 棉织物,棉布 |

jumpsuit	/ˈdʒʌmpsuːt/	n.	连衫裤
fabric	/ˈfæbrɪk/	n.	织物,布料
first-rate	/fɜːstˈreɪt/	adj.	一流的,一等的
sensitive	/ˈsensətɪv/	adj.	敏感的
brand	/brænd/	n.	品牌
wrap	/ræp/	v.	包装,包裹
scarf	/skɑːf/	n.	围巾,披巾
knitted-wear	/ˈnɪtɪdˌweə(r)/	n.	针织服装
counter	/ˈkaʊntə(r)/	n.	柜台
accessory	/əkˈsesəri/	n.	配件,饰品(如腰带、丝巾等)
stunning	/ˈstʌnɪŋ/	adj.	惊人的,抢眼的
polyester	/ˌpɒliˈestə(r)/	n.	聚酯纤维
iconic	/aɪˈkɒnɪk/	adj.	偶像的,图标的
flare	/fleə(r)/	n.	下摆略张的裙子
workmanship	/ˈwɜːkmənʃɪp/	n.	手艺,技艺
infant clothes			婴儿服
little black dress(LBD)			小黑裙
out of fashion			过时
bust measurement			胸围
dressing room			试衣间

 Dialogue 2

Joe and Beth are talking about the coming New York Fashion Week.

Joe: Beth, I'm so excited about the New York Fashion Week. It will be my first time to engage in such a big event. Please tell me more about it.

Beth: I was thrilled and flattered like you when I was invited to the show for the first time.

Joe: Who will **attend** the show?

Beth: Fashion media, buyers, **retailers**, fashion professionals, **celebrities** and socialites. Of course, designers and their **PR teams** will be there.

Joe: Wow, I can see **Karl Lagerfeld** in person.

Beth: Yeah. You'd better wear **Chanel** to the show.

Joe: Why? I planned to wear that **Gucci** black sleeveless **V-neck** silk gown.

Beth: Designers appreciate it when **attendees** wear their brand to their show. It is considered rude if you are not "appropriately" dressed in designer wear.

Joe: Oh, I see. So do you think I can wear that white and black Chanel **gown**?

Beth: Yeah, that's quite exquisite.

Joe: I'm curious about the super **models** on the **runway**. Why are they so cool and never smile?

Beth: Well, it's not that they're too cool to smile. Most high fashion designers typically ask their models not to smile while walking down the runway. The idea is that the audience will concentrate on the fashion designs instead of the model's face or personality.

Joe: Oh, I got it. Thank you so much, Beth.

Vocabulary

attend	/əˈtend/	v.	出席
retailer	/ˈriːteɪlə(r)/	n.	零售商
celebrity	/səˈlebrəti/	n.	名流
V-neck	/ˈviːnek/	n.	V形领
attendee	/ˌætenˈdiː/	n.	出席者
gown	/ɡaʊn/	n.	女裙服,女礼服
model	/ˈmɒdl/	n.	模特
runway	/ˈrʌnweɪ/	n.	T台
New York Fashion Week			纽约时装周
PR team			公关团队
Karl Lagerfeld			卡尔·拉格菲尔德
Chanel	/ʃəˈnel/		香奈儿
Gucci	/ˈɡuːtʃi/		古驰

Section B Notes

1. little black dress(小黑裙):由香奈儿设计。1926 年,香奈儿女士第一次发布了她的小黑裙。时尚鉴赏家泰斗 Didier Ludot 在他的 *The Little Black Dress* 中写道:"没有小黑裙的女人就没有未来。"小黑裙享有百搭易穿、永不失手的声誉,顺理成章地成为女士们衣橱里的必备品。

2. New York Fashion Week(纽约时装周):与巴黎、米兰、伦敦时装周(Paris Fashion

Week, Milan Fashion Week, London Fashion Week)并称全球四大时装周,每年举办两次,2月份举办当年秋冬时装周,9月份举办次年的春夏时装周。

3. Karl Lagerfeld(卡尔·拉格菲尔德):是如今在世的最著名的国际时装设计大师,他是香奈儿(Chanel)、芬迪(FENDI)两大品牌的首席设计师,被时尚界人称为"老佛爷""卡尔大帝"。

4. Coco Chanel(加布里埃·香奈儿)(Gabrielle Bonheur Chanel):1883年出生于法国索米尔。法国时装设计师,香奈儿品牌的创始人。经典名言:A woman who doesn't wear perfume has no future.(一个不喷香水的女人是没有未来的。)

5. Gucci(古驰):1921年创立于佛罗伦萨,全球卓越的奢华精品品牌之一,因其独特的创意和革新,以及精湛的意大利工艺而闻名于世,是全球时装与配饰行业的翘楚。

Section C Exercises

Ⅰ. Translate the following words or phrases into Chinese.

1. runway
2. gown
3. retailer
4. V-neck
5. jumpsuit
6. fabric
7. infant clothes
8. salesgirl

Ⅱ. Translate the following words or phrases into English.

1. 围巾
2. 针织服装
3. 品牌
4. 小黑裙
5. 包装
6. 聚酯纤维
7. 过时
8. 配件

Ⅲ. Role play.

Suppose A is a salesgirl, and B is a customer. The salesgirl is introducing the suits to the customer. Try to use the words and phrases you have learned to ask and answer questions.

Section D Related Words and Phrases

1.	designer	设计师
2.	nylon	尼龙
3.	button	纽扣
4.	stocking	长袜
5.	waterproof	防水的
6.	fur	皮毛
7.	fashion design	服装设计
8.	mandarin dress	旗袍
9.	style	款式
10.	lacing	饰花边,镶边
11.	A-line	A字形
12.	collar	衣领
13.	sleeveless	无袖的
14.	casual wear	休闲装
15.	zipper	拉链
16.	bikini	比基尼
17.	shorts	短裤
18.	embroidery	刺绣
19.	laundry	洗衣店,已洗好的衣物
20.	apparel firm	服装公司
21.	velvet	天鹅绒
22.	chiffon	雪纺,薄绸
23.	acrylic	腈纶,丙烯酸(类)纤维
24.	shoulder pad	垫肩
25.	fashion trend	流行趋势

Section E Useful Expressions and Sentences

1. The design and the color are OK, but I don't like the material.
   式样和颜色都不错,但我不喜欢这种面料。
2. Do you have chiffon materials?

你们有雪纺绸面料的吗?

3. Please rest assured, the quality is very good.

   你可以放心,质量很好。

4. What we can order from you right now are cotton goods.

   现在我们能向你订购的只有棉织品。

5. We've noticed that your orders have been falling off lately, haven't they?

   我们发现贵公司的订单最近逐渐减少了,对吗?

6. Let's go to the specialty stores. There will be some new models for sale now.

   我们去专卖店吧。现在那里该有新款上市了。

7. There will be some out-of-season clothes on discount.

   会有一些过季的衣服打折。

8. Most of the clothes here have only one average size.

   这里大部分的衣服都是均码的。

9. How about this short skirt, madam? Short skirts are in fashion now.

   这条短裙怎么样,太太? 短裙现在正流行呢。

10. She was dressed in the latest fashion.

    她穿着最新时装。

11. His mother looked ten years younger in jeans and high-heeled shoes.

    他妈妈穿上牛仔裤和高跟鞋,看上去年轻了10岁。

12. These are made of fine material.

    这些服装质地精良。

13. The color of the tie is well blended with taste.

    这条领带色彩搭配好,有品位。

14. I'm looking for some light summer business suits.

    我想买些轻便夏季商务套装。

15. Our tailoring department can make a dress for you.

    我们的制衣部可以为你定制一条裙子。

16. The first little black dress was designed by Coco Chanel.

    小黑裙是可可·香奈儿最先设计的。

17. Karl Lagerfeld is the head designer and creative director of the fashion house Chanel.

    卡尔·拉格菲尔德是香奈儿的首席设计师和创意总监。

18. If you try to choose a suit in this season, then you can choose the suit featuring with printed floral, a profiled jacket and a dress with slit design. Likewise, don't forget to wear a belt!

今季要选套装,就选全印花、有轮廓感的夹克、开衩设计的裙子,同样,别忘了系上腰带!

19. A model presents a creation at the Calvin Klein Fall/Winter 2015 collection show during New York Fashion Week.

一名模特正在 2015 纽约秋冬时装周上展示 Calvin Klein 的服装。

20. Kendall Jenner stuns in black and white Chanel gown at Cannes.

肯达尔·詹娜身穿香奈儿黑白长裙惊艳戛纳。

Topic 23 Animation and Cartoons

Section A Dialogues

 Dialogue 1

Susan：Kenny's mother   John：Susan's brother

Susan： Hi, John. Can you tell me where I can buy the **cartoon** toys? I would like to buy some for Kenny.

John： You can find a lot on Etoys. Look, here are some **animated** movie figures：Sherif Woody from *Toy Story*, the little yellow man from *Despicable Me*, Baymax from *Big Hero 6* and so on. Which one do you think my nephew will like?

Susan： They do look cute. But Kenny seems to be crazy about a Japanese cartoon image recently. Do you happen to know that blue **robot** cat?

John： You mean **Doraemon**, a **time-traveling** robot cat from the future?

Susan： Yeah. Can you search for it on the Internet?

John： Well, Doraemon has captivated children across Asia for decades but it's not so well-known in the United States, and Etoy mainly provides Disney-animated figures. But we can try Alibaba, a powerful Chinese supplier. Look, is it what you want?

Susan： Oh, yeah, that's the cat, Kenny's new favorite figure.

John： They have **stuffed toys**, **action figures**, balloons and many other choices.

Susan： Recommend one for me, John. You know what boys would love better than I do.

John： So let's buy this talking action figure. Kenny must like it!

Susan： Thanks a lot, dear.

John: You are welcome. But tell me what makes you change your attitude towards Kenny's love for cartoon. You used to think it a waste of time and money.

Susan: Um, I found it more and more difficult to communicate with this **rebellious** boy. I want cartoon to **bridge the chasm**.

John: Go and watch a cartoon feature film with your boy. Here are two tickets for you— *Big Hero 6*, the film that won the **Academy Award** for **Best Animated Feature** of 2014.

Susan: Thank you, John. Kenny will **exult** at the film, and I will try my best not to sleep in the cinema.

John: No, of course you won't. The **3D CGI animation** has high quality **visual effects** and realistic images.

Susan: Sounds fresh. But tell me what CGI means, otherwise my boy will laugh at me.

John: Computer-generated imagery. In other words, it is a new animation technique—the use of computers for creating moving images.

Vocabulary

cartoon	/kɑːˈtuːn/	n.	漫画,动画片
animated	/ˈænɪmeɪtɪd/	adj.	栩栩如生的,(似)能活动的
robot	/ˈrəʊbɒt/	n.	机器人
time-traveling	/taɪm ˈtrævəlɪŋ/	adj.	穿越时空的
rebellious	/rɪˈbeljəs/	adj.	叛逆的,反叛的
chasm	/ˈkæzəm/	n.	大差别,大分歧
exult	/ɪgˈzʌlt/	v.	欢欣鼓舞,兴高采烈
animation	/ˌænɪˈmeɪʃn/	n.	动画片制作,动画片
Toy Story			(电影)《玩具总动员》
Despicable Me			(电影)《神偷奶爸》
Big Hero 6			(电影)《超能陆战队》
Doraemon			哆啦A梦(日本动画人物)
stuffed toy			毛绒玩具
action figure			动作玩偶
bridge the chasm			弥合鸿沟

Unit 6 Art

Academy Award	奥斯卡金像奖(美国电影艺术与科学学院颁发的年度电影成就奖)
Best Animated Feature	最佳动画长片
3D (three dimensional)	三维的
CGI (computer-generated imagery)	计算机成像
visual effect	视觉效果

 Dialogue 2

Harry and Helen are talking about animation films.

Helen: Harry, are you still working on the **script** for your friend Luke's animation company?

Harry: Yes. I have finished the plot and **character design**, and now I need to write the script.

Helen: Oh, great! It's good to devote to one's hobby.

Harry: I've been in love with animation since childhood. The first cartoon film I watched was *The Wind in the Willows*. The friendship among animals touched me and I enjoyed wandering in the fairy-tale world with Mole, Rat, Badger, and Toad.

Helen: I remember that film. It was a **stop-motion animation** film **adapted from** Kenneth Grahame's classic story. My first cartoon was *Tom and Jerry*.

Harry: It's very funny, a **masterpiece** of **cel animation**.

Helen: But it seems that the traditional cartoons are not so popular nowadays. Do you think stop-motion will be replaced by CGI?

Harry: No. It has its own merits, such as low price entry and its superiority in displaying textures. It is still used by film makers. For example, the **puppet-animated** film *Corpse Bride* uses this traditional technique.

Helen: What about your movie?

Harry: It will be a 3D CGI animation with real actors.

Helen: That means a high cost, isn't it?

Harry: A local automobile company has agreed to invest in the movie on the condition that we design a cartoon image for it. Luke will handle it. I will focus on the play.

Helen: Can you tell me more about the play then?

Harry: It's a **science fiction**, and its theme is environmental protection. A boy named Potter from the Mars comes to the earth accidentally and finds a terrible secret: Monster is going to pollute all the rivers on the earth and destroy human beings. He fights against Monster and saves the people.

Helen: **Heroism** attracts boys.

Harry: Girls will also love it. There is romance in the play. Potter falls in love with a girl and she is his initial motivation to protect the earth. The girl will be a Chinese image in order to attract Chinese audience.

Helen: Imaginative! I can't wait to read your script. Where did you get the inspiration?

Harry: **Comic** books, computer games, and other cartoon movies. Actually, it is ***Kung Fu Panda*** that inspires me to use some Chinese elements in the play. It was well received in China.

Helen: You are great, Harry. I hope it will be a hit in the film market!

Harry: Thank you!

Vocabulary

script	/skrɪpt/	n.	剧本,脚本
masterpiece	/ˈmɑːstəpiːs/	n.	杰作,名作
puppet-animated	/ˈpʌpɪtˈænɪmeɪtɪd/	adj.	木偶动画的
heroism	/ˈherəʊɪzəm/	n.	英雄主义
comic	/ˈkɒmɪk/	n. & adj.	漫画(的)
character design			人物设定
The Wind in the Willows			(电影)《柳林风声》
stop-motion animation			定格动画
adapt from			改编自……
cel animation			手绘动画
Corpse Bride			(电影)《僵尸新娘》
science fiction (sci-fi)			科幻,科幻小说
Kung Fu Panda			(电影)《功夫熊猫》

📖 Section B Notes

1. Best Animated Feature(最佳动画长片):奥斯卡最佳动画片奖于2001年设立,并于第74届奥斯卡奖开始颁发。美国电影艺术与科学学院规定,动画的长度必须超过70分钟才可以参加奥斯卡最佳动画长片的竞赛。2002年,奥斯卡最佳动画片奖被细分为最佳动画长片奖和最佳动画短片奖(Academy Award for Best Animated Short Film)两个奖项。

2. 3D(three dimensional)film(三维电影):又称为立体电影。立体电影将两影像重合,产生三维立体效果,当观众戴上立体眼镜观看时,有身临其境的感觉。

3. CGI animation(计算机成像):是指采用图形与图像的处理技术,借助于编程或动画制作软件生成一系列的景物画面,采用连续播放静止图像的方法产生物体运动的效果。计算机动画可分为2D动画和3D动画。

4. character design(人物设定):常用于电影、动画、游戏等领域,即设计虚拟角色的个性特征、角色作用、造型、衣装样式、脸部特征、眼神、表情等。

5. stop-motion animation(定格动画):指通过逐格地拍摄对象,然后使之连续放映,从而产生仿佛活了一般的人物或角色。通常所指的定格动画一般都是由黏土偶、木偶或混合材料的角色来演出。Tim Burton 的 *The Nightmare Before Christmas*(《圣诞夜惊魂》)和 *Corpse Bride*(《僵尸新娘》)均为定格动画电影。

Section C Exercises

Ⅰ. **Translate the following words or phrases into Chinese.**

1. cartoon
2. stuffed toy
3. action figure
4. Best Animated Feature
5. animation
6. visual effect
7. masterpiece
8. cel animation

Ⅱ. **Translate the following words or phrases into English.**

1. 机器人
2. 穿越时空的
3. 奥斯卡金像奖
4. 三维电影
5. 计算机生成动画
6. 人物设定
7. 定格动画
8. 木偶动画的

Ⅲ. **Role play.**

A is a reporter of *Southern Metropolis Entertainment Weekly*, and B is a cartoon film fan. A is interviewing B. The topic of the interview is: Why is *Kung Fu Panda* so popular with Chinese audience? Try to use the words and phrases you have learned to ask and answer questions.

Section D Related Words and Phrases

1. animator 动画片绘制者
2. atmosphere sketch 艺术效果草图
3. camera 摄影机
4. 1st run 第一次曝光
5. 2nd run 第二次曝光
6. Ext (exterior) 外面,室外景
7. Eft (effect) 特效
8. editing 剪辑
9. mag track (magnetic sound track) 音轨
10. pose 姿势
11. post-synchronized sound 后期同步录音
12. sound effect 音效
13. modeling 模型制作
14. montage 蒙太奇
15. Ng (No Good) 不好的镜头
16. stand-in 替身
17. words and music 旁白加音乐
18. mechanical design 机器设定
19. shadow 阴影
20. character voice 配音员
21. cosplay (costume play) 角色扮演
22. video game 视频游戏
23. otaku 御宅族,计算机迷
24. animation industry 动漫产业
25. graphics software 制图软件
26. live-action film 真人电影

Section E Useful Expressions and Sentences

1. Tony studied Japanese for half an hour and then read a comic book of Hayao Miyazaki.
   托尼学了半小时日语,然后看宫崎骏的漫画书。

2. This film is a mix of animation and full-length features.
   这部电影将动画制作和长篇故事片融为一体。

3. *Snow White and the Seven Dwaves* is a Walt Disney cartoon.
   《白雪公主和七个小矮人》是一部迪士尼动画片。

4. *Transformers* is the most fun summer blockbuster this year.
   《变形金刚》是今年最精彩的暑假大片。

5. The electronic dictionary included some animations.
   电子词典中有一些动画片。

6. That film is a blend of animation and live action.
   那部影片结合了动画和真人拍摄。

7. I can't live without anime.
   我的生活离不开动漫。

8. *The Smurfs* was the creation of the cartoonist Pierre Culliford.
   《蓝精灵》是漫画家皮埃尔·库里佛的作品。

9. The fast growing Japanese cartoon industry has become an important part of Japanese economy.
   飞速发展的日本动画片产业是日本经济不可或缺的部分。

10. The sound effect is very realistic.
    音响效果十分逼真。

11. The cartoon's post-production has finished.
    该动画的后期制作已经完成。

12. More dramatic use of CGI was seen in *Big Hero 6*.
    在电影《超能陆战队》中可以看到更加生动的电脑特效技术。

13. The film was released on May 26, 2011 in Real D 3D and Digital 3D.
    该电影于 2011 年 5 月 26 日在各 Real D 3D 和数字 3D 影院上映。

14. *Naruto* has spawned many spin-off products, including feature films and video games.
    《火影忍者》已产生许多副产品，包括电影和电玩。

15. I lost myself in the blue background music of the anime.
    我沉浸在那部动画忧伤的背景音乐中。

16. ACG is short for anime, comic and game, a term frequently used by Chinese players.
    ACG 是动画、漫画、游戏的英文缩写，为华文圈玩家广泛使用。

17. Cartoon forums are a place where anime and manga lovers communicate with their unique language.
    动漫吧是动漫爱好者们用他们独特的语言进行交流的地方。

18. Smart Ikkyu-san is my favorite Japanese cartoon image.

聪明的一休是我最喜欢的日本动漫形象。
19. An animator must first understand a character's thought process for any given action.
动画师首先必须清楚一个角色对任何特定动作所做的思考处理。
20. *Afanty* is a classic Chinese stop-motion animation.
《阿凡提》是一部经典的中国定格动画。

科技英语知识

科技英语的阅读技巧

当代社会日新月异，英语科技文章在各类报刊和网络上层出不穷，其文章往往具有句子长、结构难、理解不易的特点。要想掌握最前沿的科技信息，把握时代脉搏，学习并掌握科技英语的阅读技巧非常重要。以下简要从词义、句子和段落这三个方面来概述其阅读技巧。

1. 词义方面

英语科技文章的生词普遍较多，可以使用两种技巧。

（1）将词的结构拆分成词根、前缀和后缀，从部分到整体来推测词义。例如：

The <u>maladjustment</u> of the two parts led to the problem.

maladjustment（失调）= mal（前缀，表示"错误"）+ adjust（调整）+ ment（动词变名词的后缀）

（2）结合上下文或者句中的关键词来猜词义。例如：

There existed a <u>might</u> which forced the seed to grow.

通过句中的 forced（迫使）一词可以猜测出 might 应该是 strength（力量）的意思。

2. 句子方面

（1）利用标点符号。

有些标点符号就像词一样可以传达作者的意思，尤其是破折号和冒号有解释性的作用。例如：

They lack what psychologists call a "theory of mind": they don't understand that the world looks different from another person's perspective.

在这个句子中，冒号后面的句子正好解释了 theory of mind 的含义。

（2）巧妙利用衔接词。

衔接词往往是句子与句子或者段落与段落之间意思理解的关键。常见的衔接词有以下几种。

表添加:and, besides, in addition to, as well as 等。
表转折:but, however, yet, though, although 等。
表因果:therefore, so, as a result, thus 等。
表比较:like, likewise, similarly, unlike 等。
表条件:if, unless, supposing, provided 等。

3. 段落方面

（1）找出主题句。

在阅读段落之前，首先应找出其主题句，一般位于段首、段中或段尾，少数则需要自己概括。例如：

Smoking cigarettes is harmful to your health. Experiments show that cigarette smoking can cause cancer. Besides the most serious and terrible disease (illness), cancer, cigarette smoking also can cause other health problems. Finally, studies have shown it is easy for cigarette smokers to catch colds.

本段的主题句为第一句："Smoking cigarettes is harmful to your health."

（2）找出支撑句。

支撑句就是支持主题的句子。上述段落中的支撑句有3句，分别是"Experiments show …""Besides …""Finally …"，这3个句子都是围绕主题句来写的。

总之，科技英语阅读难度较大，在阅读时有必要掌握各种阅读技巧，通过积极的思维，得出自己对作者信息的理解。

Unit 7

Computer Sciences and IT

Topic 24   Internet

Section A   Dialogues

Dialogue 1

Jimmy: Customer   David: Receptionist

David: Welcome to **China Unicom**. How can I help you?

Jimmy: Hi. I would like to get Internet access at my house.

David: Sure. We have traditional **ADSL broadband** and the more advanced **fiber-optical** broadband.

Jimmy: I'm not sure whether the fiber Internet is available in our community or not.

David: Wait a moment. Let me check for you. Emm … sorry, the fiber-optical network is not available in your neighborhood yet.

Jimmy: Then would you recommend an Internet service for me?

David: OK. For ADSL broadband Internet, we have different plans with different prices which you can choose from. The **best value** plan is RMB 60 a month. It includes a connection speed of 10 **Mbps**.

Jimmy: I have no idea what "Mbps" means.

David: Mbps is the speed of the Internet connection. Higher Mbps speeds will **load** web pages more quickly, allow more devices running the same connection **simultaneously**, and enable fast **download** speeds for music, photos, **streaming** movies and more.

Jimmy: I just want to be able to get online and chat with my friends. Oh, I could play games and watch the movies online as well.

David: Well, this connection might be suitable for your needs.
Jimmy: Do I have to pay an **installation** fee?
David: You don't need to pay for that. You only need to put RMB120 in your account now.
Jimmy: Great!
David: Do you need a **wireless router**?
Jimmy: No, I already have one.
David: All right. If you have any question, you can call our nationwide free customer service hotline at 10010 or you can get online service at www.10010.com. After **logging in**, you can check bills, customize service, change service and report failures.
Jimmy: OK, I got it. Thank you.

 Vocabulary

broadband	/ˈbrɔːdbænd/	n.	宽带
fiber-optical	/ˈfaɪbə(r)ˈɒptɪkl/	adj.	光纤的
load	/ləʊd/	v.	输入,载入,装入
simultaneously	/ˌsɪmlˈteɪniəsli/	adv.	同时地
download	/ˈdaʊnləʊd/	n.	下载
streaming	/ˈstriːmɪŋ/	n.	流动式接收,流播
installation	/ˌɪnstəˈleɪʃn/	n.	安装,设置
ADSL			非对称数字用户环线
Mbps			兆比特每秒
China Unicom			中国联通
best value			超值
wireless router			路由器
log in			登录

 Dialogue 2

Tom: User   Henry: Serviceman

Henry: What can I do for you?
Tom: The system **crashed** while I was **surfing** on the Internet.

Henry: Did you search any **illegal** website or open an e-mail **attachment** from someone unknown?

Tom: No, but does it matter?

Henry: Yes. Your computer can be easily **infected** by **virus** if you do that.

Tom: I see. I'd better never try.

Henry: That's wise.

Tom: Do you know what's wrong with my computer?

Henry: One minute. Oh, yes, it was infected by a virus as there is no **antivirus** software for prevention.

Tom: Is the antivirus software necessary for a computer?

Henry: Of course. Antivirus software **is designed to combat** a wide range of threats, including **worms**, **phishing** attacks, **Trojan horse** and other **malware**. You'd better learn something about it.

Tom: I'm afraid yes. So what should I do?

Henry: You'd better install antivirus software to protect your computer and update the **virus signature** regularly in order to gain knowledge about the latest threats. Besides, don't open e-mail attachments or click on links from people you don't know. Never click on links in e-mail messages **claiming to be** from your bank and avoid **installing programs** from sites you don't trust.

Tom: OK, I got it. What about the data I saved in the computer?

Henry: Don't worry. It should have been protected **automatically**. You should make regular **backups** of data on different media in case of the damage done by viruses. Well, I have antivirus software with me. Do you want me to install it now?

Tom: Yes, please. I'll really appreciate that.

Vocabulary

crash	/kræʃ/	v.	崩溃
surf	/sɜːf/	v.	浏览,漫游,网上冲浪
illegal	/ɪˈliːgl/	adj.	非法的
attachment	/əˈtætʃmənt/	n.	附件
infect	/ɪnˈfekt/	v.	感染,传染
virus	/ˈvaɪrəs/	n.	病毒
antivirus	/ˈæntivaɪrəs/	adj.	防病毒的

combat	/ˈkɒmbæt/	v.	防止,减轻
worm	/wɜːm/	n.	蠕虫病毒,蠕虫程序
phishing	/ˈfɪʃɪŋ/	n.	网络钓鱼,网络仿冒
malware	/ˈmælweə(r)/	n.	恶意软件
install	/ɪnˈstɔːl/	v.	安装
program	/ˈprəʊɡræm/	n.	程序
automatically	/ˌɔːtəˈmætɪkli/	adv.	自动地
backup	/ˈbækʌp/	n.	副本,备份
be designed to			目的是,被设计用于做
Trojan horse			特洛伊木马(一种计算机病毒)
virus signature			病毒特征代码
claim to be			自称,声称

Section B Notes

1. ADSL(asymmetrical digital subscriber loop)(非对称数字用户环线):一种新的数据传输方式,因为上行和下行带宽不对称,因此称为非对称数字用户线环路。它采用频分复用技术把普通的电话线分成了电话、上行和下行三个相对独立的信道,从而避免了相互之间的干扰,即使边打电话边上网,也不会发生上网速率和通话质量下降的情况。ADSL用户独享带宽,线路专用,不受用户增加的影响。

2. Mbps(megabits per second)(兆比特每秒):数据传输速率的单位。常见的数据传输速率单位还有 Kbps(kilobits per second)(千位节/秒)。

3. worm(蠕虫病毒):一种常见的计算机病毒,它利用网络进行复制和传播,传染途径是通过网络和电子邮件。最初的蠕虫病毒定义是因为在 DOS 环境下,病毒发作时会在屏幕上出现一条类似虫子的东西,胡乱吞吃屏幕上的字母并改变其形状。蠕虫病毒是自含的程序,它能传播自身功能的拷贝或自身的某些部分到计算机系统中。

4. phishing(网络钓鱼):与"钓鱼"的英语单词 fishing 发音相近而得名。攻击者利用欺骗性的电子邮件和伪造的 Web 站点来进行网络诈骗活动,受骗者往往会泄露自己的私人资料,如信用卡号、银行卡账户、身份证号码等内容。诈骗者通常会将自己伪装成网络银行、在线零售商和信用卡公司等可信的品牌,骗取用户的私人信息。

5. Trojan horse(特洛伊木马):名称来源于希腊神话《木马屠城记》。黑客程序借用其名,有"一经潜入,后患无穷"之意。该病毒没有复制能力,它的特点是伪装成一个实用工具或者一个游戏,诱使用户将其安装在个人电脑或者服务器上。中了特洛伊木马程序的计算机,因为资源被占用,速度会减慢,莫名死机,且用户信息可能会被窃取,导致数据外泄等情况发生。

6. virus signature（病毒特征代码）：又称特征码，它主要由反病毒公司制作，一般都是被反病毒软件公司确定为只有该病毒才可能会有的一串二进制字符串，而这字符串通常是文件里对应程式码或汇编指令的地址。杀毒软件会将这一串二进制字符串用某种方法与目标文件或处理程序作对比，从而判定该文件或进程是否感染病毒。

Section C Exercises

Ⅰ. Translate the following words or phrases into Chinese.

1. ADSL
2. Mbps
3. fiber-optical
4. worm
5. phishing
6. Trojan horse
7. attachment
8. virus signature

Ⅱ. Translate the following words or phrases into English.

1. 非法的
2. 流动式接收
3. 路由器
4. 下载
5. 防病毒的
6. 恶意软件
7. 程序
8. 备份

Ⅲ. Role play.

A is a serviceman for computer, and B is a user who wants to have his/her virus-infected computer repaired. Try to use the words and phrases you have learned to ask and answer questions.

Section D Related Words and Phrases

1. disk space 磁盘空间
2. script virus 脚本病毒
3. parasitic virus 寄生病毒
4. multi-partite virus 复合型病毒
5. executable file 可执行文件
6. rootkit 根程序病毒包
7. disclosure 泄露,透露
8. vulnerability 易遭攻击(性)
9. spyware 间谍软件
10. replicate 复制
11. firewall 防火墙
12. be infected with … 被……感染
13. scan 扫描
14. remove 除去
15. propagate 传播,繁殖,蔓延
16. encrypt 给……加密
17. emergency recovery disk 应急恢复盘
18. restart 重新启动
19. quarantine 隔离
20. USB flash disk U 盘
21. identity theft 身份(信息)盗取
22. confidential 秘密的,机密的
23. intrude 侵入,侵扰
24. hacker 电脑黑客
25. orifice 漏洞,孔,穴,洞

Section E Useful Expressions and Sentences

1. I would like to get Internet access at my house.
   我想给家里装个网络。
2. The fiber-optical network is not available in your neighborhood yet.

您家附近还不能安装光纤网络。

3. Then would you recommend an Internet service for me?
   那么您可以为我推荐一个网络套餐吗?

4. Do I have to pay an installation fee?
   我需要付安装费吗?

5. Do you need a wireless router?
   您需要路由器吗?

6. The system crashed while I was surfing on the Internet.
   刚刚我在上网的时候系统崩溃了。

7. Do you know what's wrong with my computer?
   您知道我的电脑出了什么问题吗?

8. Antivirus software is designed to combat a wide range of threats, including worms, phishing attacks, Trojan horse and other malware.
   杀毒软件的目的是应对各种威胁,包括蠕虫病毒、钓鱼攻击、特洛伊木马和其他恶意软件。

9. What about the data I saved in the computer?
   我储存在电脑中的数据怎么样了?

10. Well, I have antivirus software with me. Do you want me to install it now?
    对了,我带了杀毒软件,现在需要给您装上吗?

11. When you use the Internet, you should not disclose confidential information about yourself, such as your password and credit card number.
    当你在使用网络的时候,你不应该泄露你的私密信息,比如你的密码和信用卡号码。

12. Recently, I've received a lot of spam mails from companies trying to sell me goods.
    最近,我收到许多公司发来的出售商品的垃圾邮件。

13. I've been experiencing connecting problems.
    我的网络连接有问题。

14. Can you connect to the Wi-Fi?
    你能连上 Wi-Fi 信号吗?

15. Why is my Internet connection lagging?
    为什么我的网络连接延迟了?

16. You'd better change your passwords regularly.
    你最好定期更改你的密码。

17. My computer was infected by virus and restarted on its own every few minutes.
    我的电脑中病毒了,每隔几分钟就会自己重启一次。

18. You should remove the virus as soon as possible.

    你应该尽快清除病毒。

19. You can inquire with your ISP about your current Internet connection speed.

    你可以咨询你的网络供应商,了解你当前的网速。

20. You should use a combination of a variety of characters, numbers and symbols to create a password.

    你应该结合不同的字符、数字和符号来创建一个密码。

Topic 25　E-Business

Section A　Dialogues

Dialogue 1

Helen: DJ of BBC English Learning　　Jean: DJ of BBC English Learning

Helen: Today's expression is "e-business".

Jean: What is e-business?

Helen: Well, e-business is **electronic** business. It refers to any business done via the Internet.

Jean: Is that e-business?

Helen: That's right. You could say "E-business has grown very fast in China recently."

Jean: You meant that they could make money with the Internet, right?

Helen: That's right.

(*Insert*)

A: Why did you close your office?

B: Well, it's all e-business these days, so I can just work at home with my computer.

C: Do you think we should start the e-business service?

D: Why not? It could be operating in 24 hours. I'm sure our customers would love it.

Jean: So Helen, what type of companies run e-business?

Helen: Well, anything to do with computers can be e-business. A lot of travel companies use e-business too.

Jean: Yes, that's true. I have used online booking systems.

Helen: Yes. It is very easy to **book** flights or hotels online.

Jean: But you have to keep an eye on your **credit card** details.

Helen: That's a very good caution. Now let's review what e-business means.

Jean: People might have different understandings regarding this. First of all, if you want to do e-business, you need a computer, and you must be able to **log onto** the Internet easily. Many people would believe e-business is simply work with the website and e-mail to deal with the customers. For other people, e-business is a website that enables customers to order and **submit** their demands online, even though their orders may be processed manually just like a fax or telephone order. There still are some thinking that e-business means you must have advanced technology, very good customer relationship and **efficient** payment **platforms**, etc.

Vocabulary

electronic	/ɪˌlekˈtrɒnɪk/	adj.	电子的
book	/bʊk/	v.	预订
submit	/səbˈmɪt/	v.	提交
efficient	/ɪˈfɪʃnt/	adj.	有效的
platform	/ˈplætfɔːm/	n.	平台
credit card			信用卡
log onto			登录

Dialogue 2

A: Customer   B: Alibaba agent

A: I just signed an order of nasal bottles, so the new order will be made next month. Now, I just care about eye drop bottles and hand wash bottles.

B: Alibaba can offer 100% **refund** since we have this activity called trader assurance.

A: I didn't use this service before. I'm learning about it. You can send me the price and I will confirm with you later.

B: Because Alibaba will offer 5% of the discount, this means that if you place the order, we can offer you 2.5% of your order. Please be advised that this activity was launched by Alibaba this month. Some companies would not tell their **consumers**, but we do! Because we are looking forward to building a long-term business **relationship** with you.

A: Could you tell me about this activity? Is this service only **valid** in China?

B: Yes, it is right, but there is one question that Alibaba only provides unlimited chances for this campaign. We are working on it.

A: OK. Could you send me a **draft trade assurance contract**?

Vocabulary

refund	/ˈriːfʌnd/	n. & v.	退还,偿还
consumer	/kənˈsjuːmə(r)/	n.	消费者,顾客
relationship	/rɪˈleɪʃnʃɪp/	n.	关系,联系
valid	/ˈvælɪd/	adj.	有效的
draft	/drɑːft/	n.	草拟,草稿
trade assurance contract			贸易保证合同

Section B Notes

1. e-business(电子商务):是运用计算机网络技术和现代通信技术,使商务达到电子化、自动化运作的商务形式。广义的电子商务(有的也称为电子商业)包括 EDI(electronic data interchange,电子数据交换)、基于互联网的 e-commerce(electronic commerce,电子商务),以及基于企业内部的信息化系统 ERP(enterprise resources planning,企业资源计划)、SCM(supply chain management,供应链管理)和 CRM(customer relation management,客户关系管理)等。EDI 是电子商务的最初形式,20 世纪 80 年代在欧美国家发展起来,它主要通过一个内部网进行数据传递和交换,从而达到贸易过程的自动化。随着互联网技术的发明和应用,电子商务开始朝着基于 Web 的开放式平台的发展,这就是我们通常讲的 e-commerce。

2. 电子商务英语常用缩写词

缩写词	全　　称	中文注释
SEM	search engine marketing	搜索引擎营销
EDM	electronic direct marketing	电子邮件营销
CPS	cost per sales	按销售付费
CPA	cost per action	按行为付费
CPC	cost per click	按点击付费
ROI	return on investment	投资报酬率
SEO	search engine optimization	搜索引擎优化

（续表）

缩写词	全 称	中文注释
FAQ	frequently asked questions	经常问到的问题
ISP	Internet service provider	互联网服务提供商
CRM	customer relationship management	客户关系管理
C2A	consumer to administration	消费者对行政机构
B2A	business to administration	商业机构对行政机构

Section C Exercises

Ⅰ. Translate the following abbreviation into Chinese.

1. FAQ   2. CRM
3. B2B   4. B2C
5. C2C   6. O2O
7. ABC   8. M2C

Ⅱ. Translate the following Chinese into English abbreviation.

1. 企业对家庭   2. 面向市场营销的电子商务企业
3. 分享式商务或体验式商务   4. 搜索引擎优化
5. 按销售付费   6. 按行为付费
7. 按点击付费   8. 互联网服务提供商

Ⅲ. Discussion.

A and B are both doing e-business, and they are talking about the advantages and disadvantages of e-business. Try to use the words and phrases you have learned to have a discussion.

Section D Related Words and Phrases

1. B2B — 商家对商家
2. B2C — 商家对消费者
3. B2B2C — 企业对企业对消费者
4. C2B(T) — 消费者集合竞价(团购)
5. C2C — 消费者对消费者
6. B2F — 企业对家庭
7. O2O — 网上与网下相结合
8. M-B — 移动电子商务
9. B2G — 政府采购
10. G2B — 政府抛售
11. B2M — 面向市场营销的电子商务企业
12. M2C — 生产厂商对消费者
13. SoLoMo — 社交＋本地化＋移动
14. ABC — 代理商－商家－消费者
15. BAB — 企业－联盟－企业
16. P2C — 生活服务平台
17. P2P — 点对点/渠道对渠道
18. SNS-EC — 社会化网络电子商务
19. B2S — 分享式商务,体验式商务
20. SaaS — 软件服务
21. PaaS — 平台服务
22. IaaS — 基础设施服务
23. CA (certification authority) — 认证机构
24. ISP — 互联网服务提供商
25. B/S — 浏览器/服务器模式

Section E Useful Expressions and Sentences

1. E-commerce means doing business through electronic media.
   电子商务指通过电子媒介做生意。

2. Valuations of e-commerce are rising again and some of the dotcoms are making real profits.

对电子商务的评价正在再次提升,部分电子商务公司已开始盈利。

3. The other way to get noticed online is to offer goods and services through one of the big sites that already get a lot of traffic.

   在网上获得关注的另一种方法就是在一家已拥有相当访问量的网站上登载自己的商品及服务。

4. The consumers will use a search engine to find the lowest price and buy online at home.

   消费者会在家里上网查询最低售价,然后在网上订购。

5. Mr Bezos reckons that online retailers might capture 10%-15% of retail sales over the next decade. That would represent a massive shift in spending.

   Bezos 先生估计,未来 10 年网上零售业将会达到零售总额的 10%—15%,并将深刻地改变人们的消费观念。

6. To some extent, the online and offline worlds may merge.

   在一定程度上,网上和离线销售方式将会融合。

7. But often it is likely to be the website where customers will be encouraged to place their orders.

   鼓励消费者通过网站订货还是比较热衷的消费方式。

8. If the lowest prices can be found on the Internet and people like the service they get, why would they buy anywhere else?

   如果消费者在互联网上可以买到价格最低的商品,并能得到很好的服务,还有人会去其他地方购物吗?

9. One reason may be convenience; another, concern about fraud, which poses the biggest threat to online trade.

   网购一方面是便利,另一方面会面临欺诈。欺诈成为网上交易最大的威胁。

10. As long as the Internet continues to deliver price and product information quickly, cheaply and securely, e-commerce will continue to grow.

    随着互联网的发展,传递商品价格和信息迅速、价廉且安全,电子商务将继续成长。

11. Increasingly, companies will have to assume that customers will know exactly where to look for the best buy.

    越来越多的公司会设想,消费者都知道他们会在哪里做最划算的购物。

12. This market has the potential to become as perfect as it gets.

    这个网购市场可能会成为一个完善的市场。

13. The growth of the Internet has caused many new concerns for the future about protecting the privacy of the consumers.

互联网的发展已催生了许多有关保护消费者隐私权的新问题。

14. Such information has particularly become a valuable commodity that can bring jobs, businesses and customer services.

信息已成为一种有价值的商品。它可以带来更多的就业机会、商贸和客户服务。

15. Hence, these factors have created a mounting pressure to collect, hold, process and use personal data more than before.

因此,收集、保存、处理和使用个人信息比以前更困难了。

16. All these strategies have given rise to the protection of privacy issues for the future of e-commerce.

所有这些策略已经引发了关于保护隐私的问题。这为电子商务的未来做了保障。

17. When you surf the web, you should look for the privacy policies posted on the websites you visit.

当你在网上冲浪时,要注意发布在网站上的隐私政策。

18. The customer or consumer can choose to leave or back out of the site.

客户或消费者可以选择离开或退出网站。

19. The growth of e-commerce has created the potential for new risks and abuses.

电子商务的发展已催生了新的风险和潜在的弊端。

20. A useless website suggests a useless company, and a rival that is only a mouse-click away.

无价值的网站意味着公司没什么价值,竞争对手只要鼠标点击一下就能把它击倒。

科技英语知识

科技英语的翻译原则和策略

科技英语作为一种重要的英语文体,与非科技英语文体相比,具有许多鲜明的特点。科技文章大多采用较正式的文体,大量采用比较正式的长句、被动句,词性转换多,专业性强。因此,在进行科技文章的翻译时,我们应该了解相关的翻译原则和策略,在翻译上力求忠实、通顺、简洁。

1. 科技英语的翻译原则

(1) 忠实。

科技文章结构严密,语言严谨,逻辑性强,因此在翻译时,应保证译文能够准确、完整、科学地表达原文的内容,不得任意对原文内容加以歪曲、遗漏和篡改。

（2）通顺。

在进行科技文章翻译时，要弄清科技文章的文体特征，以及英汉两种语言在科技文章表达上的不同，不拘泥于原文单词或句子的语法特征，对词性、句子成分、句子类型等进行转换，使得译文通顺流畅，符合各自语言习惯，避免出现文理不通、逐词死译和生硬晦涩等现象。

（3）简洁。

科技英语的又一大特点就是简洁。因此，译者在翻译科技文章的过程中，应尽量避免冗长、累赘的句子，通过使用灵活多变的句法结构，如独立主格结构、名词化结构等方式体现该文体简洁清晰的风格。

2. 科技英语的翻译策略

（1）长句改短句。

科技英语中使用大量结构复杂的长句，而汉语则避免使用过长、结构复杂的句子。因此，将科技英语汉译时，应有意识地将英语的长句分割成短句。例如：

Its incredible power is enhanced by an M8 motion coprocessor that efficiently measures your activity from advanced sensors, including a new barometer.

M8运动协处理器让这一强大性能进一步提升。它能通过包括全新气压计在内的诸多先进传感器，来高效测量你的活动状态。

从该例可看出，译文并不拘泥于原文的句法结构，而是通过改变句式结构，将长句分割成数个短句。通过这样的调整，句子逻辑关系更加清晰，读者更易于理解。

（2）被动改主动。

科技英语中广泛使用被动语态，因为被动语态比主动语态更少主观色彩，更符合科技文献注重客观事实的特征。而汉语被动结构不那么常见。因此，在科技英语翻译时，要尽量将被动语态化为主动结构。例如：

Metal is optimized to allow the CPU and GPU to work together to deliver graphics and complex visual effects.

优化Metal技术使得CPU（中央处理器）和GPU（图形处理器）共同运作，以提供图形和复杂的视觉效果。

在上例中，我们如果将Metal is optimized翻译成"Metal技术被优化"，那么，这样的译文读起来生硬，翻译腔重，不符合汉语表达习惯，但将原文中被动语态的表达改成主动语态后，句子变得更加通顺自然。

（3）增词与减词。

在进行科技英语翻译时，译文增加或删减若干词语，可以更好地表达原文的意思，更便于读者理解原文。因此，在忠实原文的前提下，可以适当地增添或省略一些词，使译文符合汉语表达的习惯。例如：

Unit 7　Computer Sciences and IT

　　Structured programming practices gave rise to Pascal, in which constructs were introduced to make programs more readable and better structured.

　　结构化程序设计实践导致了 Pascal 语言的产生,在 Pascal 中引入的结构,提高了程序可读性,提供了更好的程序结构。

　　在上例中,在翻译"make programs more readable and better structured"时,将 make 一词相应增译成"提高"和"提供"这两个动词,这样的处理使得译文更加流畅,更便于汉语读者接受。

　　科技英语翻译是一项复杂的工作,除了上面提到的几点外,还有许多方面需要注意。我们应在不断的实践中总结经验,积累相关的科技知识。在翻译基本原则的指导下,根据需要,灵活采用各种翻译策略,准确有效地传递出原文内容。

Appendix I Words and Phrases

Words

A

absorb	v.	吸收
abundant	adj.	大量的,充足的,丰富的,富有的
accelerate	v.	加快,加速
acceptable	adj.	可接受的
accessory	n.	配件,饰品(如腰带、丝巾等)
accounting	n.	会计,会计学
accumulate	v.	积累
administer	v.	掌管,料理……的事务
advertising	n.	广告
agency	n.	代理,中介
aggregate	n.	集料
alternative	n.	可选择的东西,供替代的抉择
ambience	n.	气氛,布景,格调
animated	adj.	栩栩如生的,(似)能活动的
animation	n.	动画片制作,动画片
Antarctic	n.	南极洲
antivirus	adj.	防病毒的
appliance	n.	器具,器械
approve	v.	批准,核准
architect	n.	建筑师
arrangement	n.	安排

arrhythmia	*n.*	心律失常,心律不齐
artificial	*adj.*	人工的
asphalt	*n.*	沥青,柏油
attachment	*n.*	附件
attend	*v.*	出席
attendee	*n.*	出席者
automatic	*adj.*	自动的
automatically	*adv.*	自动地
automobile	*n.*	汽车
availability	*n.*	利用的可能性,有效性
available	*adj.*	可获得的,可找到的

B

backup	*n.*	副本,备份
bacteria	*n.*	细菌
battery	*n.*	电瓶
binder	*n.*	黏合剂
bituminous	*adj.*	含沥青的
blurred	*adj.*	模糊不清的
body	*n.*	车身
bolt	*n.*	螺钉
book	*v.*	预订
brake	*n.*	刹车
brand	*n.*	品牌
breakage	*n.*	破碎费,赔偿损失费
breakdown	*n.*	故障,崩溃
brief	*adj.*	简洁的,简短的
brittle	*adj.*	易碎的
broadband	*n.*	宽带
broaden	*v.*	使扩大,使变阔,使变宽
brochure	*n.*	手册,小册子
bug	*n.*	昆虫,瑕疵,细菌

C

calculation	*n.*	计算

calorie	n.	卡路里
camellia	n.	山茶,山茶花,山茶属植物
campaign	n.	运动,活动
cape jasmine	n.	栀子
carrot	n.	胡萝卜
carton	n.	纸板箱
cartoon	n.	漫画,动画片
carved	adj.	雕刻的
catalogue	n.	目录,目录簿
cavity	n.	腔,凹处,洞
celebrity	n.	名流
cement	n.	水泥
centerpiece	n.	中心装饰物,最醒目的(物件)
certificate	n.	证书,执照
characteristic	n.	特征,特性
charge	n.	收费
chasm	n.	大差别,大分歧
chassis	n.	底盘,底座
chlorine	n.	氯
circuit	n.	电路
classical	adj.	古典的,经典的,传统的,第一流的
cloisonné	n.	景泰蓝瓷器
coating	n.	涂层,外层
collapse	v.	倒塌,坍塌
combat	v.	防止,减轻
comic	n. & adj.	漫画(的)
compact	adj.	紧凑的
competitive	adj.	有竞争力的
compliment	v.	恭维,称赞
comply	v.	遵从,服从
comprehensive	adj.	综合的,广泛的
concept	n.	概念
concrete	n.	混凝土
conductor	n.	导体
confirm	v.	确认

consume	v.	消耗
consumer	n.	消费者,顾客
consumerism	n.	消费主义
consumption	n.	消耗
container	n.	集装箱
contract	n.	合同
convenient	adj.	便捷的,方便的
convert	v.	转变,改变
conveyor	n.	传送带,传递带
convincing	adj.	可信服的
copy	n.	副本,复制品
corporate	n.	公司的,法人的
corrode	v.	侵蚀,腐蚀
cotton	n.	棉织物,棉布
counter	n.	柜台
crash	v.	崩溃
cucumber	n.	黄瓜,胡瓜
current	n.	电流
curtain	n.	窗帘
cushion	n.	坐垫
customer	n.	顾客
customize	v.	定制,定做
cyclist	n.	骑自行车的人
cylinder	n.	气缸

D

deadly	adj.	致命的
deck	n.	桥面
deformation	n.	变形
deliver	v.	递送,交付
demand	n.	需求
delivery	n.	投递,分送,送交
demonstrably	adv.	可论证地,明确地
deviate	v.	偏离,背离
device	n.	装置,设备

diagonal	n.	对角线,斜线符号,斜构件
diagonally	adv.	对角地,斜对地
diet	n.	饮食
diminish	v.	减少,减小,减弱
direct	vt.	导向,指向
discerning	adj.	眼光敏锐的,有识别力的,有洞察力的
discount	n.	折扣
displacement	n.	排量
distressing	adj.	令人苦恼的
documentary	n.	纪录片
dome	n.	穹顶
domestic	adj.	国内的
doorway	n.	出入口,门道
download	n.	下载
draft	n.	草拟,草稿
dramatic	adj.	巨大的
dreadful	adj.	可怕的
ductility	n.	延展性
due	adj.	预定应到的,预定的
durable	adj.	耐用的,持久的
dwindling	adj.	减少的,逐渐变小的
dynasty	n.	王朝,朝代

E

efficient	adj.	有效的
Egyptian	adj.	埃及的
ejection	n.	喷出,射出,喷出物
electronic	adj.	电子的
embassy	n.	大使馆
enchanting	adj.	令人着迷的,迷人的
engine	n.	发动机
engineer	n.	工程师
enterprise	n.	公司,企业
era	n.	时代
ergonomic	adj.	人类工程学的

exaggerated	adj.	夸张的,言过其实的
exchange	n.	交换,交易
exhibition	n.	展览会
expand	v.	扩大,扩张
exquisite	adj.	精致的,细腻的,优美的
extract	n.	提取物,萃取物
exult	v.	欢欣鼓舞,兴高采烈
eye-catching	adj.	引人注目的

F

fabric	n.	织物,织品,布料
fantastic	adj.	极好的
fertilize	v.	使肥沃,使受孕,施肥
fiberglass	n.	玻璃纤维
fiber-optical	adj.	光纤的
finish	n.	涂层,保护层
firm	n.	公司
first-rate	adj.	一流的,一等的
fixture	n.	装置器,固定装置
flare	n.	下摆略张的裙子
floral	adj.	花的
fold	v.	折叠,合拢
foldable	adj.	可折叠的
formula	n.	公式
foundation	n.	地基,基础
fragrance	n.	香味
fructose	n.	果糖
fruity	adj.	有果味的,水果的
fuel	n.	燃料
fuel-efficient	adj.	节油的
fund	v.	投资,拨款给
furniture	n.	家具

G

garage	n.	汽车保修行,汽车修理店

gasoline	n.	(美)汽油
gene	n.	基因
gene-edited	adj.	基因编成的
glucose	n.	葡萄糖
gown	n.	女长裙,女礼服
graphic	adj.	绘画的,图案的
gravity	n.	重力
green	adj.	绿香调系的
guarantee	n.	保证,保障
guardrail	n.	栏杆,护轨,护栏
guidebook	n.	指南

H

handwriting	n.	手写
hardware	n.	硬件
heroism	n.	英雄主义
hinge	n.	铰链
horrible	adj.	可怕的
humanized	adj.	人性化的

I

iceberg	n.	冰山
iconic	adj.	偶像的,图标的
illegal	adj.	非法的
illustration	n.	说明,阐释
imperial	adj.	皇帝的
inch	n.	英寸
indicate	v.	表明,反映
indispensable	adj.	必不可少的
infect	v.	感染,传染
ingenious	adj.	精巧的,新颖的,独特的
inform	v.	通知,告知
injured	adj.	受伤的
innovative	adj.	革新的,新颖的
insert	n.	镶嵌物,镶块

inspiration	n.	启发
install	v.	安装
installation	n.	安装,设置
intact	adj.	完整的
interior	adj.	内部的
intern	n.	实习生
interzum	n.	木工机械、家具及家具配件展
intuitive	adj.	凭直觉得到的,直观的
investigative	adj.	调查研究的
invisible	adj.	无形的,看不见的
invoice	n.	发票
irrevocable	adj.	不可撤销的,最终的

J

jasmine	n.	茉莉
jumpsuit	n.	连衫裤

K

knitted-wear	n.	针织服装

L

landscape	n.	风景,风景画
lane	n.	车道
lavender	n.	薰衣草
lawn	n.	草地,草坪
layout	n.	安排,设计,布局
lettuce	n.	莴苣,生菜
lighten	v.	使照亮
load	v.	输入,载入,装入
location	n.	位置
lotion	n.	洗剂,润肤乳
lubrication	n.	润滑

M

magnificent	adj.	宏伟的,壮丽的

magnitude	n.	震级
maintain	v.	维修,维护
maintenance	n.	维修,维护
malware	n.	恶意软件
manual	adj.	手动的
manufacturer	n.	生产者,制造者
marine	adj.	海产的,海洋的
masterpiece	n.	杰作,名作
maximize	v.	最大化
measurement	n.	尺寸,大小
mechanic	n.	机修工
mechanical	adj.	机械的
membrane	n.	薄膜
merchant	n.	商人,店主
meter	n.	米
model	n.	模型,模特
moderation	n.	适度,节制
modification	n.	修改,修正
motivate	v.	刺激,使有动机,激发……的积极性
mould	n.	模具
multi-axis	adj.	多轴的
mutual	adj.	共同的,相互的,彼此的

N

narcissus	n.	水仙,水仙花
neat	adj.	整洁的,干净的
negotiate	v.	谈判,商议
nonskid	adj.	(轮胎等)不滑的
nickel-plated	adj	镀镍的

O

offspring	n.	后代
open-plan	adj.	开放式的,敞开式的
optimal	adj.	最佳的
optimize	v.	使优化,使最佳化

optional	adj.	可选择的
organic	adj.	有机的
oriental	adj.	东方的
original	n.	原件,原型,原作
originally	adv.	起初,原来
ornamental	adj.	装饰的,装饰用的
outcome	n.	结果
outlook	n.	外观
overcharge	v.	收费过高

P

packaging	n.	包装
paperwork	n.	表单
parameter	n.	参数
parlor	n.	客厅,起居室,(旅馆中的)休息室
particle	n.	微粒
parts	n.	零部件
passenger	n.	乘客
patch	n.	补丁,补片,斑点,小块
patent	n.	专利
pavement	n.	人行道,硬路面
pavilion	n.	亭,阁楼
payment	n.	支付,付款
pcs (pieces)	n.	件
pedestrian	n.	步行者,行人
pepper	n.	胡椒,辣椒,胡椒粉
perennial	adj.	终年的,长久的,多年生的
permission	n.	许可
permit	v.	允许
phishing	n.	网络钓鱼,网络仿冒
piping	n.	绲边
piston	n.	活塞
platform	n.	平台
polish	n. & v.	抛光,上光
polishing	n.	抛光

polybag	n.	胶袋
polyester	n.	聚酯纤维
pontoon	n.	（架设浮桥用的）浮舟
porter	n.	服务员，行李搬运工
post	v.	宣布，公布
potential	adj.	潜在的
power	n.	电源
practical	adj.	实践的，实际的，实用的
precaution	n.	预防措施，预防
prescribe	v.	规定，指定
pre-stress	v.	预加应力
primarily	adv.	主要地
program	n.	程序
programmable	adj.	可编程序的
pulley	n.	滑轮
puppet-animated	adj.	木偶动画的
pursuit	n.	追求

Q

qualified	adj.	合格的，有资格的
quarter	n.	四分之一
quit	v.	停止，放弃

R

ratio	n.	比例
raw	adj.	生的，未加工的
real estate		房地产，不动产
real-time	adj.	实时的
rear	adj.	后面的
rebellious	adj.	叛逆的，反叛的
reception	n.	感受，反应
recession	n.	（经济的）衰退
recognizable	adj.	可辨认的，可认识的
recommend	v.	推荐，介绍
refund	n. & v.	退还，偿还

register	v.	登记,记录,给……注册
relationship	n.	关系,联系
reliable	adj.	可靠的
remodel	v.	改造,改变
render	v.	使成为,使变得
renowned	adj.	著名的,知名的
replicate	v.	复制,重复
representative	n.	代表
requirement	n.	要求
resistor	n.	电阻
retailer	n.	零售商
revitalize	v.	使复兴
rib	n.	骨状物,翼肋
rip-off	n.	索要高价,敲竹杠
robot	n.	机器人
runway	n.	T台
rushed	adj.	匆忙的
rust	n.	铁锈

S

sag	v.	中间下垂,弯曲
salesgirl	n.	女售货员
satisfy	v.	使满意
sample	n.	样品
scale	n.	水垢,水锈
scarf	n.	围巾,披巾
scent	n.	气味
script	n.	剧本,脚本
seam	n.	线缝,接缝
seaming	n.	缝合
self-cleaning	adj.	自洁式的,自动清洗的
seminar	n.	研讨会,研讨班
semipermeable	adj.	半渗透的
sensitive	adj.	敏感的
shear	n.	切断,修剪,剪断

showroom	n.	展厅
simultaneously	adv.	同时地
slide	n.	行位,滑板,滑道
smooth	adj.	光滑的
smoothly	adv.	平稳地
software	n.	软件
solution	n.	溶液,溶剂
sophomore	n.	大学二年级学生
span	n.	跨度,墩距
specialize	v.	专门从事,专门研究
species	n.	物种
specification	n.	规格,详述
spectacular	adj.	壮观的
sponsor	v.	赞助
sprawl	v.	蔓延,杂乱无序地拓展
stabilize	v.	使稳定,保持……的稳定
staff	n.	职员
stain	v.	污染
stand	n.	货摊,展位
standard	n.	标准配置
steer	v.	驾驶,行驶,引导
stevia	n.	甜菊
streaming	n.	流动式接收,流播
strengthen	v.	加强
stunning	adj.	惊人的,抢眼的
styling	n.	造型,款式
submit	v.	提交
sugarholic	n.	嗜甜食者
suitcase	n.	手提箱
sunroof	n.	顶窗
superb	adj.	极好的,华丽的
supervisor	n.	监督人,管理人
surf	v.	浏览,漫游,网上冲浪
swatch	n.	样品,布样
sweetener	n.	甜味剂

swelling	adj.	逐渐增加的,突出的

T

tap	v.	敲击
target	v.	把……作为目标
tasteful	adj.	高雅的,有滋味的
taxpayer	n.	纳税人
tend	v.	照料,照顾,护理
tensile	adj.	可伸展的,可拉长的,张力的
texture	n.	晒纹
thousandth	n.	千分之一
timber	n.	木材
time-travelling	adj.	穿越时空的
traditional	adj.	传统的
transgenic	adj.	转基因的
transmission	n.	转动装置,变速器
transparent	adj.	透明的
transportation	n.	交通
trend	n.	趋势
tweak	v.	对……做微调

U

ultimately	adv.	最终,最后
ultrafiltration	n.	(化学)超滤
undercut	n.	底切,底部掏槽
unique	adj.	唯一的,独一无二的,独特的

V

valid	adj.	有效的
vehicle	n.	交通工具,车辆
versatile	adj.	多用途的
version	n.	版本
virus	n.	病毒
V-neck	n.	V形领

voltage	n.	电压
volume	n.	量,额
vivid	adj.	生动的

W

warehouse	n.	仓库
warranty	n.	保证,担保
weed	n.	杂草,烟草
	v.	给……除杂草,除(草)
welding	n.	焊接
withstand	v.	经受,承受
woody	adj.	木质的,木本的
workmanship	n.	手艺,技艺
worm	n.	蠕虫病毒,蠕虫程序
wrap	v.	包装,包裹

Z

zinc	n.	锌

Phrases

3D (three dimensional) film	三维电影
3D drawing	三维绘图

A

ABS (anti-lock braking system)	防抱死制动系统
Academy Award	奥斯卡金像奖（美国电影艺术与科学学院颁发的年度电影成就奖）
action figure	动作玩偶
adapt from	改编自……
ADSL	非对称数字用户环线
air pollutant	大气污染物
alloy steel	合金钢
aluminum alloy	铝合金
an advertising campaign	广告宣传活动
anchor bolt	地脚螺栓
anchor nut	地脚螺母
angle lifter	斜顶
annual revenue	年收入
appeal to	呼吁
Apple concept store	苹果概念店
application form	申请表
application program	应用程序
apply for patents	申请专利
artistic beauty	艺术美学
ASAP (as soon as possible)	尽快
assembly line	装配线
assembling operation	装配业务
automobile battery	汽车电瓶

B

base on	基于

be designed to	目的是,被设计用于做
be familiar with	熟悉
be willing to ...	愿意,乐意
bending strength	抗弯强度
Best Animated Feature	最佳动画长片
best value	超值
Big Hero 6	(电影)《超能陆战队》
branch office	分公司,分店
brick and concrete structure	砖混结构
bridge the chasm	弥合鸿沟
business card	名片
business certificate	营业执照
business tax	营业税
bust measurement	胸围

C

CAD (computer-aided design)	计算机辅助设计
carbon steel	碳素钢
cardboard box	纸箱
CCD (charge coupled device)	电荷耦合装置
cel animation	手绘动画
center of gravity	重心
CGI (computer-generated imagery)	计算机生成动画
Chandigarh Convention Center	昌迪加尔会议中心
character design	人物设定
check in	报到,登记入住
check out	退房,结账离开
China Daily	《中国日报》
China Unicom	中国联通
claim to be	自称,声称
color scheme	配色方案,色彩设计
complaint call	投诉电话
concept of design	设计理念
constructive material	建材
contemporary design	当代设计
continuous arc welding & spot welding	连续电弧焊和点焊

contribute to	是……的原因之一
conveying system	输送系统
Corpse Bride	(电影)《僵尸新娘》
counter space	灶台空间
credit card	信用卡
cruise control system	巡行车速控制系统
cutting drum	切割滚筒
cutting operation	切割作业
CV(curriculum vitae)	履历

D

date stamp	日期戳,邮戳
Despicable Me	(电影)《神偷奶爸》
Doraemon	哆啦A梦(日本动画人物)
double action door	双向平开门
double room	双人间
dove white	鸽子白
draft angle	拔模角
dressing room	试衣间
dynamic design	动态设计

E

Egyptian pyramid	埃及金字塔
electrical system	电气系统
electrical winch	电动绞车
engage in	从事,参加
erection drawing	安装图
exhibition hall	展览厅

F

fashion color	流行色
fee- and interest-free policy	费率双零政策
feng shui	风水
figure out	计算,解决
filter cartridge	滤芯

fossil fuel burning	矿物燃料燃烧
FPY (first pass yield)	直通率,一次性通过的成品率
fragrance blotter	试香卡
freight forwarder	货运代理商
frosted glass	磨砂玻璃,毛玻璃
fuel filter	燃油滤油器
full-view visual parking support system	全方位可视泊车辅助系统

G

gas station	加油站
gating requirement	浇口要求
gating system	浇注系统
general drawing	总规划图
genetic engineering	遗传工程
genetically modified	转基因的
gentle beauty	柔美
GM food (genetically modified food)	转基因食品
grey marble	云灰大理石

H

high efficiency	高效
higher efficiency	更高效
high-strength low-alloy steel	高强度低合金钢
hit back	回击,反击
hotel reservation	酒店预订
household water filter	家用净水器
Humble Administrator's Garden	拙政园
hydraulic fluid	液压油
hydrogen-boosted gasoline engine	氢助燃汽油发动机

I

in more detail	更详细地
infant clothes	婴儿服
initial order	首次订单

inner space	内在空间
intake valve	进气阀
interior design	室内设计

J

Jack of all trades	万事通

K

KDF55	高纯度铜锌合金55
Kung Fu Panda	(电影)《功夫熊猫》

L

laws and regulations	法律法规
LED(light emitting diodep)	发光二极管
less emission	更少排放
light composite material	轻型复合材料
light up	照亮,点亮
liquid fund	流动资金
little black dress(LBD)	小黑裙
log in	登录
log onto	登录
lung function decrease	肺功能降低

M

macromolecular organic component	大分子有机物
machine loading	机器装载
material transfer	物料传送
make a reservation	预订
make the best use of	最大限度利用
market research	市场调研
marine creature	海洋生物
Marketing Department	市场营销部
Marseille Apartments	马赛公寓
masonry building	砖石建筑

material removal	物料去除
masonry building	砖石建筑
Mbps	兆比特每秒
mechanical automation	机械自动化
mechanical engineering	机械工程
mechanical structure	机械结构
mineral filler	矿物质填料
mix with	混合
mould machine	注塑机
MRN(multimedia radio navigation)	多媒体收音机导航

N

National Day	国庆节
national tax authorities	国家税务机关(国税局)
New York Fashion Week	纽约时装周

O

Ohm's Law	欧姆定律
on the edge of	在……的边缘
ocean acidification	海洋酸化
organic contaminant	有机污染物
out of fashion	过时

P

part inspection	部件检验
part sorting	零件筛选
part cleaning	零件清洗
part polishing	零件抛光
particulate matter (PM)	颗粒物
parting line	分型线
passenger car	小客车
perpendicular tolerance	垂直偏差
Phoenix Bike Company	凤凰自行车公司
photo navigation	实景导航

place an order	订购,下单
placing, finishing and caring	浇筑、饰面(抹光)、养护
plate glass	平板玻璃
plate number(= number plate)	车牌号
polyaromatic hydrocarbons (PAHs)	多环芳烃
polyurethane foam	聚氨酯泡沫
power unit	动力设备
PR team	公关团队
premature death	过早死亡
private bathroom	独立卫生间
product design	产品设计

R

rack up	累积,聚集
raw material	原材料
reception room	接待室
reduce plastic	减胶
regional tax authorities	地方税务机关(地税局)
regular check-up	定期保养
reinforced concrete structure	钢筋混凝土结构
residual chlorine	余氯
return flight	往返航班
road milling machines	路面铣削机
RO (reverse osmosis)	逆渗透技术
rotating-drum batch mixer	间歇式转筒搅拌机
run out of	用完,耗尽
rush hour	上下班高峰期

S

saddle leather strap	鞍皮带
sales contract	买卖/销售合同
science fiction (sci-fi)	科幻,科幻小说
seismic force	地震力
seismic performance	抗震性能
semi-aniline leather	半苯胺真皮

senior mechanical engineer	高级机械工程师
set up	建立
settle on	选定
show ... around	带领……参观
single room	单人间
Small Flying Rainbow Bridge	小飞虹
spare key	备用钥匙
spare part	备用零件
spark plug	火花塞
special economic district	经济特区
spray coating	喷涂,油漆
stained glass	彩色玻璃,有色玻璃
stainless steel	不锈钢
state of mind	心态
steel structure	钢结构
stock up	贮备,备足
stop-motion animation	定格动画
sulfured hydrogen	硫化氢
switch to	转变,(使)改变

T

tactile sensory	触觉传感器
tax authorities	税务登记,税务机关
tax registration	税务登记
technical title	技术职称
test drive	试驾
the Canton Fair	广交会
the Forbidden City	紫禁城
Louvre Pyramid	卢浮宫金字塔
the tip of the marketing iceberg	市场营销的冰山一角
The Wind in the Willows	(电影)《柳林风声》
Window of the World (WOTW)	世界之窗
tinker with	小修补,小修理
tour package	旅行套餐
Toy Story	(电影)《玩具总动员》

trade assurance contract	贸易保证合同
treatment amount	处理水量
Trojan horse	特洛伊木马（一种计算机病毒）
turn down	关闭

U

Ultra Low Emission Zone (ULEZ)	超低排放区
ultra-sized retractable full-view roof	超大尺寸可伸缩全景天窗
urban traffic conditions	城市交通路况

V

value added tax	增值税
Villa Savoye	萨伏伊别墅
virus signature	病毒特征代码
visual effect	视觉效果
visional sensory	视觉传感器
voltage dropping resistor	降压电阻

W

water feature	水景
WeChat ID	微信号
wire rope	钢丝绳，钢索
wireless router	路由器
working current	工作电流
working hour	工作时间
working parameters	工作参数
working voltage	工作电压

Appendix Ⅱ   Keys to Exercises

Unit 1

Topic 1   Automotive Design and Manufacturing

Ⅰ. 1. 汽车   2. 底盘,底座
    3. 气缸   4. 电气系统
    5. 安排,设计,布局   6. 可折叠的
    7. 偏离   8. 回击,反击

Ⅱ. 1. indispensable   2. high efficiency
    3. displacement   4. concept of design
    5. interior   6. passenger car
    7. gravity   8. make the best use of

Ⅲ. （略）

Topic 2   Car Sales

Ⅰ. 1. 标准配置   2. 防抱死制动系统
    3. 巡行车速控制系统   4. 造型
    5. 顶窗   6. 全方位可视泊车辅助系统
    7. 直观的   8. 紧凑的

Ⅱ. 1. fuel-efficient   2. multimedia radio navigation
    3. urban traffic condition   4. ultra-sized retractable full-view roof
    5. photo navigation   6. fee- and interest-free policy
    7. humanized   8. reliable

Ⅲ. （略）

Topic 3   After-Sale Service and Repairing

Ⅰ. 1. 发动机   2. 机修工
    3. 刹车   4. 维修
    5. 汽车保修行   6. 故障
    7. 索要高价   8. 火花塞

Ⅱ. 1. piston   2. spare key
    3. overcharge   4. part

Appendix Ⅱ　Keys to Exercises

5. smoothly
6. reception room
7. complaint call
8. plate number

Ⅲ．（略）

Unit 2

Topic 4　Product Design

Ⅰ．1. 最佳的　　　　　　　2. 计算机辅助设计
3. 聚氨酯泡沫　　　　4. 绲边
5. 样板　　　　　　　6. 定制
7. 小修补　　　　　　8. 玻璃纤维

Ⅱ．1. manufacturer　　　　2. showroom
3. mould　　　　　　　4. product design
5. gas station　　　　　6. available
7. device　　　　　　　8. aluminum alloy

Ⅲ．（略）

Topic 5　Mould Machining

Ⅰ．1. 抛光　　　　　　　2. 喷出
3. 三维绘图　　　　　4. 斜销
5. 规格　　　　　　　6. 底切,底部掏槽
7. 许可　　　　　　　8. 备用零件

Ⅱ．1. automatic　　　　　2. texture
3. gating system　　　　4. draft angle
5. insert　　　　　　　6. date stamp
7. reduce plastic　　　　8. welding

Ⅲ．（略）

Topic 6　Electrical Automation

Ⅰ．1. 工作电压　　　　　2. 工作电流
3. 导体　　　　　　　4. 欧姆定律
5. 降压电阻　　　　　6. 机器人
7. 视觉传感器　　　　8. 触觉传感器

Ⅱ．1. light up　　　　　　2. spot welding
3. circuit　　　　　　　4. cutting operation
5. packaging　　　　　6. assembling operation
7. part sorting　　　　　8. part polishing

Ⅲ．（略）

Topic 7　Automation Equipment

Ⅰ．1. 机械工程　　　　　2. 证书
3. 核心业务　　　　　4. 自动化机械设备

209

5. 制造 6. 可编程序的
7. 技术职称 8. 订购,下单

Ⅱ. 1. theory foundation 2. innovative
3. mechanical engineer 4. operation interface
5. customize 6. optimize
7. assembly line 8. apply for patents

Ⅲ.（略）

Unit 3

Topic 8　Civil Engineering

Ⅰ. 1. 大学一年级新生 2. 钢筋混凝土结构
3. 抹光 4. 混凝土
5. 水泥 6. 不锈钢
7. 地基,基础 8. 木材

Ⅱ. 1. sophomore 2. supervisor
3. placing, finishing and caring 4. high-strength low-alloy steel
5. pre-stress 6. general drawing
7. thousandth 8. rotating-drum batch mixer

Ⅲ. 1. C　2. A　3. F　4. I　5. E　6. G　7. J　8. B　9. H　10. D　11. K

Ⅳ.（略）

Topic 9　Building Structural Design

Ⅰ. 1. 抗震性能 2. 砖混结构
3. 抗弯度 4. 砖石建筑
5. 柔美 6. 透明的
7. 建筑师 8. 可辨认的

Ⅱ. 1. injured 2. collapse
3. brittle 4. tensile
5. ductility 6. renowned
7. pursuit 8. Jack of all trades

Ⅲ.（略）

Topic 10　Architectural Design and Decoration

Ⅰ. 1. 改造 2. 当代设计
3. 灶台空间 4. 家具
5. 双向平开门 6. 彩色玻璃
7. 平板玻璃 8. 窗帘

Ⅱ. 1. interior design 2. color scheme
3. open-plan kitchen 4. in more detail
5. show … around 6. at a diagonal to the doorway

Appendix Ⅱ Keys to Exercises

    7. face the door directly   8. state of mind

Ⅲ．（略）

Topic 11　Transportation Construction

  Ⅰ．1. 完成   2. 维修，维护

    3. 人行道，硬路面   4. 量

    5. 壮观的   6. 专家

    7. 浮舟   8. 车道

  Ⅱ．1. asphalt   2. mineral filler

    3. smooth   4. deck

    5. conveying system   6. transportation network

    7. road milling machine   8. marine traffic

Ⅲ．（略）

Unit 4

Topic 12　Food Engineering

  Ⅰ．1. 遗传工程   2. 复制

    3. 转基因的   4. 健康饮食

    5. DNA 字符   6. 物种

    7. 基因   8. 日常饮食

  Ⅱ．1. gene-edited   2. transgenic

    3. fructose   4. glucose

    5. alternative   6. sugarholic

    7. artificial sweetener   8. raw honey

Ⅲ．（略）

Topic 13　Environmental Engineering

  Ⅰ．1. 更少的排放   2. 纪录片

    3. 大气污染物   4. 肺功能降低

    5. 超低排放区   6. 吸收

    7. 侵蚀   8. 结果

  Ⅱ．1. ocean acidification   2. fossil fuel burning

    3. pH level   4. marine creature

    5. appeal to   6. reduce the availability of carbonate ions

    7. dreadful outcome   8. build the shells and skeletons

Ⅲ．（略）

Topic 14　Chemical Engineering

  Ⅰ．1. 薄膜   2. 花的

    3. 薰衣草   4. 织物

    5. 水垢   6. 氯

7. 锌　　　　　　　　　　　　8. 润肤乳

Ⅱ. 1. warranty　　　　　　　　 2. extract
   3. fragrance blotter　　　　　4. household water filter
   5. ultrafiltration technology　6. KDF55
   7. filter cartridge　　　　　　8. green

Ⅲ. (略)

Unit 5

Topic 15　Management

Ⅰ. 1. 财务部　　　　　　　　　2. 人力资源部
   3. 研讨会　　　　　　　　　4. 专利权
   5. 工资,工钱　　　　　　　　6. 装配线
   7. 广告宣传活动　　　　　　 8. 操作系统

Ⅱ. 1. Marketing Department　　2. Production Department
   3. advantage　　　　　　　　4. technician
   5. software　　　　　　　　 6. overtime work
   7. regular training　　　　　8. mutual benefit

Ⅲ. (略)

Topic 16　Finance and Economics

Ⅰ. 1. 中小型零售商　　　　　　 2. 年收入
   3. 家用电器　　　　　　　　 4. 经济衰退
   5. 国内需求　　　　　　　　 6. 是……的原因之一
   7. 消费习惯　　　　　　　　 8. 首次公开募股

Ⅱ. 1. shop online　　　　　　　2. potential demand
   3. tap the domestic demand　4. e-commerce site
   5. merchant　　　　　　　　 6. stock up
   7. Black Friday　　　　　　　8. somebody

Ⅲ. (略)

Topic 17　Logistics

Ⅰ. 1. 手工制作　　　　　　　　 2. 底价
   3. 支付条款　　　　　　　　 4. 提前
   5. 流动资金　　　　　　　　 6. 准时到达
   7. 展厅　　　　　　　　　　 8. 销售合同

Ⅱ. 1. irrevocable L/C　　　　　2. freight forwarder
   3. sign a contract　　　　　 4. insurance value
   5. the Canton Fair　　　　　6. cover insurance
   7. precaution　　　　　　　　8. beyond the expectation

Ⅲ. (略)

Appendix Ⅱ　Keys to Exercises

Topic 18　Marketing Management

Ⅰ．1. 交换,交易　　　　　　2. 使满意
　　3. 导向　　　　　　　　4. 代理,中介
　　5. 谈判　　　　　　　　6. 市场营销的冰山一角
　　7. 分公司,分店　　　　　8. 市场调研

Ⅱ．1. advertising　　　　　2. firm
　　3. corporate　　　　　　4. contract
　　5. expand　　　　　　　 6. target
　　7. laws and regulations　8. advertising campaign

Ⅲ．(略)

Topic 19　Tourism

Ⅰ．1. 小册子　　　　　　　2. 行李搬运工
　　3. 皇帝的　　　　　　　4. 宏伟的
　　5. 登记入住　　　　　　6. 旅游套餐
　　7. 往返航班　　　　　　8. 结账离开

Ⅱ．1. guidebook　　　　　　2. dynasty
　　3. business card　　　　4. make a reservation
　　5. single room　　　　　6. private bathroom
　　7. the Forbidden City　　8. rush hour

Ⅲ．(略)

Unit 6

Topic 20　Industrial Design

Ⅰ．1. 精巧的　　　　　　　2. 规格
　　3. 机械构造　　　　　　4. 需求
　　5. 高质量　　　　　　　6. 轻型复合材料
　　7. 动态设计　　　　　　8. 很受欢迎

Ⅱ．1. engineer　　　　　　2. convenient
　　3. nonskid　　　　　　　4. durable
　　5. discount　　　　　　6. raw material
　　7. stable demand　　　　8. partner

Ⅲ．(略)

Topic 21　Environmental Art Design

Ⅰ．1. 亭子　　　　　　　　2. 栀子花
　　3. 黄瓜　　　　　　　　4. 装饰的
　　5. 护栏　　　　　　　　6. 开花
　　7. 风景　　　　　　　　8. 精致的

Ⅱ．1. perennial flower　　　2. Small Flying Rainbow Bridge

213

3. fertilize 4. narcissus

5. camellia 6. weed

7. classical garden 8. water feature

Ⅲ．(略)

Topic 22　Dress and Costume

Ⅰ．1. T台 2. 女裙服,女礼服

3. 零售商 4. V形领

5. 连体衣 6. 布料

7. 婴儿装 8. 女售货员

Ⅱ．1. scarf 2. knitted-wear

3. brand 4. little black dress

5. wrap 6. polyester

7. out of fashion 8. accessory

Ⅲ．(略)

Topic 23　Animation and Cartoons

Ⅰ．1. 动画片,卡通 2. 毛绒玩具

3. 动作玩偶 4. 奥斯卡最佳动画长片

5. 动画 6. 视觉效果

7. 杰作 8. 手绘动画

Ⅱ．1. robot 2. time-travelling

3. Academy Award 4. 3D movie

5. computer-generated imagery 6. character design

7. stop-motion animation 8. puppet-animated

Ⅲ．(略)

Unit 7

Topic 24　Internet

Ⅰ．1. 非对称数字用户环线 2. 兆比特每秒

3. 光纤的 4. 蠕虫病毒

5. 网络钓鱼 6. 特洛伊木马(一种计算机病毒)

7. 附件 8. 病毒特征代码

Ⅱ．1. illegal 2. streaming

3. wireless router 4. download

5. antivirus 6. malware

7. program 8. backup

Ⅲ．(略)

Topic 25　E-Business

Ⅰ．1. frequently asked questions 的缩写，意思是"经常问到的问题"
2. customer relationship management 的缩写，即"客户关系管理"
3. 商家对商家
4. 商家对消费者
5. 消费者对消费者
6. 网上和网下结合
7. 代理商—商家—消费者
8. 生产厂商对消费者

Ⅱ．1. B2F
2. B2M
3. B2S
4. SEO
5. CPS
6. CPA
7. CPC
8. ISP

Ⅲ．（略）

Appendix Ⅲ　Translation of Dialogues

Unit 1

Topic 1　Automotive Design and Manufacturing

Dialogue 1

莫顿：工程师　　亨利：设计师

莫顿：众所周知,柳州是一座汽车城。虽然大街上有很多的出租车,但是,老百姓还是希望拥有自己的小汽车,这现在已然成为一种潮流。

亨利：每次来柳州,我都感觉车越来越多了,而且路况也是越来越好了,所以,汽车肯定会成为我们生活中不可缺少的一部分。

莫顿：随着社会的发展,你的设计理念也在改变。

亨利：设计理念会因时代而异,但是,满足客户需求这个基本原则是不会改变的。

莫顿：顾客们所期望的是能反映时代精神的汽车款式。现在奥迪 A8L 的理念是什么?

亨利：是制造最好的车。现在让我详细地介绍一下。这一次的设计除了保留了近几年热销的车款以外,还加上了"经济环保、高效、时尚、安全"等全新的设计理念。

莫顿：我们都知道,汽车是由发动机、底盘、车身和电气系统四大部分组成的,那么,请问您都在哪几个部分进行了改造呢?

亨利：首先,我们从发动机开始说起。在石油资源日趋紧张的环境下,我们应当开发全新的发动机,使之能最高效地利用燃料,"1.0 升 EcoBoost"三缸发动机,也是排量最小的发动机。

莫顿：听上去好极了!那么它的价格怎样呢?

亨利：这你大可放心!为了增强吸引力,提高市场份额,福特汽车公司已经和我们签了合同,在这款车发行前半年,他们将会为我们提供投资和赞助。

莫顿：我明白了。我有一个简单的问题,此款汽车是采用手动挡还是自动挡呢?

亨利：为了更适应客户的需求,我们提供两种选择,即手动挡与自动挡,按照 5∶1 的比例制造。

莫顿：你们的设计理念真不错!

亨利：非常感谢!

Dialogue 2

詹姆士：工程师　　大卫：设计师

詹姆士：您好,大卫,最近在忙什么呢?

大卫： 我在研究设计一款新的汽车。

詹姆士：太好了!进展得怎么样?

大卫： 外观基本设计好了,不过,我在内饰空间的布置上遇到了点问题。

詹姆士：噢,什么问题?

大卫： 我想设计成七人座小客车,可是这样内在空间就非常小,不方便携带行李。您能帮我解决这个问题吗?

詹姆士：我有一个建议。可以将后两排的座椅设计成折叠式,同时在座椅下方设计一个储存空间。这样在携带很多行李时,可以将座椅折叠,并放置在存储空间里;在行李少的时候,放出座椅,可以搭载更多的乘客。

大卫： 太棒了,真是太感谢了!

詹姆士：不客气!(检查了汽车)您设计的气缸存在问题。气缸设计在这个位置的话,汽车在转弯的时候会产生严重的倾侧,因而会降低汽车的安全性。

大卫： 我所设计的气缸位置是根据汽车的有限空间设计的,这样设计会更好地利用汽车的空间,有效降低汽车的生产成本,使汽车空间更加紧凑,使用效率更高。

詹姆士：至于那个倾侧问题,不如我们制造一台试验车来试验一下,看看是否存在问题,然后再解决?

大卫： 好的,我们试试。

(一个小时后,这两人完成试驾回来了。)

大卫： 虽然汽车的设计不错,可是每当汽车在转弯的时候,汽车的重心确实会偏离,没有位于汽车的中心。

詹姆士：考虑汽车倾侧问题是由于重心偏离问题造成的,我们可以重新设计一下气缸的位置,使汽车的重心不再侧偏。

大卫： 是的,您给我提了一个很好的建议。非常感谢您!

詹姆士：乐意效劳!

Topic 2　Car Sales

Dialogue 1

凯文：客人　　艾利克斯:销售经理

凯文： 我喜欢上次你介绍给我的那部福特福克斯。它比较符合我的需求。

艾利克斯：好的,先生。你选对了。福特在新福克斯的设计上做了很多改进。

凯文： 基本配备是什么呢?

艾利克斯：我们新车的基本配备包括空调、防抱死制动系统、双气囊、收音机及DVD播放器。另外,福克斯还配有巡行车速控制系统。

凯文： 与老款相比较有什么不同?

艾利克斯：这辆车的新款在外观设计和涂层上都有了改进。它更加舒适,更加醒目。

凯文： 不错。那么天窗呢?是基本配备吗?

艾利克斯：对不起,先生,天窗是选装的。

凯文： 这样啊。另外一个重要的问题是什么时候可以拿车。我需要尽快拿到车子。

艾利克斯：如果你现在订购,需要两周时间,我们5月可以交车。

凯文： 那还不错。新款福克斯都有什么颜色?

艾利克斯：新款的颜色有红色、白色、蓝色、灰色和银色。这些都是标准颜色。当然，你也可以特别指定其他的颜色。

凯文：   我同事有一辆去年的福克斯，是银灰色的。我很喜欢那个颜色，我是否可以选那个颜色？

艾利克斯：我知道你说的颜色。先生，是这个吗？

凯文：   是的，我想就是。我可以选这颜色吗？

艾利克斯：可以。这颜色在我们客户中很受欢迎，所以，我们接受指定这种颜色。

凯文：   那么，我想订购一辆福克斯的新款车。看起来像是很棒的车子。

艾利克斯：你选对了。我自己也开福克斯的车，紧凑、坚固又可靠。

凯文：   是的。我认为福特是路面上最可靠的车子。我不会改变心意的。我现在开的福特几乎没有维修的问题，它跑得像丝绸一样平顺。

艾利克斯：好的，我帮你准备资料，请稍等。

Dialogue 2

乔什：客人　　艾伦：销售经理

艾伦：早上好，先生。有什么可以帮您的吗？

乔什：早。我想买一辆车。你能给我推荐一辆吗？

艾伦：年轻的你该开更有科技感的车。

乔什：我最近想买辆这样的车，有没有什么好的建议啊？

艾伦：哈哈，算你找对人了。我带你转转。我们这里展示了很多款式。

乔什：太好了，谢谢。

艾伦：我们4S店现在有款新3008，动力、外观都很出色。

乔什：我想一定是辆不错的车，快具体说说。

艾伦：嗯，它配备的时断时续发动机智能启停系统很省油，据说城市路况最多可以节省15%的油耗，超大尺寸可伸缩全景天窗倍儿爽。当然，还有我很满意的多媒体收音机导航系统，对于我们这些天天玩iPhone、iPad的人来说，显示和操作都很直观便捷。这款车还集成了3D实景导航和全方位可视泊车辅助系统。考虑中国人的操作习惯，这个系统还支持手写和拼音输入，十分方便。总的来说，很人性化。

乔什：听起来不错，我也想去试驾了。

艾伦：当然可以。你可以在这预约试驾，而且现在还有费率双零的政策。如果你现在购买的话，各种颜色都有现货。

乔什：哈哈，那我赶紧挑个自己中意的颜色。

Topic 3　After-Sale Service and Repairing

Dialogue 1

A：4S店的接待员　　B：车主

A：早上好。有什么问题吗？

B：没什么问题。我将要开车行驶很远的路程，我想确保车子状况良好。

A：明智的决定。您上次是什么时候保养车子的？

B：时间不长，我想是4个月前。

A：我们通常建议您每行驶完5000千米就来保养下车子。

B：为什么？我是说，为什么要经常检查车子？你们是如何来保养车子的呢？

A：首先，我们更换机油和滤油器。如果您不换这个，这会导致您的发动机耗损过快，也就是说您必须得更换活塞和进气阀。

B：我明白了。还有别的吗？

A：我们还会检查火花塞、燃油滤油器和其他油的指数，比如液压油。我们还会检查离合器和刹车来判断您的车是否需要更换新的零件。

B：好吧，你们那样做的话，看起来不像是浪费时间和金钱。

A：相信我，定期保养，会让您的车子驾驶起来没有任何问题，而且能避免故障。

B：有道理。

A：请拿出您车里的贵重物品，请把车子的备用钥匙给我。我带您去我们的接待室，请在表格中填写您的车牌号、姓名和电话号码。

B：我要多久才能来取车？

A：您可以明天下午两点来取车。这是我的名片，上面有我的电话，随时为您服务。

B：非常感谢。

A：不客气。

Dialogue 2

A 和 B 都是车主。

A：你到哪儿去？

B：我把汽车送到修理店去。它需要润滑和换机油，而且刹车也吱吱作响。我打算把它留下让机修工检查一下。

A：我想你刚送去修理过。

B：那是上个月。我换了一个变速器。这车我才买了 6 个月，已经花了一大笔钱修理。

A：我认为买车容易保养车难。更糟糕的是，我不相信那些汽车维修店。有时，他们收费过高，或者不给换我付过钱的那些零部件。上周，他们甚至试着劝我买根本不需要更换的新零部件。你知道的，我的车才买了半年，还是名牌。我对所有这些都很怀疑。

B：有这样一些店以卖零部件为生。我也不喜欢他们的服务。他们要的是你的钱。但是从长远来说，他们会失去客户。无论如何，汽车服务业在中国还是新行业。我们都必须控制我们的行为。否则，他们不会改进的。

A：有人被索要高价时，有没有可能打电话去某个机构投诉？

B：有可能。有那样的机构。如果你需要法律援助，你可以打电话寻求法律援助。

A：对一些小问题，没必要去修理店去修。修理店利润很高。我们自己需要了解一些修车的基本知识。

Unit 2

Topic 4　Product Design

Dialogue 1

艾伦：面试官　　张强：求职者

艾伦：请进。

张：早上好，先生。

艾伦：早上好,请坐,您是张先生?
张：是的,我是张强。
艾伦：我看过您的简历。您为什么选择机械工程专业呢?
张：许多因素导致我做出这样的选择。其中一个因素是我很喜欢摆弄机械。
艾伦：您已经工作两年了。对于机械工程,您对哪些方面最感兴趣?
张：我最喜欢设计产品,我设计的作品曾经还得过奖。而且,我熟悉 CAD 软件。我相信如果我被录用,我会做得很好。
艾伦：据我了解,CAD 是一款有用的产品设计的软件。您能简单地介绍下这个软件吗?
张：好的。计算机辅助设计(computer-aided design)简称 CAD。它是利用计算机及其图形设备帮助设计人员进行设计工作。在设计中,通常要用计算机对不同方案进行大量的计算、分析和比较,以决定最优方案。
艾伦：很精彩。您刚才介绍说您的作品得过奖,可以说下您的设计吗?
张：好的。我曾经设计了一个氢助燃汽油发动机,可以提高车辆的燃油利用率。因为目前加油站还不能供应氢,所以这款强大的发动机还没推广到市场上。然而,我相信消费者在不久的将来会看到这款发动机。
艾伦：太好了。关于工作,您还有问题要问吗?
张：没有问题了。
艾伦：非常感谢,张先生。我会尽快告诉您面试结果,再见。
张：谢谢,再见。

Dialogue 2

马克：顾客　　盖瑞：销售人员

盖瑞：下午好,先生。有什么可以帮您的?
马克：下午好,我想了解下你们公司的情况。
盖瑞：好的。我们是家设计公司,和一些专业的家具制造商合作,比如木制、五金器具、玻璃纤维等。
马克：挺好的。你们的产品有图册吗?
盖瑞：有的。除了图册外,我们还有网站。您还可以登录因特网详细了解我们的产品。
马克：好的。有机会能看下你们的设计室吗?
盖瑞：合作之后会有,但是,您可以在我们的展厅看到所有的设计样品。您对什么产品感兴趣呢?
马克：我想定制一套真皮沙发。这套看起来不错。皮质比你们的竞争对手要好。
盖瑞：您确实很专业。沙发和靠垫都是半苯胺真皮。
马克：这个坐垫看起来不是很厚,坐垫下面的材质为什么用布的呢?
盖瑞：坐垫是由 PU 海绵制成,非常舒服。另外,这个坐垫和鞍皮带之间的角度是符合人体曲线标准的。这个设计还申请过专利。请您试坐一下。
马克：很不错。我可以看下沙发的背面吗?
盖瑞：好的。这里用的是热压缝合技术,而且这个模具是铝合金一次成型的。您看下五金抛光,还有这些线条。
马克：好的。木纹清晰,接口干净。还可以做其他颜色吗?
盖瑞：一共可以做 10 种颜色,我们官网上面有色板。

马克：好的。这套沙发质量很好。我非常满意。我明天会告诉你是否订货。
盖瑞：谢谢,我希望结果是顺利的。

Topic 5　Mould Machining

Dialogue 1

乔：教授　　格蕾丝：制造商

乔：　　关于这套模具加工还有什么问题吗?

格蕾丝：是的,还有些问题需要问您。目前,我们有这套模具的基本信息,如注塑机型号、型腔数量、产品材料和浇注系统等。但是,我们还不知道浇口要求、产品表面要求和备用件标准。首先,您能告诉我产品表面是否为可视面? 表面做什么处理,晒纹还是抛光?

乔：　　是外观面。请在产品的这个面上做晒纹处理。

格蕾丝：好的,我知道了。您提供的二维绘图和三维绘图不一致,请问以哪一个绘图为准?

乔：　　请用三维绘图。我之前已经把模具规格、三维绘图和顾客资料抄送给你们组长了,你们收到了吗?

格蕾丝：是的,我们收到了。我们发现您提供的三维绘图里有的地方没有拔模角,有的地方胶位太厚。所以,我们需要跟您再次确认一下。

乔：　　是吗? 我记得图里面除了骨位以外,大部分都加了拔模角。但是,这也不会影响模具结构。你们是根据最新版本的三维绘图来加工的吗?

格蕾丝：对不起,我不确定。我需要检查下稍后再告诉您,好吗?

乔：　　好的。另外,模具能否全自动运行?

格蕾丝：不一定。产品可能会挂在斜销上。需要时,我们会考虑二次喷出。不过,后面我们还会做一些图片,与您再次确认。

乔：　　好的。还有其他问题吗?

格蕾丝：没有了。谢谢您,教授。

乔：　　不客气。

Dialogue 2

彼得：教授　　史蒂文：学生

史蒂文：教授,您现在有空吗? 我可以问一些关于我课程设计的问题吗?

彼得：　当然,有什么可以帮到你?

史蒂文：下面是我将要设计的模具的信息,请帮我确认下是否正确。这个产品的长度是 310.02 mm,宽度是 68.47 mm,高度是 36 mm,胶厚是 1.8 mm,重量是 59.93 kg,注塑机的规格是是 230 吨,胶料颜色是黑色,产品外表面做晒纹处理,内表面做抛光,需要日期印。

彼得：　信息是正确的。

史蒂文：请问这个模具尺寸的测量单位是英寸还是米? 另外还需要备用件吗?

彼得：　我想应该是米制。你最好准备一套备用零件以备不时之需。

史蒂文：好的。另外,产品的这个位置有底部掏槽,所以,我打算在这个位置做斜销或行位,您认为可以吗?

彼得：　可以的。做完后,你会发现在此面上会有分型线。

史蒂文：这个筋骨位的胶太厚,而且位置偏低,注塑时很难填充这个筋位,我可以减少这个筋骨位的厚度吗?

彼得: 减胶有两种做法,那就是做镶件和烧焊。

史蒂文: 遗憾的是,产品的这个面我已经做了晒纹处理,如果需要减胶,这个面重新做晒纹大约需要 5 天时间。那么我就不能按时交作业了,我可以得到您的允许吗?

彼得: 这个问题我需要同其他教授商量后再答复你。

史蒂文: 谢谢您,教授。

Topic 6　Electrical Automation

Dialogue 1

艾比: 我有一个发光二极管,你能帮我设计一个电路点亮它吗?

贝蒂: 当然。你的电源电压是多少伏?

艾比: 我有一个 12 伏的汽车电瓶。

贝蒂: 你能告诉我你的发光二极管的工作参数吗?

艾比: 让我看看。哦,工作电压是 2 伏,工作电流是 10 毫安。

贝蒂: 那我们需要安装一个降压电阻。

艾比: 那(降压电阻)是什么? 怎么工作的?

贝蒂: 阻碍电流运动的就是电阻,它通常用字母 R 表示。电阻的单位是欧姆,通常用 Ω 表示。欧姆定义为:一段电路两端的电压为 1V,通过的电流为 1A 时,这段电路的电阻为 1Ω。

艾比: 那电阻值是多少呢? 怎么计算出来?

贝蒂: 你学过欧姆定律吗?

艾比: 知道的。由于电阻和二极管是串联,所以电阻和二极管上的电流就都是 10 毫安。但是电阻的电压应该是多少伏呢?

贝蒂: 电阻的电压应该用电源的电压减掉发光二极管的工作电压。

艾比: 是的。那就应该是 2 伏(12 伏 − 2 伏)。

贝蒂: 完全正确。根据欧姆定律,我们可以用公式 $R = U/I$,得到的电阻值应该是 1000 欧姆。

艾比: 我学到了很多。谢谢你对我的帮助。

贝蒂: 你太客气啦。

Dialogue 2

加里: 你好! 你在干什么?

保罗: 我在看关于机器人的书籍。

加里: 哦,我对机器人也很感兴趣。

保罗: 真的吗? 书上说机器人在工业上帮助很大。有些事情机器人比人类的效率还高。你同意吗?

加里: 是的,比如说机器人从来不会生病,也不需要休息,一天工作 24 小时,一周工作 7 天。

保罗: 明白了。当从事一些人类认为危险和冒险的工作时,机器人可以代替人类。

加里: 你还从书上学到了什么?

保罗: 我还学到了虽然机器人不能从事每一项工作,但它在很多领域上都得到了广泛应用,如装配业务、连续电弧焊和点焊、包装、喷涂、物料去除、机器装载、物料传送、切割作业、部件检验、零件筛选、零件清洗和零件抛光。

加里: 真让人难以置信! 你能在机器人焊接上说详细一点吗?

保罗：当然。焊接是工业机器人所从事的最常见的工作。机器人焊接的车能提高安全性，因为机器人从来不会错过一个焊接点，而且会一整天都有同样精确的表现。

加里：真是一个努力工作的机器人。那么，机器人又是如何区分零件筛选的呢？我真无法想象！它是怎么区分不同零件的呢？

保罗：好的，让我们先来谈谈视觉传感器吧。有了它，机器人就能够决定位置、方向，并辨别所要选取的零件。

加里：视觉传感器是多么神奇啊！那么，触觉传感呢？它是怎么工作的？

保罗：这是一个复杂的问题。为了模拟人手的触觉，接触传感系统必须完成一些基本操作，比如：(1) 关节检测，检测加在机器人的手、腕和臂关节上的力量；(2) 触觉检测，检测加在手平面各个点上的力。

加里：哦，我明白了。感谢你的耐心和介绍。我和女朋友还有个约会，下次详谈。

保罗：很乐意。再见。

Topic 7 Automation Equipment

Dialogue 1

A：面试官　　B：应聘者

A：请进。

B：早上好，先生。

A：早上好。请坐。我是面试官，约翰·怀特。

B：谢谢。我叫李军。

A：我看了你的履历。你为何会选择机械自动化专业？

B：有很多因素导致我选择这个专业，其中最重要的一个是我一直怀揣着一个梦想，那就是有一天让大家使用我设计出来的机器。

A：你认为你能胜任这项工作吗？

B：是的。我在机械工程系读了4年，打下了坚实的理论基础。而且我正在另一家公司工作了4年，积累了很多经验。我来这里是为了寻求更大的发展空间。

A：那么，你了解我们公司吗？

B：当然。锦源科技公司创建于2003年，致力于综合制造服务，例如机器人、机械设计、定制装配线、自动化设备等。由于拥有丰富的经验，锦源已成为中国研发和定制自动化设备方面的领导者。

A：很好，看来你为今天的面试做了充分准备。你是什么职称呢？

B：我是高级机械工程师。

A：带证书了吗？

B：在这儿。还有，这些是我的设计，其中一些已经获得了专利。

A：能简单介绍其中一项吗？

B：好的。这是我最喜欢的——四工作站集成设备。它由一个12轴机械臂、4个供料器和8个托盘组装而成，定位精准。同时，它还装载了自动推送器和中英文操作界面。

A：听起来非常棒。你对自己的职业发展有什么看法？

B：我希望能在积累足够经验和专业知识后，成为研发部的管理人员。

A：很好。

Dialogue 2

A：客服人员　　B：客户

A：你好！这是泰东科技公司。有什么能效劳的？

B：你好！我正为我的装配线寻找一些设备。有人跟我推荐了你们公司，但我对你们公司和产品都不太了解。

A：让我为你简单介绍一下。泰东创立于2003年，专门为电脑和通信行业设计和制作最先进和最具创新的自动化设备。我们拥有2000多名员工和200套加工设备。

B：我想了解一下你们的核心业务和服务。

A：泰东公司一直专注于新技术的研究，在机器人、机械设计和自动化设备专业领域首屈一指。我们还能为你定制全自动装配线。

B：事实上，因为我在筹备装配线，所以对你们的自动化设备比较感兴趣。我需要一些机器。

A：那么，泰东就是你最好的选择啦。我们配置最新CCD检测系统、激光测量系统和多轴机器人，实现精确、高速的组装。你需要哪种设备呢？

B：我想要能够取代手工劳动，把小型散光片装载到屏幕上的设备。

A：我们的散光片自动贴合设备能满足你的要求。它是泰东全新的产品。

B：能详细介绍一下吗？

A：该设备配置有一个四轴机械臂、两个传送带和三个能精确定位的CCD摄像机。该机器的运动控制系统可编译，应用程序易于优化，还可以随时更新数据。它不仅节省了劳动力，还大大提高了生产力和直通率。

B：你刚刚提到CCD摄像机，它有什么优点？

A：集成CCD视觉系统可以精准监控机器人实时运动。

B：好的。我现在就想订购！

Unit 3

Topic 8　Civil Engineering

Dialogue 1

凯文：工头　　乔：监理

凯文：乔，下午好！

乔：　下午好！今天下午，我们的任务是安装这台接收塔。你的团队应该遵循安装说明。安装前，请认真阅读安装说明和图纸。这是这座塔的安装说明和总规划方案图。

凯文：谢谢。我想先跟您核对一下接收塔的一些信息，如重量、高度和重心。

乔：　这里显示塔的重量是40吨。

凯文：好重哦。高度如何？高度超过50米了吗？

乔：　是的。

凯文：监理，我看不懂图纸上这条虚线是什么意思。

乔：　它是塔的重心，重心离塔基20米。

凯文：好的，谢谢。

乔：　请牢记彻底检查一下下面的工具：电动绞车、钢丝绳、滑轮等，确认它们都处于良好状态。同时，不要忘记进一步对照图纸检查一下地脚螺栓。

凯文: 谢谢提醒。

乔: 这是应该的。

凯文: 呃,这部分我看不清楚,这张安装图修改过吗?

乔: 我看一下。哦,这是复印件,这些字母和尺寸都模糊不清了。

凯文: 你能核对一下这些字母和尺寸吗?

乔: 我来核对一下。这是原版的图纸,给你。

凯文: 谢谢监理。一切就绪,我们已经全部检查好了。

乔: 好了!准备工作了。

凯文: 大家请注意一下,听我的指令……很好,塔已经安装到位了,垂直偏差小于高度的千分之一。合格。

乔: 好的,请拧紧地脚螺帽。请休息吧!

凯文: 多谢!

Dialogue 2

乔什:大二学生　　艾伦:大一新生

艾伦: 你好,我叫艾伦。我是大学一年级新生。

乔什: 你好,我叫乔什。我是这所大学大二的学生。很高兴认识你!

艾伦: 我这么幸运啊,您是我的师兄哦!您是什么专业呢?

乔什: 我是土木工程专业。你呢?

艾伦: 我也是哦。您能告诉我一些关于这个专业的知识吗?

乔什: 好的,首先我要告诉你的是我们土建工作包括建造道路、建筑物、基础和钢筋混凝土结构。

艾伦: 那么建房子需要什么样的材料呢?

乔什: 通常用的材料是沙、砖和石头。

艾伦: 懂了,我知道混凝土是建筑中非常重要的材料之一,建造工人是如何获得混凝土的呢?

乔什: 混凝土是一些建筑公司在工作现场通过间歇式转筒搅拌机搅拌而得的。

艾伦: 这样哦。那我们如何评估混凝土的质量呢?

乔什: 混凝土的质量主要取决于适当的浇筑、饰面、抹光和养护。

艾伦: 如果我们想要增加混凝土的强度,该怎么办呢?

乔什: 混凝土一般可以通过预加应力得到增强。

艾伦: 请告诉我一些关于工程材料方面的知识。土建中最重要的建造材料是什么?

乔什: 水泥、钢和木材是土建中最重要的建造材料。据我所知,钢大致分为以下4种:碳素钢、合金钢、高强度低合金钢和不锈钢。

艾伦: 多谢了,师兄。我学到了很多东西。我能记一下您的手机和微信号吗?

乔什: 我的手机号码是18878020006,微信号是445566@hotmail.com。

艾伦: 真的很感谢您,师兄。希望下次再与您相见!

Topic 9　Building Structural Design

Dialogue 1

凯文:大学生　　乔:同学

凯文：乔,晚上好!

乔：凯文,晚上好!我听说昨晚我们吃晚饭时日本发生了6级地震。

凯文：是的,很多人伤亡了,许多建筑物和房子在晚间都毁于一旦了。

乔：真痛心啊!我听说日本政府正在采取提高房屋性能的方法,为什么还有如此多的建筑和房屋都倒塌了呢?你知道原因吗?

凯文：关于日本地震,我知道得甚少,但我和室友做了很多有关四川汶川地震的调研。

乔：真的吗?再告诉我多一些。

凯文：经过很多的调研和数据分析,我们发现具有钢结构建筑物的抗震性能最好;同时,在地震发生的整个过程,这种钢结构房屋的地震力最小,因为钢的质量很轻。

乔：哦,我开始理解为什么位于极震区的北川县城的3幢钢框架厂房都在轻微破坏和基本完好之间了。

凯文：是的,孺子可教。

乔：多谢夸奖。我还看到了很多钢筋混凝土结构的建筑,它们的抗震性能和钢结构相比怎么样呢?

凯文：问得好,你发现映秀镇这些混凝土结构的建筑破坏严重并倒塌了吗?

乔：抱歉。

凯文：没关系。尽管钢筋混凝土结构比较重,但它们的延展性比较好,这使得它们能承受较大的变形,所以钢筋混凝土结构的抗震性能比砖混结构建筑物的抗震性能要好。

乔：你的意思是说,钢结构建筑物的抗震性能比钢筋混凝土结构建筑物的抗震性能好,钢筋混凝土结构建筑物的抗震性能比砖混结构建筑物的抗震性能好,是吗?

凯文：是的,非常正确。

乔：但是,我不明白为什么砖混结构建筑物的抗震性能比钢筋混凝土结构建筑物的抗震性能差呢?

凯文：因为砖比较重且脆,其抗拉、抗剪、抗弯强度均较低,所以,砖石结构房屋的抗震性能相对较差。

乔：懂了。

Dialogue 2

乔什：总经理　　艾伦：商人

艾伦：你好,乔什。好久没有见你了。暑假你去哪里了?

乔什：你好,艾伦。见到你很高兴。我去深圳旅游去了。

艾伦：深圳?一个漂亮、发达的经济特区。你参观世界之窗了吗?

乔什：是的,我女儿吵着说要去世界之窗。

艾伦：是吗?她为什么如此喜欢世界之窗呢?

乔什：她说她想仔细看看埃及的金字塔。

艾伦：真有主见!你认为埃及的金字塔如何?

乔什：它们非常漂亮——一种力量美,这正是设计师们所想表达的。你知道法国的马赛公寓和印度的昌迪加尔会议中心吗?它们有着类似的设计风格。

艾伦：我从来没参观过。但是我见过美籍华人贝聿铭设计的巴黎卢浮宫金字塔和上海的苹果概念店,它们都是以柔美闻名,这些建筑完全是用透明玻璃建成的。

乔什：是的,你说得对。如今,许多日本建筑师比如妹岛和世、石上纯也都追求柔美。

艾伦：你好像一个万事通。

Appendix Ⅲ　Translation of Dialogues

乔什：谢谢夸奖。艾伦，你听说过法国的萨伏伊别墅吗？
艾伦：嗯，我从法国的商界朋友那里听到一些。他们曾经邀请过我参观这座最易辨认的具有国际化风格的著名建筑。
乔什：你让我眼界大开。
艾伦：哈哈，有点夸张了。
乔什：明年春节你有何出行计划？
艾伦：有啊，你愿意加入我们的计划吗？
乔什：太好了！我和我妻子都期望能和你家人共度一个长途旅行呢。
艾伦：我们也早就期待了。我们下个月做一个具体计划吧！

Topic 10　Architectural Design and Decoration

Dialogue 1

卡尔文：设计师　　艾利克斯：客人

卡尔文：下午好，欢迎光临 PC 室内设计。
艾利克斯：你好，我看到外面的广告说你们承包各类室内设计工程。
卡尔文：是的，请问您有什么需要？
艾利克斯：嗯，我想改造我的厨房。
卡尔文：您有什么特别的要求吗？
艾利克斯：我现在的厨房是传统式的，而我想要一个开放式的厨房。
卡尔文：听起来不错。您介意我毛遂自荐吗？
艾利克斯：不介意，那样就太好了。
卡尔文：那么，我们现在谈一下关于您期望的厨房的细节。您对新厨房有什么要求呢？
艾利克斯：我希望有一个宽敞的厨房，厨房有很大的灶台空间供准备食物时使用，还要有一个大桌子招待朋友们。
卡尔文：好主意。您喜欢什么特定的设计风格呢？
艾利克斯：我比较喜欢现代化一点的设计。
卡尔文：您选好喜欢的配色方案了吗？
艾利克斯：还没有。我的厨房需要弄得明快一些。这是关于我厨房的一些图片。黄色和红色的色调如何？
卡尔文：我认为那样的色调和您的家具不相配。黄色和红色的色调太复杂了。
艾利克斯：您能给我推荐一款和我的家具相配的配色方案吗？
卡尔文：我觉得鸽白色和云灰大理石色会令房间显得明亮，而且和您的家具配起来也很协调。
艾利克斯：鸽白色和云灰大理石色？嗯……听起来不错。
卡尔文：那您希望您的厨房能营造出哪种氛围呢？
艾利克斯：我希望它看起来简单、干净且轻松舒适。
卡尔文：明白了。

Dialogue 2

乔什：设计师　　艾伦：客人

乔什：下午好，艾伦。我带您看一下您的办公室。

艾伦：谢谢。我希望我的办公室可以有个好风水。

乔什：没问题。风水会告诉你环境可以影响你的心态。

艾伦：是的,风水在当今很重要,尤其是对于商人而言。

乔什：您说得对。这个是应您要求设计的双向平开磨砂玻璃门。

艾伦：很好。可以在那里也加一个门吗?

乔什：最好不要。办公室有两个门对风水不好。因为您的能量会从一个门进入房间,然后从另一个门溜走。

艾伦：天呐,听起来太糟了。

乔什：这边请。底层的窗子是彩色玻璃的,而其他楼层是平板玻璃窗。

艾伦：底层用彩色玻璃,而其他楼层用平板玻璃。好的。什么时候可以安装窗帘呢?

乔什：明天,如果没有任何需要改动的地方的话。

艾伦：您准备选用什么颜色的窗帘呢?

乔什：我认为蓝色的窗帘很适合您的办公室,您认为呢?

艾伦：我想应该很不错。

乔什：这是您的办公室。桌子放在门口的斜对面。根据办公室风水学,桌子必须面朝门。

艾伦：噢,我明白了。我可以把办公桌挪到正对门口而椅子背靠墙的位置吗?

乔什：当然可以。稍后我会把办公桌挪到那个位置。

艾伦：谢谢你。我觉得您设计得很棒。

乔什：我很高兴您喜欢我的设计。

Topic 11 Transportation Construction

Dialogue 1

乔治：建筑公司工程监理　　马克：建筑公司实习生

马克：监理,早上好。您今天来得真早。

乔治：早,马克。我今天要到工地看看沥青路面的养护进行得怎么样。

马克：哦,我能和您一起去吗? 我想向您请教有关沥青的知识。

乔治：行啊,我们边走边谈吧。通常说的沥青是指沥青黏合剂与集料的混合物,有时还会添加矿物填充物。

马克：监理,与其他路面材料,比如混凝土路面相比较,沥青路面有什么好处呢?

乔治：问得好! 除了顺滑、耐用、安全和安静外,沥青是用途最广的路面材料。可以在沥青路面行驶从客车到重型卡车等任何类型的车辆。

马克：我听说在很多国家,比如中国和澳大利亚,沥青路面主要用于城市交通或者是交通繁忙的路线。

乔治：是的。沥青有很多用途,既可以用来建设新的道路,也可以巩固已有道路,纠正已有道路的不规则之处,以及对已有道路进行维修。

马克：哇! 沥青真是道路建设的好材料。

乔治：是的,没错。

马克：监理,既然今天我们是检查沥青道路的维护,您能否说说维护的重要性和必要性体现在哪里呢?

乔治：在很多情况下沥青道路的使用寿命都比原来预期的要低。这主要是因为交通流量的增加以及商业运输车辆的载重不断加大,这两个因素的叠加往往导致严重的问题。

Appendix Ⅲ　Translation of Dialogues

马克：所以，全国每年需要立即维护的道路都在增加。有没有什么机器设备可以帮助延长沥青道路的使用寿命？

乔治：现在大型的路面铣削机是道路维护的主要设备。通常，路面铣削机是由三个系统组成的：动力系统、截割滚筒和输送系统。路面铣削机的使用，可以大大降低沥青道路的维护费用。到了工地，你可以看看这个设备是如何操作的。

马克：谢谢，监理。非常感谢您的解答。

乔治：不客气哦。

Dialogue 2

乔丹和斯坦芙妮是交通土建专业的大学生。他们正在谈论桥梁工程的话题。

乔丹：　　斯坦芙妮，你在做些什么呢？

斯坦芙妮：没啥。我在网上查些资料。

乔丹：　　什么资料？我瞧瞧。威廉·R.班尼特大桥。哇，这座桥真壮观！

斯坦芙妮：班尼特大桥建成于 2008 年 5 月，是繁忙的奥肯娜干湖公路交通枢纽引人注目的一座大桥。

乔丹：　　斯坦芙妮，你听起来像个行家。

斯坦芙妮：你太过奖了。坦率地说，我还真对桥梁工程感兴趣。

乔丹：　　威廉·R.班尼特大桥是座浮桥，对吗？

斯坦芙妮：是的。大桥全长 1060 米，有桥柱支撑的部分长达 690 米。

乔丹：　　一共有多少个浮舟？

斯坦芙妮：9 个混凝土浮舟。像原来的老奥肯娜干湖桥一样，它是北美为数不多的浮桥。新桥之所以命名为威廉·R.班尼特大桥是为了纪念第 27 任英属哥伦比亚州长。桥面是 5 车道，桥下可以有船只通过，自行车与行人都更为便利了。

乔丹：　　真了不起。我想知道建这座桥花了多少钱？

斯坦芙妮：由于建材费用，包括钢筋、水泥和燃料以及人力成本的大幅上涨，建桥的费用由原来的 1 亿加元增加到 1.44 亿加元。

乔丹：　　尽管花费巨大，我想有了这座桥，当地的交通大大改善了。

斯坦芙妮：是的。现在威廉·R.班尼特大桥设计的车流量是每天 8 万辆。

Unit 4

Topic 12　Food Engineering

Dialogue 1

艾尔莎和安娜是同学，现在在超市。

艾尔莎：安娜，我们可以走了吗？购物清单上的东西都差不多买完了。

安娜：　嘿，等一下。我还要去买些甜味剂，这边走。

艾尔莎：甜味剂？你经常吃吗？

安娜：　没错呢。我喜欢甜食，但是糖会让人肥胖。所以甜味剂是一个完美的替代品，它的卡路里也没这么高。有了它，我的饮食很健康。

艾尔莎：真的吗？我几天前碰巧看了一篇文章。这位作者好像有不同的意见。

安娜：　是吗？文章里是怎么说的？

229

艾尔莎：简单来说，糖不好，但是甜味剂是致命的。

安娜： 这听起来有点可怕了。我想再多了解些。

艾尔莎：我认为这个研究的结果是令人信服的。研究人员做了一个为期10周的研究。

安娜： 这个研究具体是什么？

艾尔莎：有两组志愿者，在10周的时间里，研究人员在他们的饮食中分别加入葡萄糖和果糖。

安娜： 好的，这下我明白了。但是研究者是如何得出了结论，说糖糟糕，甜味剂更致命的？

艾尔莎：第一组志愿者吃的是定量的甜味剂。他们身体里产生了新的肥胖细胞，这些细胞包围在他们的心脏、肝脏和其他的消化器官周围。

安娜： 另外一组呢？

艾尔莎：他们身上貌似没有这些变化。

安娜： 这太让人震惊了。我一直认为甜味剂比糖健康多了。我还是把这些甜味剂放回架子上吧。但是我没了甜食不行呢。我真的很喜欢甜食。那我该怎么办？

艾尔莎：第一，避免人工甜味剂，它们对我们身体健康的损害速度比果糖要快得多。接下来，适量食用一些有机蔗糖或者是未加工过的蜂蜜。另外，甜菊也是一个选择。

安娜： 非常感谢。这个推荐非常实用。我觉得我可以很轻易地在超市里某个角落找到它们。

艾尔莎：这个决定非常聪明。哦，顺便提一下，你最好戒了甜味的饮料，例如苏打水。多吃一些水果和蔬菜来摄取葡萄糖而不是果糖。

安娜： 那好吧。我会严格遵从你的建议，变得更健康的。

Dialogue 2

泰勒：学生　艾利：教授

泰勒：早上好，教授。我在为我关于转基因食物的毕业论文收集资料。您能告诉我一些这方面最新的信息吗？

艾利：当然。我非常高兴看到像你一样的年轻人想知道更多关于转基因工程方面的信息。

泰勒：那么，据我所知，大众关于转基因的蔬菜，例如玉米、大豆等有激烈的讨论。但是，我关心的是科学家们是否在关注转基因动物。

艾利：这是当然。研究者们已经在近几年里饲养了一些转基因动物，包括猪、鸡、三文鱼和山羊。

泰勒：转基因动物和传统的动物有什么区别？

艾利：具体来说，它们是基因组成动物。它们不单与传统的动物不同，与转基因动物也不同。转基因动物携带有从不同物种身上提取的基因。然而，基因编成动物身上携带的DNA字符是从相同物种身上调整或者复制过来的。这样的话，就安全得多。

泰勒：哦，我这是第一次听说"基因编成动物"这个词。

艾利：是的，这非常特别。但是，我们仍在等待大众对此的积极反应。我们确信基因编成动物的好处明显，不容我们忽视。这是解决资源短缺问题的一个有效的方法。不然，不断减少的资源怎么能养育不断增长的人口？

泰勒：非常合理。我们需要使用所有我们能用的工具来解决全球性的问题，基因工程应该是其中之一的工具。

艾利：的确。希望这些能帮到你。

泰勒：非常感谢您，教授。您给了我很多启发。

Appendix Ⅲ　Translation of Dialogues

Topic 13　Environmental Engineering

Dialogue 1

凯莉：记者　　蒂姆：市长

凯莉：早上好，市长先生。欢迎来到我们今天的电台节目。

蒂姆：这是我的荣幸。

凯莉：几天前我们在网上看到一个叫《穹顶之下》的纪录片，是由一位中国的记者投资、调查、拍摄的。她的行为让我想到了我们自己的大气污染问题。所以，市长先生，能请您为大家介绍一下"大气污染物"的话题吗？

蒂姆：好的。当它第一次在18世纪的伦敦出现时，是个很严重的问题。幸运的是，现在伦敦的空气污染问题在逐步改善。

凯莉：您有一次提出要让伦敦成为"超低排放区"。那听起来非常棒，您能告诉我们一些细节吗？

蒂姆：提到这个，我想先说说柴油车的事。这是主要的污染物。我们一旦解决了这个问题，就能轻松地实现超低排放区。

凯莉：好的。柴油车有什么问题？与汽油相比，柴油的效率更高，并且二氧化碳的排放量也更少，以前政府不是高度赞扬过吗？

蒂姆：是的，从效能和二氧化碳的排放方面来说，柴油相对于汽油来说有明显的优势。但是，我们忽略了一件事，即它同时带来二氧化氮这个污染物。二氧化氮是导致肺功能降低和其他相关严重心脏疾病的诱因。

凯莉：我明白了。所以，一些组织呼吁政府升级他们的柴油发动机。

蒂姆：是的，我们也意识到了这个。但是，我们政府倾向于采取另外一个更严格的规定来加快超低排放区的实现。

凯莉：您是指向每一辆驶入伦敦中心的柴油车征收20英镑的事吗？

蒂姆：是的，我们希望这个奏效。

凯莉：市长先生，您认为这个可行吗？我们有大量的柴油车。

蒂姆：我们注意到了推行新规定的难度。但是，我们同时也意识到了柴油带来的危害。柴油的燃烧严重威胁人们的健康。例如，它燃烧释放了颗粒物、臭氧、二氧化氮和多环芳烃。潜在的后果可能是肺病、心脏病、心律失常，甚至是过早死亡。

凯莉：这让我印象深刻。或许下次我们可以邀请另外的专家告诉我们一些由于大气污染物带来的严重疾病有哪些。

蒂姆：是的，如果污染物得不到有效控制，后果将会很可怕。所以，我呼吁大众更关心环境和自己的后代。

凯莉：的确。谢谢您，市长先生。

Dialogue 2

詹姆：海洋科学家　　李：记者

李：　很高兴见到您，詹姆斯。我读过您一篇关于海洋酸化的报道。我希望了解更多相关的内容。这对呼吁大众保护环境方面一定会有一些启发。

詹姆：嗯，我非常乐意帮忙。你希望知道一些什么呢？

李：　您最近做了一个关于海洋蜗牛的研究？

231

詹姆：是的。结果显示，南极洲海洋里面的蜗牛正在受海洋酸化的影响。

李： 您的意思是……

詹姆：蜗牛的壳正在被侵蚀。

李： 海洋酸化究竟是什么？

詹姆：它是矿物燃料燃烧的结果。

李： 矿物燃料燃烧？在海洋里？

詹姆：哈哈哈，不是这样的。矿物燃料燃烧产生二氧化碳。海洋吸收大气中的二氧化碳。海洋吸收了大气中一半的二氧化碳。这个吸收的过程让海洋酸化，而且这个海水酸碱度的变化对海洋生物和生态系统产生了严重的后果。

李： 似乎很严重。但是，酸化究竟是如何影响海洋生命的呢？

詹姆：你真的很关心这个问题，我很欣赏。酸化减少了碳酸根离子的可用性。碳酸根离子是海洋生物外壳和骨架生长的一个重要因素。

李： 现在我明白您的研究和一些海洋科学家呼吁之间的联系了。他们要求稳定排放量，最后是减少排放。

詹姆：是的，那是正确的。二氧化碳不单单影响大气，同时还影响海洋。不控制二氧化碳的排放，后果会是致命的。

Topic 14　Chemical Engineering

Dialogue 1

格蕾斯：顾客　　南希：销售人员

格蕾斯：我想要一瓶香水，你能帮忙吗？

南希： 当然。您喜欢哪种香型？

格蕾斯：哦，说实话，我以前没用过香水，我也不确定哪种香型比较适合我。你们有哪些香型？

南希： 差不多所有不同香型的各类款式香水我们都有，有花香型的、果香型的、木质香型的、绿香型的、东方型的等。你可以根据自己的个性选择适合不同场合和天气的多款香水。

格蕾斯：我想选一款适合我这周末约会的香水。哪一款比较合适？

南希： 那样的话，花香型系列的香水对您来说可能是个不错的选择。它们含有茉莉花、薰衣草、玫瑰等鲜花的萃取物，能散发花香，香味能带来纯洁和浪漫的感觉。这类香水我们有倩碧心悦繁花、范思哲浮华传奇、香缇卡仲夏派对和瑰珀翠铃兰百合几款。

格蕾斯：有这几款香水的试香卡吗？

南希： 有。但是，香水在纸上闻起来和喷在身上的味道不太一样。我们有试用装，你可以喷一些在你的手腕内侧，等 10 分钟再闻闻香味。这样，这些香水的整体香味就会呈现出来，你再决定是不是喜欢它们的香味。

格蕾斯：我喜欢 Petales 的香味。我觉得这就是我想要的。你能告诉我怎么用香水吗？我还没用过呢！

南希： 好的。喷香水之前，先沐浴，涂润肤乳。因为皮肤干净湿润的话，香水的香味保持的时间会更长一些。

格蕾斯：好的。那我该把香水喷哪里呢？

南希： 喷在您脉搏跳动的地方，如耳后、胸前、肘部内侧、膝盖，因为这些地方血流最强，皮肤最暖和。喷的时候离自己的身体 5～6 英寸。

Appendix Ⅲ　Translation of Dialogues

格蕾斯：好的,还有什么是我要注意的吗?
南希：香水也可能会弄脏某些织物,在用的时候要小心衣物。另外,将香水放置在阴凉干燥的地方,这样它的香味才能更持久。
格蕾斯：好的。非常谢谢你给的这些详细的建议。

Dialogue 2

米雪儿：顾客　　吉米：销售经理

米雪儿：你们有家用净水器吗?我想买一台净水器。
吉米：　有。我们有很多种类供您挑选,您有心仪的款式吗?
米雪儿：我想要一台自洁式的。
吉米：　好的。我认为这款是个不错的选择。它使用超滤净水技术,这是目前最受欢迎的净水技术。
米雪儿：这种技术有什么优势?
吉米：　超滤净水技术使用水压将含盐的水通过滤膜变成淡水。它使用一种半渗透的超滤膜来去除饮用水中的较大颗粒。这款净水器使用的是中空纤维超滤膜,这种滤膜能去除铁锈、沙子、一些大分子有机物以保证经净化后的水更纯净、清洁,口感更好。另外,这款净水器带有两个备用滤芯。
米雪儿：很好。那这款净水器使用什么滤料?我听说高纯度铜锌合金55(KDF55)在净水器中广泛使用。这款净水器也用这种滤料吗?
吉米：　是的。这种材料能有效去除重金属、余氯、硫化氢,能抑制细菌和水垢。
米雪儿：好的。这款净水器的处理水量多大?保修期多长?
吉米：　能处理37吨水,我们为您提供终身保修。
米雪儿：容易安装和保养吗?我很怕这种技术性的活儿。
吉米：　别担心,我们提供上门服务。如果您需要帮助,请随时联系我们。我们的服务电话在使用手册里。
米雪儿：太好了!

Unit 5

Topic 15　Management

Dialogue 1

A：总经理　　B：秘书　　C：生产部经理

A：让我们来看看目前各部门的项目吧。就财务部来说,我认为他们正转换会计系统。
B：是的,没错。我们的旧系统存在一些问题,所以他们正在考察一个新的系统。
A：好的。让我们转到市场部。他们现在进行什么特别的项目吗?
B：没什么,但他们正为我们的新产品策划一场新的广告宣传活动。
A：很好。我很期待。生产部呢?
B：嗯,您知道的,他们正在装配新的自动装配线。
A：当然,那他们肯定很忙。还有人事部呢?
B：他们现在正尝试招募新的毕业生。
A：进展如何?

B：挺好的。

A：管理服务部怎么样了？

B：好像他们正忙着准备下个月一系列的质量培训班。

A：对，马上就要到时间了。另外，新项目进行得怎么样了？

C：很好！我们正开发新生产线。

A：我们能很快申请到专利吗？

C：我希望如此。我正在准备新的图纸。我们仍在测试产品。

A：还有市场调研情况如何？

C：嗯，好像目前形势还不错。

A：我们必须进行一场很好的广告宣传活动。

C：那是一定的。

A：有了专利，那也必将会成为我们的优势。

C：当然，我们必须小心、仔细。在新产品投放市场前，我们必须进行完整的测试。

A：肯定的。我们希望成功。

C：价格已经定了吗？

A：还没有。我们得要谨慎行动。

Dialogue 2

A：人力资源部经理　　B：总经理　　C：培训中心主管

场景一

A：既然我们有如此多的优秀技术员，我想给他们更合理的工资。

B：这能够让我们在这个区域内成为最好的雇主吗？

A：可能不会。但是一定能吸引很多寻求更高报酬和更好老板的技术人员。

B：是的，一些公司提供很有竞争力的工资。但总的说来，高薪水会让人止步不前。

A：你的意思是，我们应该付合理的工资来得到我们想要的技术人员，而不是付过高的工资。

B：就是这样。工资政策能让我们控制经营的主要方面，同时还能让我们节省费用。

A：那你的意思是加班？

B：是的。一部分通过加班，一部分通过其他的方式。

A：我明白了。但通常的情况不是雇主而是员工他们自己控制加班。

B：一定有办法来解决这个问题。

A：回到薪水影响力的问题上来，你不认为高薪水是激励员工的重要因素吗？

B：这其实真的是个复杂的问题。高薪水可能会鼓励我们生产更多，但我不确定它是否能让我们更具有竞争力。

A：那让我们一起想一个更好的政策并讨论其中的细节。

场景二

C：我们讨论一下培训项目的细节好吗？

A：好的。根据我们的协议，我们将派送销售人员去你们中心接受技术培训。他们将学习操作最新的产品和你们研发的软件。

C：没问题。我们很高兴能这么做。

Appendix Ⅲ　Translation of Dialogues

A：还有我们上次讨论的用户培训呢？

C：哦,是的,我差点忘了。

A：很多用户不知道如何正确地使用我们的操作系统。所以,希望你能给我们的用户开办常规培训班。

C：好的。我们会给你送去最新的用户培训班的时间安排表。

A：谢谢。我们还想让公司的实习生在你们中心使用设备来做他们的研究。

C：没问题。这对他们未来的职业生涯很好。

A：是的。他们需要提前经历这种实践。

C：这也会帮助扩大你们在中国的影响。

A：那是重点。这是互惠互利,不是吗？

Topic 16　Finance and Economics

Dialogue 1

简：纳税人　　山姆：税务工作人员

简：　早上好！我们是一家外企公司,获批准从事房地产开发,兼营建材销售。请问如何办理税务登记？

山姆：早上好！你公司涉及营业税和增值税等不同税种的业务,须分别到地税局和国税局申请登记。

简：　这两个局有什么区别吗？

山姆：主要区别就是负责的税种不同。

简：　我知道了。税务登记在时间上有什么要求吗？

山姆：在领取营业执照后30日内提出申请。

简：　需要什么手续？

山姆：领取并填写申请表。此外,根据不同的经济类型提交不同的资料。

简：　复印件可以吗？

山姆：可以。

简：　多长时间能够办完登记？

山姆：大约在受理申请的30日内。核发登记证时我会通知您。

简：　费用是多少？

山姆：80元。

简：　顺便问一下你们的工作电话和时间。

山姆：我们的电话号码是68945790。登记时间为上午8：30到12：00,下午2：00到5：30。

简：　谢谢！

山姆：不客气！

Dialogue 2

简：经济学专业大一学生　　林：简的舍友、同学

简：哇,你又在网上买窗帘了！

林：挺好的啊！优惠活动很吸引人！明天就是"双十一"啦！商店和网店都推出很多优惠活动。

简：哎,中国的"光棍节"变成消费狂欢节了。

林：我认为"光棍节"最初是瞄准那些在寒冷的11月宅在家里的单身无聊的人们,鼓励他们在网上购物。但后来,因为促销太吸引人,所有的人都参与进来了。

简：阿里巴巴宣布"双十一"当天销售额超过90亿美元,打破了之前59亿美元的纪录。相比之下,美国

235

消费者在感恩节后的"黑色星期五"促销活动中只花费了12亿美元。

林：京东网在"光棍节"当天前10小时的销售额是去年同期的2.4倍,而其他一些中小型零售商称其年收入的15%到20%来自于这一天的销售。

简：简直太疯狂了!

林：很多买家,就像我,是为家里存货。就是一些小东西,比如搅拌机或者家用电器。你现在可以在网上买到任何东西,很方便!

简：确实! 电商提供的方便的送货上门服务和安全的第三方支付系统,改变了中国人的消费习惯。

林："光棍节"和电商网站确实影响着中国经济! 消费支出的急剧膨胀发生在中国经济增长放慢之际。去年第三季度的经济增长是7.3%,那是2009年经济衰退以来的最低涨幅。中国国家主席习近平承诺进行全面深入的经济改革,把国内需求作为未来经济增长的驱动力。

简：哟呵! 阿里巴巴及其网站上的25000个商户可以帮助促进这一转变啦!

林：习主席确实说"拉动内需是非常必要的,阿里巴巴非常幸运有能力发掘这种需求"。

简：好吧! 他确实厉害。阿里巴巴初始股在美国上市时,创造了250亿美元的筹集纪录。它庞大市值的基础就是巨大的中国消费者潜在需求啊!

Topic 17　Logistics

Dialogue 1

简：忙碌的物流经理,她负责将货品送到广交会　　　山姆：货运代理商员工

简：　请问你能帮忙运这些去广交会吗?

山姆：当然!

简：　我想请你将这些展销品直接从仓库运到展厅,展后再从展厅运回仓库。

山姆：没问题!

简：　那什么时候可以送到?

山姆：一般是展会前两天。

简：　展会从10月10日到15日,我们这批展品要求10月9日就位。

山姆：那10月6号我们开始运送,因为考虑将有公路和铁路运送,必须要提前点时间。

简：　当然。谢谢。

山姆：不用谢! 还有什么可以帮你?

简：　请问你们有没有大箱子能装得下这个东西?

山姆：让我看看……我们有5×4×6的大箱子。

简：　太棒了! 这件250磅的箱子也需要运到那里呢!

山姆：需要多快送到?

简：　两周后必须到广州! 这是我们第一次参展,我想确保它们能及时送到。

山姆：没问题!

简：　这对于我们公司意义重大,我希望你能确保一定准时送到!

山姆：包您满意! 我们等会儿会签一份合同的。

简：　好!

山姆：现在来谈谈费用吧……

Dialogue 2

简：顾客　　林：销售经理

Appendix Ⅲ　Translation of Dialogues

简：你们的景泰蓝花瓶太漂亮了，我想定一些，可是你们的定价有点超出我的预计。

林：您想要哪一个型号的呢？需要订购多少件呢？

简：80件，CHZ01。

林：每件80美元，纽约到岸价。

简：我觉得你们的价格有点高，如果以这个价格进货，我们将很难促进销量。

林：你知道，它们是纯手工制作的。

简：必须承认它们真的很令人赞不绝口！我们知道这些东西很不错，但老实说，市场上有很多类似产品，而我们是新公司，需要在价格上更有竞争力。

林：我相信在你市场上会很受欢迎。

简：嗯，真希望这次首订单能打开市场。

林：嗯，我们也只能以每件75美元给你了，这是底价。

简：也许，我们先谈一谈支付条款吧？

林：好的。我们通常是即期不可撤销信用证支付。

简：啊？信用证支付对于我们不是很方便，它将增加我们的成本，并且资金很难回笼。能不能破例一次，电汇行吗？这个对于我们来说要相对简单点。

林：这样的话，我们只接受提前支付。请理解我们，这样毕竟有保障一些。

简：好的！我还想知道保险是否包括破碎险？

林：我们会在人寿保险按照发票金额的110%投保所有险。

简：好的。包装上，我想纸板箱恐怕不够结实，经受不住装这么重的货物。

林：放心吧。我们会尽一切可能保障我们货物的运输安全。现在我拟一份销售合同，您看好吗？

简：好。

Topic 18　Marketing Management

Dialogue 1

萨拉：市场营销英语学习节目DJ　　罗杰：嘉宾，某公司市场营销部经理

萨拉：早上好。欢迎收听我们的节目。今天，我们邀请到的嘉宾是罗杰，他是一个公司的市场营销部经理。您好，罗杰，感谢您做客我们的节目。

罗杰：您好，萨拉。很荣幸能来参加节目。

萨拉：今天我们的节目主要讨论市场营销的概念。大部分人认为市场营销仅仅是销售和广告。您的看法如何呢，罗杰？

罗杰：我可以告诉你，销售和广告仅仅是市场营销的冰山一角。虽然它们很重要，但只是市场功能中的两项不是特别重要的组成部分。

萨拉：如果是这样，那什么是市场营销呢？

罗杰：简单来说，市场是指利用恰当的沟通将合适的商品和服务在合适的时间和地点提供给合适的人群。

萨拉：通常，我们认为市场是购买者和销售者聚集来交换他们的产品和服务的地方。

罗杰：是的。但更重要的是，市场是一系列针对实际的和潜在的购买者的产品和服务。

萨拉：从您的解释中，我注意到这些关键词：顾客需要、欲望和需求。那在市场上是不是那个说法，"顾客就是上帝"永远是对的？

罗杰：噢，差不多是这样。所有的市场最终的目的还是人群。即使我们说一个公司购买一台联想电脑，我们也是指公司的一个或几个人决定购买它。

萨拉：谢谢您的生动阐释，罗杰。我已经更好地了解市场的概念了。现在可以请您对市场的概念做个小结吗？

罗杰：本质上来说，市场是指给一个公司成功创建和导向其销售其产品或服务的过程，在这个过程中消费者不仅有需求，并且乐意去消费。

萨拉：谢谢您耐心的解释，罗杰。希望您下次能继续来参加我们的节目。

Dialogue 2

詹妮和伊莱亚斯是商业合作伙伴，他们在讨论分公司如何开办运营得更好。

詹妮：你认为我们应该做些什么来保证我们的分公司能更好地运营呢？

伊莱亚斯：首先，我要确保我们有个好的当地的公司法务律师。他/她精通当地所有的法律法规。

詹妮：那是非常重要的。我朋友推荐了一个很好的律师事务所。另外，我们需要一个人负责招聘员工。

伊莱亚斯：我认为我们应该派人力资源部的人去做这项工作，而不是利用代理机构，因为他们不熟悉我们要雇用哪种类型的职员。顺便问一下，我们分公司的选址决定了吗？

詹妮：是的，我们决定了。我们选了城市的东北部，距离机场不远，在商务中央区的边上。

伊莱亚斯：为什么我们不选在商务中央区呢？

詹妮：那个区域的租金太贵了。我们有没有洽谈到合同呢？

伊莱亚斯：有的。因为我们之前在这个国家做了市场调研，我们已经和当地的公司签了两份合同。这个月我们有望签下第三个。

詹妮：太棒了。什么时候能正式开分公司呢？

伊莱亚斯：希望下个月吧。所有的事情都比较匆忙。我们应该能够建立起分公司，并很快扩大我们的业务。

詹妮：我们已经准备了广告宣传活动了吗？

伊莱亚斯：是的，我们打算通过商业杂志把商业界作为目标。

詹妮：好的。我已经在上次的调研中通过大使馆拟定了很多商务合同。我们在那里应该会获得很多顾客群。

Topic 19　Tourism

Dialogue 1

托尼：旅行社职员　　贝蒂：顾客

托尼：早上好，有什么能帮您的？

贝蒂：我想了解一下去欧洲旅游的信息。

托尼：很乐意为您服务。我们有好几种欧洲旅行的套餐供您选择，时间从 10 天到两个星期。10 天的这个旅行套餐是非常受欢迎的。

贝蒂：我对 10 天的比较感兴趣，这个套餐花费是多少呢？

托尼：最低花费是每人 9999 元。

贝蒂：我知道了。那这个套餐包括哪些项目呢？

托尼：这个套餐包括往返机票费用、9 天的住宿费和每天的早餐。

Appendix Ⅲ　Translation of Dialogues

贝蒂：还算合理。小孩子怎么收费呢？我儿子只有7岁,他可以跟我睡一起。这样会便宜一些吗？

托尼：对不起,即使你儿子不单独占用一张床的话,价格也与成人价一样。你们计划什么时候开始这个旅行呢？

贝蒂：大概在国庆节。

托尼：我们还有一个10天的套餐可以订,是9月30日从北京出发的,可以吗？

贝蒂：好啊。这个时间对我太好了。因为那天我正好不用上班。我考虑一下,然后尽快给你们打电话预订。

托尼：好的。您最好快点做决定,否则就订满了。国庆节很多人去国外旅游的,尤其是欧洲行。

贝蒂：我会尽快决定的。我能拿张您的名片吗？

托尼：当然可以。这是我的名片,您可以打上面的电话。

贝蒂：谢谢。您能给一些关于欧洲旅行的小册子吗？

托尼：如果您想进一步了解这方面信息的话,在咨询台有一本指南,上面用好几种语言介绍了欧洲行。

贝蒂：谢谢。再见。

托尼：再见。

Dialogue 2

玛丽：接待员　　约翰：旅行者

玛丽：晚上好,先生,有什么可以帮您的？

约翰：晚上好,我想登记入住。

玛丽：先生,您有预约吗？

约翰：是啊,我昨天预约了4个晚上。

玛丽：请问您的名字？

约翰：约翰·史密斯。

玛丽：等等,是的,根据记录,您有一个预约,4晚的单人间。

约翰：但是,如果可以,现在我想要一间带独立卫生间的双人间。

玛丽：现在是旺季,我看看是否还有您想要的房间。(一分钟后)对不起,今晚没有双人间了。

约翰：明天有人要退房吗？

玛丽：请稍等。是的,明早有两位客人要退房。正好是带独立卫生间的双人间。

约翰：好啊,我今晚就住单人间。请等这两位客人明天走后就给我换成双人间。

玛丽：您打算待多久？4天吗？

约翰：可能更久。

玛丽：这是您的房卡。服务员会帮您把箱子提到房间。

约翰：谢谢。我需要明天7点的叫醒服务。

玛丽：没问题。您需要在房间用早餐吗？

约翰：是的,请给我送一份早餐和一份《中国日报》。

玛丽：好的。

约翰：顺便问一下,紫禁城离这儿远吗？

玛丽：上下班高峰期时坐公交车大约需要20分钟。

约翰：每天紫禁城人多吗？

玛丽：肯定很多。它是明清时期的皇宫，非常壮丽，所以每天都有众多游客参观。
约翰：谢谢。
玛丽：不客气。

Unit 6

Topic 20　Industrial Design

Dialogue 1

琳达：凤凰自行车公司代表　　克拉克：美国一家公司代表

克拉克：下午好。我是克拉克。我来自美国，这是我的名片。

琳达：谢谢。很高兴认识你，克拉克先生。我是琳达，是凤凰自行车公司的公司代表。这是我的名片。

克拉克：谢谢。很高兴认识你，琳达小姐。这是我第一次来中国参加展会，我对贵公司的产品很感兴趣。你能简要介绍一下你们的最新产品吗？

琳达：当然可以。这就是我公司的新款自行车。它放在展厅的正中间。

克拉克：好的。我今早有看到。我觉得那款自行车设计得非常精美。

琳达：是的，我公司工程师设计的新款自行车非常精巧、实用。这款自行车可以半折叠，方便携带，尤其在交通堵塞中或旅行时特别方便。而且这款自行车的轮胎具有在潮湿路面不打滑的特点。

克拉克：好的，都有哪些规格呢？

琳达：如果您看一下手册的第6页，就会在那儿找到所有的规格。

克拉克：很好。

琳达：这款自行车由于机械的构造简洁，所以很少有故障，易于保养。这款自行车在国外很受欢迎，需求量一直很大。

克拉克：好的。非常感谢，琳达小姐。如果我还须进一步了解你们的产品，我会联系您的。

琳达：不客气，希望尽快听到您的消息。

克拉克：我想会的，琳达小姐。

Dialogue 2

爱丽丝：售货员　　弗兰克：售货员

爱丽丝：早上好，弗兰克。很高兴见到你！

弗兰克：早上好，爱丽丝。很高兴见到你！我来向你介绍我们的新手提箱。请看！

爱丽丝：嗯。这款手提箱很精美。

弗兰克：是的，这款手提箱品质优良，很具艺术美感。它的表面耐用并容易清洗。与其他手提箱相比，该产品使用了轻型复合材料和动态设计，使之适用于不同人群，更高效、经济和实用。

爱丽丝：很好。这款产品有哪些颜色？

弗兰克：这款手提箱有多种颜色，包括亮黑、纯白、太空灰、亮银、亮红、金色及玫瑰金。这些都是最近的流行色。这款产品精美、高雅，在国内外久享盛誉。该产品很受欢迎，在欧洲多国销量很快。这款手提箱在市场中一直保持稳定的需求量。

爱丽丝：不错。每个多少钱？

弗兰克：45美元。

爱丽丝：有点贵。你能给我一个折扣吗？

Appendix Ⅲ　Translation of Dialogues

弗兰克：嗯,你知道原材料价格从上季度以来就上涨了10%。我们的产品是亚洲最好的,在价格上完全可以跟日本竞争。我们通常让利指标为5%。你是我重要的合作伙伴,我给你让利8%,但那还需要根据订货的多少来决定。

爱丽丝：好,我订500只。明天把货送到这里来。

弗兰克：没问题。

Topic 21　Environmental Art Design

Dialogue 1

戴维和辛迪：绿色城市公司的景观设计师

辛迪：嗨,戴维,这些天你去哪里了?

戴维：我才从中国苏州回来。

辛迪：苏州,让我想起那里的古典园林。

戴维：是啊,那里有很多园林,我去了拙政园。

辛迪：这是什么意思?

戴维：园林的名字,翻译成英语是 Humble Administrator's Garden,是苏州最大、最负盛名的园林。

辛迪：那一定好漂亮。

戴维：是啊,很迷人,水景和自然景观都令人印象深刻。

辛迪：水景? 是中国园林的特色吗?

戴维：是啊,中国园林素有"无水不成景"之说。

辛迪：真好玩,那有水一定也有桥咯。

戴维：对啊,我记得朱色雕花护栏的小飞虹,非常雅致。园林建筑也是绕水而建。

辛迪：水对园林还真重要。那陆上风景呢?

戴维：自然风景有小树林、小山,还有人造亭子、回廊和休息室。

辛迪：和我的小园真不一样。

戴维：当然了,那里占地5.2万平方米,你的就是个迷你园。

辛迪：哪天我也要去参观参观,或许能从中获得灵感,把我的小园设计得更美些。

戴维：好呢! 期待你的迷你中国园。

Dialogue 2

梅吉：园艺爱好者　　蒂娜：梅吉的同事

梅吉：我们去购物吧。你明天有空吗?

蒂娜：对不起,我没有空呢,到了园子耕种的时候了。

梅吉：你真幸运。我都没有花园。你要种什么?

蒂娜：我通常种点蔬菜和花草。

梅吉：哇,这样既实用又美观。你要种哪些菜?

蒂娜：我要种胡萝卜和莴苣。已经有种子了,它们很容易就长出来的。我也总会种些西红柿。

梅吉：花园里新鲜的西红柿特别美味。你还会种什么?

蒂娜：去年,我们种了一小片黄瓜。长得很好,但到处疯窜,今年就不打算种了。

梅吉：噢。你要种豌豆还是辣椒? 我最爱这两样。

蒂娜：不,种豌豆活儿太多了。而且,我种的辣椒总死掉。

梅吉：哦，亲爱的，那你要种什么花？
蒂娜：我想我种些花木或是宿根花卉，因为太忙没太多时间打理。
梅吉：栀子花和茶花怎么样？很漂亮的。
蒂娜：好，我会种一些。此外，我会种植百合、玫瑰和水仙。一定会是个完美的花园。
梅吉：你会为汤姆种草坪给他放玩具吗？
蒂娜：好主意，但这意味着更多活儿。如果你能帮我，我会考虑。
梅吉：好的。但你下周得帮我设计下我的花园。你要去哪里买这些东西？
蒂娜：这儿的超市前面有一个园艺中心。
梅吉：愿花儿都为你绽放。听起来好像得干很多活。
蒂娜：是啊，得翻土、挖洞、种花、播种、浇水，但是，这仅仅是个开始。
梅吉：真的吗？打理花园很难吗？还需要做什么？
蒂娜：我必须定期给花园除草，浇水施肥，还得防虫。打理花园有很多的工作。
梅吉：但为了那漂亮的庭园也值了。

Topic 22　Dress and Costume

Dialogue 1

奥莉薇亚：顾客

售货员A：早上好。我能帮您的忙吗？

奥莉薇亚：我在给我的宝宝找婴儿服。

售货员A：请跟我来。看这些衣服都是全棉的。

奥莉薇亚：这件连体衣好可爱。

售货员A：是啊，这是我们店最畅销的衣服之一，布料很柔软。除了粉色还有蓝色和黄色。

奥莉薇亚：蓝色很漂亮，我的孩子喜欢。但是这件有点短了。有没有80厘米的？

售货员A：等等，我帮你查一下。哦，有的。

奥莉薇亚：多少钱呢？

售货员A：125块。

奥莉薇亚：啊，太贵了！

售货员A：但是女士，看看衣服的质量，这是一等品。孩子的皮肤很敏感的。我们的衣服最合适宝宝。

奥莉薇亚：倒是，这个牌子很有名。好吧，我要了，可以帮我包起来吗？

售货员A：当然了，女士。

奥莉薇亚：我还想给自己想买裙子和丝巾，在哪里有卖呢？

售货员A：女装、针织品专柜在二楼，饰品在三楼。

奥莉薇亚：谢谢。

（奥莉薇亚上楼去。）

售货员B：早上好，有人接待您了吗？

奥莉薇亚：还没有。我想找条裙子，一条很漂亮的在聚会上穿的裙子。

售货员B：噢，明白，您看这条蓝色连衣裙怎么样？

奥莉薇亚：款式挺喜欢，但涤纶料子不够好。我更喜欢真丝的。

售货员B：那这件小黑裙怎么样？这是奥黛丽·赫本款。这种经典明星同款是永不过时的。

Appendix Ⅲ　Translation of Dialogues

奥莉薇亚：我挺喜欢这蓬蓬裙型和它简洁的设计。做工看着也精湛。好吧,我试试看。

售货员 B：您穿多大码?

奥莉薇亚：以前穿中码,但生孩子后变胖了些。

售货员 B：我帮您量一下尺寸吧。您的胸围是 42 英寸,腰围 28 英寸,臀围 45 英寸。大码应该合适您了。

奥莉薇亚：好的,试衣间在哪里呢?

售货员 B：就在那,咖啡色沙发后面。

(奥莉薇亚试裙子。)

售货员 B：您穿上身太漂亮了。

奥莉薇亚：你觉得我需要买条围巾来搭配吗?

售货员 B：白色真丝丝巾可以搭配的。但是,配珍珠项链或者钻石项链会让您在聚会上显得更优雅时尚。

奥莉薇亚：谢谢你的建议,那我就买这条小黑裙吧。

Dialogue 2

乔和贝丝正在讨论纽约时装周。

乔　：贝丝,要去参加纽约时装周我好兴奋。我还是第一次参加这么大型的活动。能多告诉我一些信息吗?

贝丝：我第一次受邀参加的时候也和你一样受宠若惊。

乔　：都有谁参加时装周呢?

贝丝：时尚媒体、时尚买手、零售商、时尚专家及社会名流。当然,还有设计师和他们的公关团队。

乔　：哇,那我可以见到老佛爷本人了!

贝丝：是啊,你最好穿香奈儿品牌的服装出席。

乔　：为什么啊?我还想着穿那条古驰的黑色无袖 V 领真丝长裙呢。

贝丝：设计师更喜欢出席者穿设计师的品牌服饰。如果你不穿设计师的服饰,会被认为穿着不当,不礼貌。

乔　：噢,我明白了。那你觉得我可以穿那件香奈儿黑白长裙吗?

贝丝：可以啊,那件挺精致的。

乔　：我还很好奇,那些 T 台上的超模怎么都是酷酷的从来不笑?

贝丝：呃,不是他们太酷不会笑。大多数高级时装设计师会特别要求模特走 T 台时不要笑。这样,观众的注意力就会集中在服装设计上,而不是去关注模特的外貌或个性。

乔　：啊,我懂了。太谢谢了,贝丝。

Topic 23　Animation and Cartoons

Dialogue 1

苏珊：肯尼的妈妈　　约翰:苏珊的弟弟

苏珊：嗨,约翰,你能告诉我在哪可以买到卡通玩具吗?我想给肯尼买些玩具。

约翰：在 Etoy 网就有很多啊。看,这些都是电影动画玩具:《玩具总动员》的胡迪,《神偷奶爸》里的小黄人,《超能陆战队》的大白等。你觉得我外甥会喜欢哪个?

苏珊：看起来都可爱。但是,肯尼最近好像对一个日本动画形象很着迷。你知道那只蓝色机器猫吗?

约翰：你说的是哆啦A梦？那只来自未来的机器猫？
苏珊：是啊，你能在网上搜一下吗？
约翰：嗯，哆啦A梦几十年来在亚洲都很受小孩喜欢，但在美国就没那么出名。Etoy主要是卖迪士尼动画玩偶的。不过，我们可以试试阿里巴巴，这个网络供应商很强大。看，是你想要的吗？
苏珊：嗯，正是那只猫，肯尼的新宠。
约翰：这里有毛绒玩具、动作玩偶、气球，还有很多其他选择。
苏珊：那你给我推荐一个吧，约翰。你更了解男孩喜欢什么。
约翰：那就买这只会说话的机器猫动作玩偶吧。肯尼一定会喜欢的！
苏珊：太谢谢了，亲爱的。
约翰：不客气，姐姐。不过，你得告诉我，你对肯尼的卡通爱好态度怎么变了，以前你老说那是浪费时间浪费钱呢。
苏珊：呃，我发现越来越难和这个叛逆的小家伙沟通了。希望卡通能帮我弥合这一鸿沟。
约翰：带孩子去看部动漫电影吧。给，这是《超能陆战队》的两张票，2014年奥斯卡最佳动画长片得主。
苏珊：谢谢了，约翰舅舅。肯尼一定高兴坏了。我尽量不在电影院睡着。
约翰：你不会睡着的。三维电脑动画视觉效果惊人，形象逼真。
苏珊：听起来挺新鲜。不过你得告诉我什么是CGI，不然我的小家伙又要笑我了。
约翰：计算机成像，就是一种用电脑来制作动画形象的新技术。

Dialogue 2

哈利和海伦正在谈论动画电影。

海伦：哈利，你还在为你朋友卢克的动漫公司写剧本吗？
哈利：是啊。我已经完成剧情设计和人物设定了，现在需要写剧本了。
海伦：噢，真不错！能投身于自己的爱好真是好事。
哈利：我从童年时期就爱上动画了。我看的第一部动画电影是《柳林风声》。动物们的友谊深深打动了我。鼹鼠、鼠、獾和蟾蜍带我畅游童话世界，真享受。
海伦：我记得那部电影。那是肯尼斯·格林厄姆经典故事改编的定格动画电影。我看的第一部动画却是《猫和老鼠》。
哈利：那部动画很好玩，是手绘动画的杰作。
海伦：但好像传统制作动画如今没有那么受欢迎了。你觉得定格动画会被电脑生成动画所取代吗？
哈利：不会。它有自己的优点，比如成本低，纹理表现优异。一些电影制作人还在使用定格动画。比如木偶动画《僵尸新娘》用的就是这一传统技术。
海伦：那你们的电影呢？
哈利：我们的电影是电脑三维动画真人电影。
海伦：那成本很高，是吧？
哈利：一家当地汽车公司已经同意投资了，条件是我们要为他们设计一个卡通形象。卢克会搞定的。我主要负责剧本。
海伦：能多谈谈你的剧本吗？
哈利：我写的是科幻片，主题是环保。一个来自火星的男孩波特意外来到地球，发现了一个可怕的秘密。妖怪要把地球上的河流都投毒，消灭人类。波特和妖怪打斗，把人类拯救出来。

Appendix Ⅲ　Translation of Dialogues

海伦：英雄主义很吸引男孩。
哈利：女孩也会喜欢的,剧中有爱情故事。波特爱上一个女孩,那个女孩是他保护地球的最初动力。为了吸引中国观众,我会把她设计成中国女孩。
海伦：真有想象力!真想看你的剧本!你的灵感来自哪里?
哈利：漫画、电脑游戏和其他卡通电影。实际上,是《功夫熊猫》提醒我在本剧加入中国元素。那部电影在中国票房很火。
海伦：你真棒,哈利。祝你们的动画在电影市场一炮打响。
哈利：谢谢!

Unit 7

Topic 24　Internet

Dialogue 1

吉米：客户　　大卫：接待员

大卫：欢迎来到中国联通,您需要什么服务吗?
吉米：你好,我想给家里装个网络。
大卫：好的。我们有传统的ADSL宽带和更高级的光纤宽带。
吉米：我不确定我们小区是否可能安装光纤网络。
大卫：您稍等,我来为您查看一下。嗯……很抱歉,您家附近还不能安装光纤网络。
吉米：那么您可以为我推荐一个网络套餐吗?
大卫：好的。对于ADSL宽带网络,我们有不同价格的套餐供您选择。最超值的是每月60元的套餐,它的连接速度可达10兆比特每秒。
吉米：兆比特每秒是什么意思?
大卫：兆比特每秒是指网络连接速度。该速度越快,那么加载网页的速度就越快,还可以允许更多的设备同时运行,高速下载音乐、图片、电影等。
吉米：我就只是想上网,和朋友聊聊天。噢,我也打游戏和在线看电影。
大卫：那么这个网速比较适合您的需求。
吉米：我需要付安装费吗?
大卫：我们不收安装费,您只要在您账户里存120元。
吉米：太好了!
大卫：您需要路由器吗?
吉米：不,我已经有一台了。
大卫：好的。如果您有任何疑问,可以拨打我们的全国免费客服热线10010,或者您可以登录www.10010.com获取在线服务。在上面您可以查询账单、定制服务、更改服务和报修故障。
吉米：好的,我知道了,谢谢您!

Dialogue 2

汤姆：用户　　亨利：维修员

亨利：有什么需要我做的吗?
汤姆：刚刚我在上网的时候系统崩溃了。

亨利：您有没有浏览什么非法网站或是打开了陌生人的电子邮件附件？

汤姆：没有。这有什么关系吗？

亨利：是的，如果您那样做，您的电脑很容易感染病毒。

汤姆：我知道了，我不会那样做的。

亨利：那是明智之举。

汤姆：您知道我的电脑出了什么问题吗？

亨利：请稍等。噢，是的，电脑中了病毒，而且您没有安装杀毒软件。

汤姆：电脑必须得装杀毒软件吗？

亨利：当然了。杀毒软件的目的是应对各种威胁，包括蠕虫病毒、钓鱼攻击、特洛伊木马和其他恶意软件。您最好要了解一些。

汤姆：恐怕是这样的。所以，我应该怎么做呢？

亨利：您最好安装杀毒软件来保护您的电脑，并且定期更新病毒特征代码来了解最新的威胁。除此之外，不要打开陌生邮件的附件及陌生人发来的链接。绝不要点击那些声称是您开户银行发来的邮件中的链接，并且避免从您不信任的网站安装程序。

汤姆：好的，我了解了。我储存在电脑中的数据怎么样了？

亨利：别担心，它应该已经被自动保存了。为了防预病毒造成的损害，您应该定期把数据备份在不同的媒质上。对了，我带了杀毒软件，现在需要给您装上吗？

亨利：好的，请给我装吧，非常感谢。

Topic 25　E-Business

Dialogue 1

海伦：BBC 英语学习节目主持人　　珍妮：BBC 英语学习节目主持人

海伦：今天我们学习的词汇是电子商务。

珍妮：什么是电子商务呢？

海伦：电子商务就是电子业务，通过互联网来做的业务。

珍妮：那就是电子商务了。

海伦：是的，你可以说"最近中国的电子商务发展得很快"。

珍妮：你的意思是他们能够通过互联网挣钱，对吗？

海伦：是的。

（切换场景）

A：为什么你关了你的办公室？

B：嗯，现在都是电子商务，我可以只在家里电脑上工作。

A：你认为我们应该开启电子商务服务吗？

B：为什么不呢？这将给我们带来 24 小时的销售，我相信我们的客户会喜欢的。

珍妮：那海伦，什么类型的公司要用电子商务呢？

海伦：嗯，任何与电脑有关的都可以做电子商务。很多旅游公司也用电子商务。

珍妮：是的，确实如此。我已经用了在线预订系统。

海伦：是的。网络买飞机票或预订酒店房间很容易了。

珍妮：但是，你必须小心你的信用卡信息。

Appendix Ⅲ　Translation of Dialogues

海伦：真是个很好的提醒啊。现在让我们概括一下电子商务意思是什么吧。
珍妮：不同的人会给出不同的理解。首先，如果你想做电子商务，一台电脑是必不可少的，而且，你必须能够很容易上网。许多人认为，电子商务只是简单的网站和有能够通过邮箱下订单、报价或是做预约的功能。另一些人认为，电子商务就是能够让客户下单和在线提交信用卡信息的网站，即使他们的订单可以人工处理，就像传真或是电话订单。仍然有一些人认为，做电子商务意味着你必须有先进的技术，非常好的顾客关系，以及高效的付费方式，等等。

Dialogue 2

A：顾客　　B：阿里巴巴代理商

A：我刚签下一个鼻瓶的订单，那么新的订单下个月订。现在我关心的是眼滴瓶和洗手瓶。
B：因为阿里巴巴有一个活动叫贸易保证，可以给予你100%的赔偿。
A：在这之前我没有用过这个服务，我正在学习它。你可以报个价给我，我将晚点和你确认。
B：因为阿里巴巴将提供5%的优惠，意味着如果你和我们下单，我们可以给你订单价格的2.5%。这就是我想告诉你的。这次活动仅仅是这个月由阿里巴巴组织的。一些公司都不告诉顾客，但是我们告诉！因为我们也期望与您建立长期的业务关系。
A：你能告诉我这个活动吗？这项服务仅仅只是面向中国的公司吧？
B：是的。但是，阿里巴巴可以为你们提供无限机会得到资金偿还。我们在努力。
A：好，把草拟的贸易保证协议发给我，好吗？